THE BUDDHIST LANDSCAPE OF VARANASI

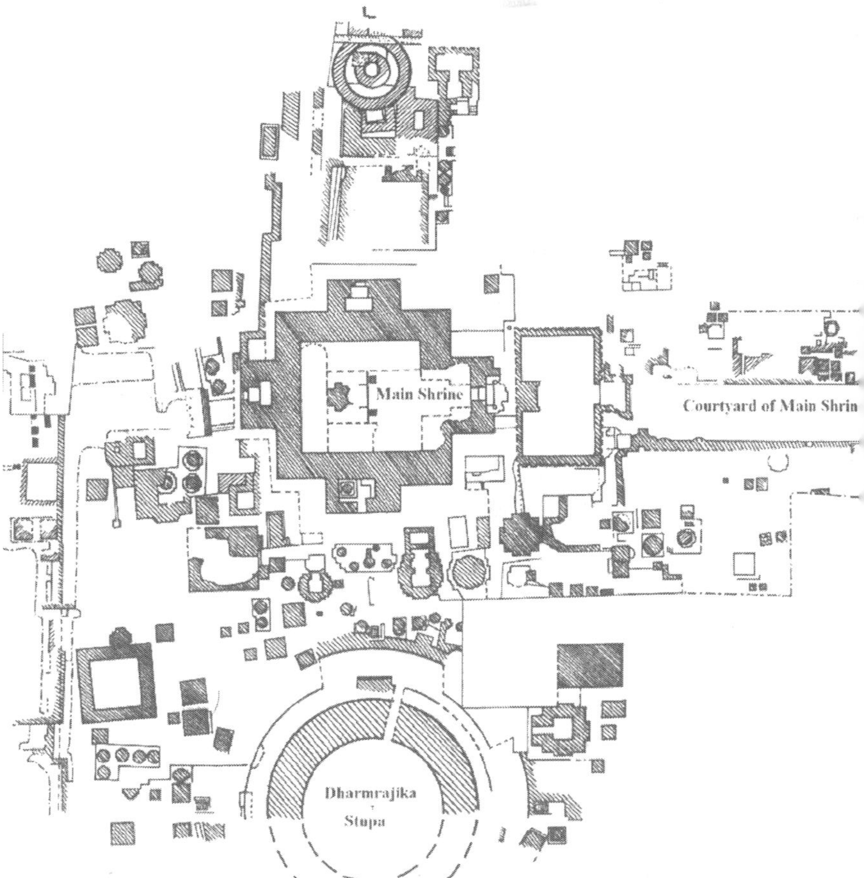

Sacred Landscapes of South and Southeast Asia

South and Southeast Asia has been homeland of diverse cultures since prehistoric times. Despite the varied histories and religions of societies here, there is a common understanding that terrestrial units imbibe a distinct celestial meaning. The present series seeks to examine the 'sacred landscapes' of the region.

In social sciences, including cultural anthropology and archaeology, the understanding of what constitutes 'sacred' involves beliefs, traditions, migrations, practices and rituals, as also related material remains including artefacts, structures and icons. Drawing on archaeological and historical research, each volume of the series would explore the relationship among the nature, culture and built landscape of a region, where heavenly and earthly energies blend in perfect harmony creating vibrant sacred landscapes.

THE BUDDHIST LANDSCAPE OF VARANASI

Vidula Jayaswal

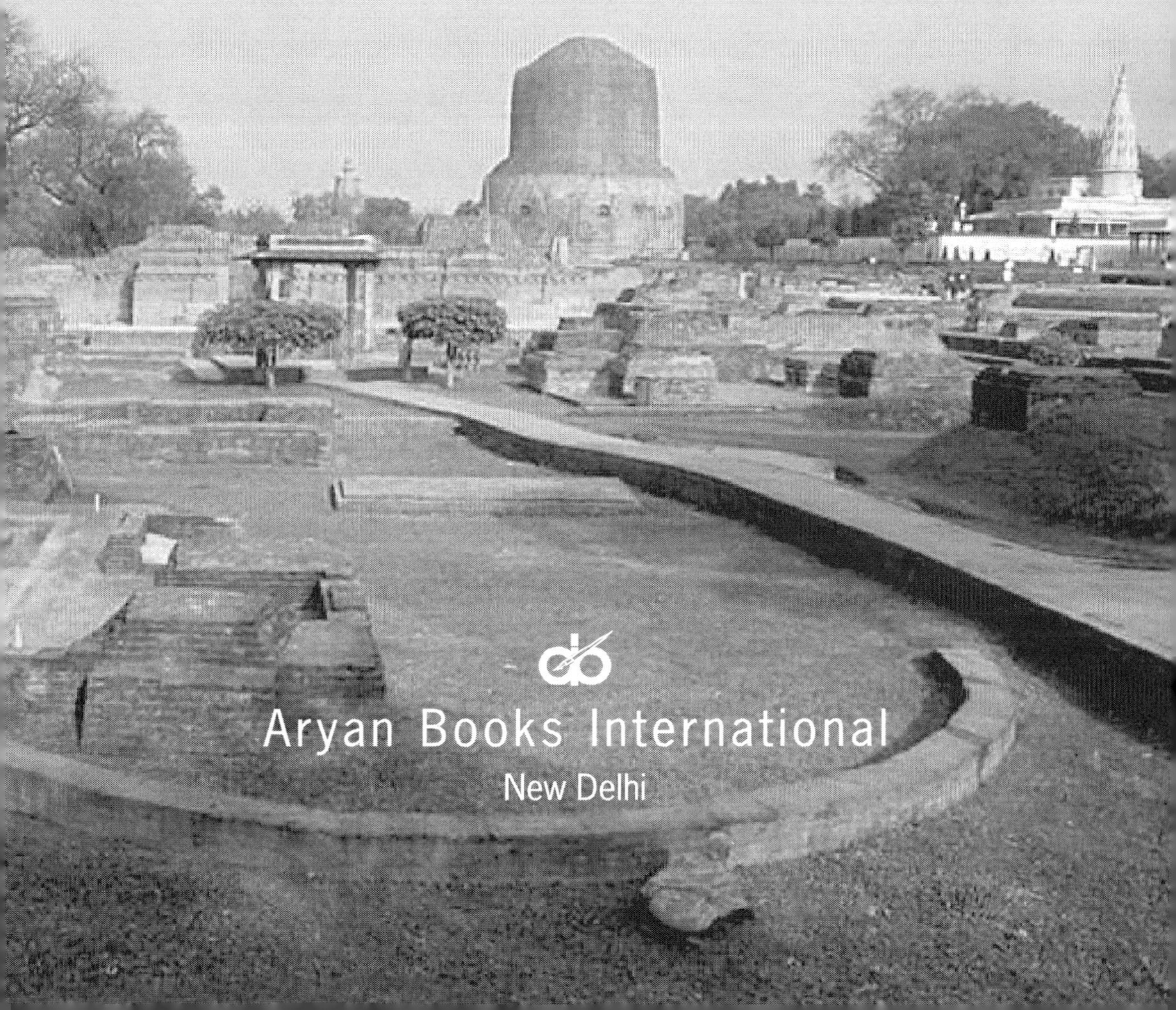

Aryan Books International
New Delhi

THE BUDDHIST LANDSCAPE OF VARANASI

ISBN: 978-81-7305-541-6

Published in **2015** by
Aryan Books International
Pooja Apartments, 4B, Ansari Road
New Delhi-110 002 (India)
Tel.: 23287589, 23255799
Fax: 91-11-23270385
E-mail: aryanbooks@gmail.com
www.aryanbooks.co.in

Designed and Printed in India by
ABI Prints & Publishing Co., New Delhi

Preface

Lord Buddha came to Sarnath, and delivered his First Sermon, and paved a stable foundation for Buddhism. Following of his preaching grew, generation by generation, century by century and over millennia, undisrupted. The place of the First Sermon, the Mrigadaya of Buddhist scriptures, obviously became the most holy place, and a famous Buddhist pilgrimage. Buzzing with multifaceted activities of pilgrims, donors, artisans, and supporting communities for more than one and a half millennium, the boundaries of this sacred place kept expanding beyond its nucleus. As a result, a large Buddhist landscape came up with Mrigadaya at the centre. The western side of it was occupied by the learned and wise immigrants, the residents of Rishipattana. While, the small villages to its east were supporting the Buddhist establishment in various ways, including supplying of stone carvings and icons to adorn the monuments. It is possible to say so because a chain of ancient workshop sites have been identified and excavated in the vicinity and a dense concentration of structures at Sarnath.

The Buddhist landscape of Varanasi has a long (6th century BCE–till this date) and chequered history. But, its origin is vague, its growth little known, and its shrinkage sudden. In fact, for some centuries the place was abundant, as to accumulate a thick cover of earth, burying the ruins of yester centuries. This forgotten pilgrimage was discovered by non-archaeological activities, accidentally. Jagat Singh, the builder of Varanasi, probed the area with the intention to obtain building material from this deserted Buddhist site. As a result, Sarnath caught the attention of archaeologists, who soon brought to light the remnants of its glorious past. Remembrance of the pilgrimage by a number of modern Buddhist organisations has partly revived the religious landscape of Sarnath, in terms of building temples, monasteries, educational and social institutions. Revival of this pilgrimage naturally attracts a large number of devotees and tourists. As in the past, Sarnath, the heritage site of international repute, is gaining momentum through donations in modern times.

There are a number of unanswered questions related to the Buddhist landscape of Varanasi, e.g. why did the Lord choose to deliver his First Sermon at Sarnath? Also, when Varanasi was the famous city, why was periphery selected by him? The nature and successive growth of the landscape created around the place of First Sermon also is obscure. The old and recent archaeological investigations carried out in the vicinity of Sarnath have brought to light evidence which provide answers to some of the above questions, and also outline the chronology and growth of this Buddhist landscape. Identification of Rishipattana, for instance, was possible after the excavation of Aktha site, which is located in the vicinity of Sarnath. Similarly, the chain of supporting rural settlements on the east and south-east of Sarnath, when exposed, demarcated the eastern boundaries of this landscape. This area was meeting the requirements of the pilgrimage.

It may be confessed that the theme of the present monograph emerged from a number of short articles, which were presented by me in national and international seminars on Buddhist art, archaeology and culture. This gave me the opportunity to develop a number of facets of the theme, such as: correlation of Jataka stories and archeological remains of Varanasi, Buddhist archaeology of Varanasi and Mauryan columns, sacred landscape of Varanasi, and contribution of donors to the Buddhist landscape, etc. All these fragmentary attempts are woven together along with additions of other important aspects which were essential for the reconstruction of Buddhist landscape of Varanasi in the present volume.

This book is aimed at reaching a larger section of society, which is interested in Buddhism and Buddhist sites. Although archaeological and other scientific data has been utilised, technical jargon has been avoided. The work is also aimed to promote such specialised attempts in the historical studies, when interpretation of archaeological findings of a holy place is envisaged in its geo-cultural totality.

I shall be failing in my duty if I do not mention the support and help received from individuals and institutions in the preparation of this manuscript.

Dr. Meera Sharma has not only helped me with literary references, but she has also been working with me on some important themes. Conclusions of our joint studies, like the one on Vedic ritual objects, have helped interpretation of archaeological contexts of Aktha, the Rishipattana. Shri Ajai Kumar Chakrawal has prepared line drawing illustrations, and Shri Samrat Chakravarti took some photographs for this manuscript. Some of the photographs were obtained from the photo archives of Archaeological Survey of India, Janpath, New Delhi. Views of recent digs were provided by Dr. B.R. Mani, Director of Excavation, Sarnath (2014) and Additional Director General, Archaeological Survey of India. While the other photographs of Sarnath were exposed by me with the permission of the Archaeological Survey of India. A few pictures of Buddha images are taken from the collection of American Institute of Indian Studies. The staff of the library of Jnana-Pravaha, the Centre for Cultural Studies and Research, Samneghat, Varanasi, extended all possible support in finding and acquiring the required publications.

Last, but not the least, I appreciate the efforts put in by Shri Vikas Arya of the Aryan Books International, for quality publication of this volume.

To each one, I wish to record my sincere thanks.

Vidula Jayaswal

Contents

Preface	*v*
List of Illustrations	*xi*
1. Backdrop: Political and Cultural	1
2. Aktha: The Rishipattana	21
3. Sarnath: The Mrigadaya	53
4. Donors and Donations	121
5. Sculpturing Workshops and the Sarnath School of Art	149
6. The Intangible Boundaries Drawn by the Jatakas	177
7. The Buddhist Landscape of Varanasi: Origin, Growth and Shrinkage	195
Bibliography	203
Index	211

List of Illustrations

1. Northern Black Polished Ware dish in situ, Oriyaghat, Ramnagar. 4
2. Location of ancient sites in Varanasi. 8
3. Dhamek Stupa viewed by the earlier explorers. 10
4. Unexcavated mound in front of Dhamek Stupa, Sarnath. 11
5. Excavation at Sarnath (2014). (Courtesy: Dr. B.R. Mai, ASI). 12
6. Excavation at Rajghat (1940). (Courtesy: ASI). 13
7. Excavation at Ramnagar (2006). 14
8. Excavation at Locality-1, Aktha (2002). 15
9. Excavation at Kotwa (1994). 17
10. Site plan of Aktha. 24
11. View of Locality-1 with cluster of sculptures, Aktha. 26
12. View of exposed floor of Later Vedic period, Aktha. 29
13. Reconstruction of Shala. 30
14. Vedic *patra/kapalas* from Aktha. 31
15. Potsherds obtained from Later Vedic Period, Aktha. 39
16. Kiln for baking red pots. 40
17. Kiln for baking black pots. 41
18. Main shapes of Black-and-Red Ware pots, Aktha. 42
19. Bowls and dishes in Black Slipped Ware, Aktha. 43
20. *Ghata* and storage pots in Red Ware, Aktha. 44

21. Hay impressed gritty ware pottery, Aktha. 45
22. Painted Black-and-Red Ware bowl, Narhan. 46
23. Iron objects of Later Vedic times, Aktha. 47
24. Bone tools of Later Vedic times, Aktha. 48
25. Terracotta model of a *Rishi*, Aktha. 50
26. Miniature ritual pots, Aktha. 51
27. Sarnath and other sites of Varanasi (after Cunningham). 55
28. Site plan of Sarnath monuments. 56
29. Geo-physical map of Sarnath (after Cunningham). 57
30. Excavation of 20th century with Dhamek stupa at the background. 60
31. Plan of structures exposed by Kittoe. 61
32. Fragments of Asokan pillar and other structures from excavation of the western side of the temple area. 62
33. View of monuments of main shrine area from the top of Dhamek stupa. 63
34. Location and Plan of the structures of Mauryan times. 65
35. Sandstone *hermika* with Mauryan polish, Sarnath. 67
36. Fragments of Asokan pillar, under the canopy, Sarnath. 68
37. Lion capital of Asokan pillar, Sarnath. 69
38. Railing post found in association with Asokan pillar. 71
39. View of inscribed shaft of Asokan column in the process of exposure. 71
40. Kushan and Gupta inscriptions on Asokan column. 72
41. Exposed view of base of Asokan pillar (early 20th century). 75
42. Mauryan pillar inset in a brick structure, southern chapel of main shrine. 77
43. Railing posts discovered from Mulagandhakuti Vihara. 84
44. Close-up view of railing post bearing Sunga-Kushan motifs. 85
45. Location of plan of structures of Kushan times. 91
46. Bodhisattva image donated by Bala Bhikhu, Sarnath. 93

47. Carved *chhatravali* found with Bala Bhikhu Boddisatva image, Sarnath. 95
48. Locally carved Boddhisttava image of Kushan period, Sarnath Museum. (Courtesy: American Institute of Indian Studies). 96
49. An exposed stair case of Dharmarajika Stupa, Sarnath 2014. (Courtesy: Dr. B.R. Mani, ASI). 98
50. Plan of monuments of Gupta and early medieval times. 101
51. Doorjambs, Post Gupta period, Sarnath. 104
52. Carved architectural fragment, early medieval period, Sarnath Museum. 105
53. Preaching Buddha image of Gupta period, Sarnath. 112
54. Standing Budha image in *abhaya mudra*, Gupta period, Sarnath. 113
55. Copy of the Asokan inscription on the shaft of the lion capital, Sarnath. 127
56. Inscription in Mauryan Kharoshti (reading ativaoshah) on the block of Chunar sandstone. 129
57. Inscription on a Sunga rail-stone in Brahmi script, Sarnath. 131
58. Copy of the inscription in Kushan Brahmi on Boddhisattva image donated by Bala Bhikhu, Sarnath. 133
59. Inscriptions (Āchāryaṇṁ sarvvāstivā- and dinaṁ parigrāhe) in Brahmi script of 3rd/4th century CE on the Mauryan railing surrounding the southern chapel of main shrine. 135
60. Inscription in Brahmi script recording donation of Buddha image by Abhayagupta, Gupta Period, Sarnath. 137
61. Copy of inscriptions on a Sunga railing in Brahmi script of 2nd century BCE and Gupta period, recording donation of the same rail-stone twice. 140
62. Inscription of Gahadvala Queen Kumaradevi recording donation of monuments at Sarnath. 146

63. Inscriptions in Brahmi of 11th century CE recording donation and restoration of monuments at Sarnath by Sivapala and Vasantapala, Sarnath. 147
64. View of ancient quarry at Chunar. 155
65. Cylindrical sandstone blocks in and around the quarry, Chunar. 156
66. Cylindrical sandstone blocks in the process of transportation, Chunar. 157
67. Evidence for navigation of sandstone blocks through Ganga. 158
68. Map showing route of transportation from Chunar to Varanasi. 159
69. General view of modern sculpture carving workshop, Varanasi city. 160
70. Master craftsman at work, at Lallapura, Varanasi. 161
71. Initial dressing of an image, Lallapura, Varanasi. 162
72. Exposed Kushan chiselling floor at Kotwa. 165
73. Exposed Gupta chiselling floor at Kotwa. 166
74. Map of Asokan pillars of the middle Ganga Plain. 167
75. General view of mound at Kotwa, with rich chiselling debris. 170
76. Split cylindrical sandstone block for carving two images. 171
77. Back view of Buddha image, Sarnath. 172
78. Standing Buddha image, Gupta period, Sarnath. 173
79. Buddha bust with classic Gupta features, Sarnath. 174
80. Buddha head of Gupta Period, Sarnath. 175
81. View of Ramnagar mound from Ganga. 182
82. Exposed NBPW workshop at Oriyaghat, Ramnagar. 183
83. NBPW shards found at Oriyaghat, Ramnagar. 184
84. Engraved NBPW shards, Oriyaghat, Ramnagar. 185
85. Profile of embankment, Oriyaghat, Ramnagar. 187

1

BACKDROP

Political and Cultural

Backdrop: Political and Cultural

It is of significance that the earliest description of Kashi and Varanasi as territorial units is available in the Buddhist literature. Varanasi in the scriptures is said to be the capital of Kashi kingdom, and Kashi is included in the group of *Sodasa*-Mahajanpadas listed in the *Anguttar-Nikaya* (Law 1968: 1). Though formation of states and their governance in India is dated to a couple of centuries (c. 800 BCE) earlier than the time of the historical Buddha (6th century BCE), the detailed recording of the socio-political format of Kashi Janpada is available in the Buddhist literature, particularly the Jatakas. The boundaries of Kashi kingdom is said to be... "From Varanasi the eastern boundaries of Kashi measured 100 miles and northwest limit 250 miles", which has been calculated to lie between Kanpur (western end) and Ballia (eastern end) (Altekar 1937). *Tandulkar-Jataka* (No. 5), describes the capital of Kashi, Varanasi, as a fortified city (Cowell 1895: Pt. IV: 22). The fortification of the city is said to measure 12 Li, while its periphery is mentioned to be 300 Li. This is estimated to be 85 and 900 miles, respectively (Rhys Davids 1903: 181). The said dimension of the city is an exaggerated estimation. But it highlights the socio-cultural significance of Varanasi in the minds of Buddhist followers.

The time of Mahajanpadas (7th/6th century BCE) is significant for the history of India for more than one reason. Divided into sixteen main states

(*Sodasa*-Mahajanpadas), north India in this period was governed by more than one political system—monarchical, the Janapadas, and republican, the Ganas. Kashi state, for instance, was ruled by kings, while the home region of Buddha, the foothills of the Himalayas, was governed by the clan of Shakyas (Law 1968: 2, 4 & 16). In spite of the diverse governance of Ganas and Janapadas, the region is marked by cultural unity (Jayaswal 2013 a). The middle Ganga plain was the nucleus of many of these states. To name the important ones, mention may be made of Kosala, Vatsa, Kashi, Magadha, Vriji, Anga, etc. Each of the states had a capital.

A number of capital cities of the Mahajanpada times, like Varanasi, Kaushambi, Vaisali, Patliputra, Champa, etc., have been excavated. Besides representing the succeeding stage of socio-political history, these sites are also significant for bringing to light the process of urbanisation in the Ganga Valley. It is important to note that all these sites are characterised by uniform techno-typological features seen in the artefacts, like, punch-marked coins, semi-precious stone beads, iron tools for various activities, temporary structures, etc. A fine variety of pottery with thin shining and black surface (Fig. 1), addressed as Northern Black Polished Ware (NBPW), is the diagnostic artefact type, after which this archaeological culture gets its name. The excellence of potting technology characterising NBPW was accepted as a precious commodity at the time of Mahajanpadas. Treated as table ware of deluxe quality, it was repaired when broken and was also a traded item. Affluent sections of society contemporary to the Shakya Muni was using this ceramic. That the economic status at the time was high is also attested by the occurrence of large quantities of beads of semi-precious stone, copper vessels and iron implements, which associate the remains of the Mahajanpada period.

A state without a capital is hard to comprehend. Similarly, a capital of a governance unit has to be a city. It is therefore in the fitness of circumstances that the time of Mahajanpadas is parallel to the emergence of urban settlements in the Ganga plain. But, one finds discrepancy

1. Northern Black Polished Ware dish in situ, Oriyaghat, Ramnagar.

between the time of the establishment of Mahajanpadas and their capital, the cities. As was mentioned above, *Sodasa*-Mahajanpadas came into existence by 6th/7th century BCE. But the first influx of cities in the Ganga plain has been assessed on archaeological grounds, around 4th/3rd century BCE (Ghosh 1990: 84). This would mean that the cities in the Gangetic plain flourished about two to three centuries later than the historical Buddha. However, the ancient texts provide elaborate description of the capital cities. These cities are said to be composed of rich traders and royal persons, who were toeing the path of Dhamma, shown by the Lord by visiting him and the places visited by him.

It was this scenario in which two prophets, the Buddha and the Mahavira, were born, who laid the foundation of new religious thoughts and ideologies. Both these spiritual leaders came to Varanasi. For Shakya Muni, Varanasi was the place to spell out his acquired wisdom for the benefit of humanity. So he delivered his First Sermon in the periphery of the capital city of Kashi. The question is why did he select Varanasi for this pious act? The answer to this question requires review of politico-cultural format of Kashi and Varanasi.

I had noted the following facts in one of my earlier publications (Jayaswal 2009: 1), which is useful to repeat here. Varanasi, for more than a century now has been accepted as one of the oldest settlements of the 'Aryan Culture' of the Ganga valley (Havell 1905: 14). Kashi is mentioned in the Pippalad Samhita of *Atharva Veda* (Winternitz, 1933. V.22.14: 261), while Varanasi is listed with other flourishing capital cities, Kausambi and Hastinapur (Rhys Davids & Carpenter 1982: 146) of the Janapada period. Buddhist texts say that Kashi was ruled by the Brahmadatta dynasty. It is also known from historical accounts that sometime around 650 BCE, the kingdom of Kashi was included in Kosala. Its subsequent inclusion in the kingdom of Magadha too is well attested (Rhys Davids 1903: 12). Rhys-Davids concludes, for instance, that "The Kasis are of course the people settled in the district around Benares. In the time of the Buddha this famous old kingdom of the Bharatas had fallen to so low a political level that the revenues of the township had become a bone of contention between Kosala and Magadha, and the kingdom itself was incorporated into Kosala" (Rhys Davids 1903: 12-13). Later, around the first century BCE, this city came under the governance of Asvaghosh, a king of Kaushambi. During the Kushan and Kstrapa rule it became an important administrative centre. The city then passed on successively under the domain of the Guptas, the Maukharies and the Gahadavalas, respectively (Altekar 1937). During its historical existence, Kashi-Varanasi experienced political instability. It went in the hands of one to the other kingdoms indicating that it was not nurtured directly as a seat of political power.

The political instability does suggest that the cultural growth of Varanasi was not the result of dynastic patronage. City is never claimed, for instance, to be established by some king, as was the case with Kaushambi. Nor is it recorded anywhere that the arts and crafts were run by royal owners. But, there are a number of references which record excellence of crafts and textiles produced at Varanasi, which were recommended for use at special and auspicious occasions. *Digha Nikaya* (Vol.II. 3.24.103), for instance, mentions that

> The cloth of Varanasi enjoyed special fame during the period, which is confirmed by the fact that the dead body of Buddha was covered with it and this cloth was so fine that it did not absorb oil.

Paradoxic to political instability, Varanasi experienced a continuous and multi-dimensional growth culminating in the centre for Indian culture. In due course, the city earned the reputation of being a seat of learning and centre of Indian arts and crafts. Be it the origin and development of religious thoughts and ideologies, or intricacies of skilled handicrafts and performing arts or trade and commerce, this city has been in the forefront since ancient times. The reputation of Varanasi as one of the oldest living cities of the world, and with rich inheritance of Indian culture traits, was perhaps an outcome of a natural growth of peoples' endeavour, not influenced by political ideologies. In such a situation there is freedom to put forward new ideologies and thoughts, and likewise, innovate new technologies and craft skills at one's own will. The long freedom for creativity and expression helped the region to attract artisans, literates, sages and saints from other parts of the continent. Particularly, those learned persons found the ambience of Varanasi encouraging who were seeking a suitable platform to spread their newly acquired wisdom and knowledge. Gautama Buddha was one of them. Besides, the geography of Kashi-Varanasi too was supportive as the region was located between the 'Aryan homeland' of the west, and the 'non-Aryan region' of the far east, which came under Aryan cultural expansion later. This would also imply that the region under consideration was free from any strong religious bias, and was an open space receptive to diverse ideologies and techno-material expressions.

Varanasi, the centre of Kashi state, demarcated the boundary between the Aryan and non-Aryan regions. But, technically it formed part of the region which was awaiting expansion of Aryan culture. It is to be noted that Pippalad Samhita of *Atharva Veda* says that "like security persons are sent to guard wealth of Gandhara, Munjavan and Anga, to Magadha and Kashi, the *jwara* or the fever is also being sent to these regions" (Satvalekar 1983: 92), suggesting that the last two states of the above-quoted text, though known, were not looked upon with respect because these were located outside the culture zone of the Later Vedic people. It may be interesting to note that even today, Varanasi lies between the western and eastern culture-zones of the Ganga plain.

Varanasi lies between the Varuna (east) and Assi (west) rivers, and the Ganga (south) to Sarang-tal (north). This geomorphic unit is marked by two prominent ancient settlements—the city area at and around Kashi-Rajghat, on the left bank of the Ganga river, and the Buddhist pilgrimage Sarnath, which is about 5 to 6 kilometres north of the Ganga river, cluster around Sarang-tal (Fig. 2). The cultural landscape of Varanasi accordingly is marked by two religious landscapes—the Buddhist and the Saivite. But, both of these were incorporated in one way or the other by each. This is testified by the mythology and intangible interactions between the two. In view to acquire a holistic picture, the canvas of this monograph has been stretched to the entire Varanasi region.

One of the useful approaches to studying archaeological settlements could be identification and mapping of cultural landscapes. As is implied in the theme of the present series reconstruction of sacred landscapes is being attempted in this volume. Archaeological remains on account of Buddhist material remains, both over and underground, reflecting activity-

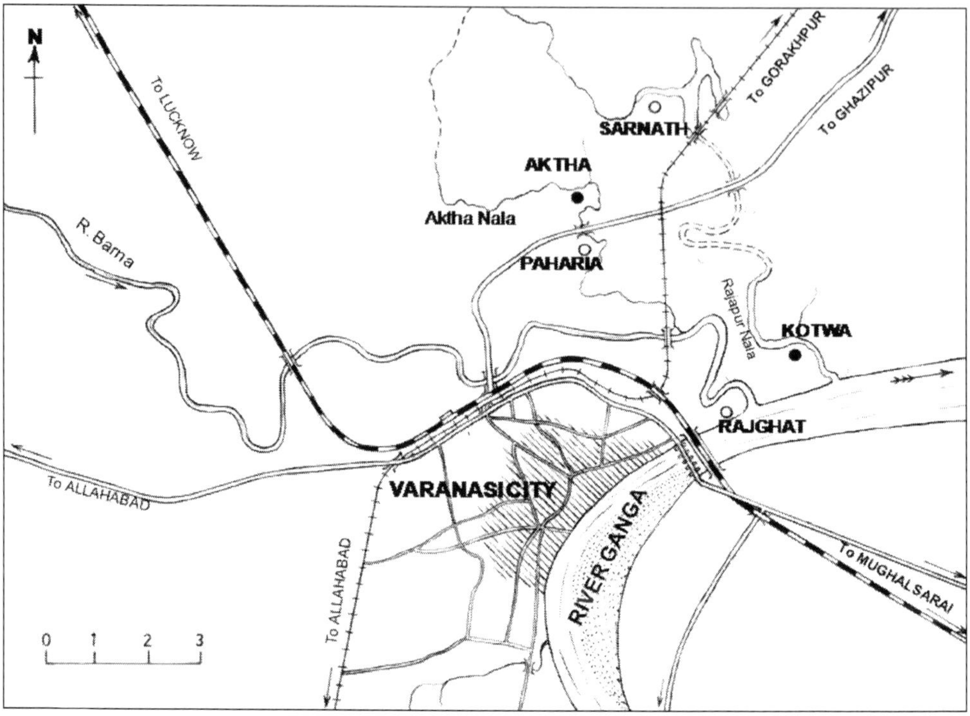

2. Location of ancient sites in Varanasi.

based needs of the contemporary society obviously becomes major source. The nature of structures, theme of icons and at times contexts of objects in dwellings convey their utility. The religious usage of objects, floors and contexts in archaeological records were noted. Take, for instance, the stupas and Buddha images of Sarnath. These are distinct reminiscent of Buddhist followings and form integral part of the sacred landscape. Along with these tangible examples, the intangible boundaries of this landscape could be identified on the basis of descriptions of ancient literature and mythology. Drawing conclusions from these, the proposed reconstruction of the Buddhist landscape of Varanasi is attempted which may be complimentary to the other, the Saivite landscape of Varanasi.

It may be admitted at the very outset that the proposed exercise is complex, and may not be foolproof. Varanasi, the longest living cities of the world has long undisrupted history. In the process, it reached the stage where multi-layered religious and cultural components integrated in a way to make it one of the most holy cities of the mankind. It is practically a small composite model of India, where communities of different provinces, religions, faiths and customs reside. In spite of this, the city over the years has gained fame for its Buddhist and Saiva followings. This reputation has historical basis. The twin geo-cultural units of Varanasi, the Buddhist and Brahminical, have more or less independent history of their occupation and expansion. One lying north of the main channel of the Ganga river, for instance, has strong Buddhist bias. While the other, the main city area, located along the left bank of the Ganga, between the rivers Varuna and Assi, may be demarcated as retaining Saivite hue (Fig. 2). Though there are numerous localities where followers of other religious communities reside, the monuments and mythology suggest the city to be a Saivite settlement. This reputation of the city is since ancient times. Even foreign travellers like Xuanzang described the citizens of Varanasi as followers of Maheshwara (Siva), and the city having large statues of the deity and *devalayas* of the God (Beal 1884: 291). Large numbers of Siva temples, which dot the region and the mythology associated with various places, bear testimony to the present Saivite prominence of Varanasi. The Buddhist landscape is located away from the bank of the Ganga river. Its location inland, amidst small streams and natural water reservoirs, is also marked by altogether different settlement pattern. The Saivite settlement has dense concentration of dwellings, which are dotted with temples and religious structures. In contrast to this, the Buddhist complex located north of Ganga is marked by a pronounced cluster of monuments in the worship area. The nature and extent of these two sacred landscapes of Varanasi have come to us as a result of independent historical processes. In the growth of these landscapes, diverse geomorphologic features were adapted. In view to project a focussed picture, it is logical to deal with the two in separate volumes. The twin prominent culture landscapes of Varanasi, thus, could be—the Buddhist Landscape and the Hindu Landscape. The present book dwells upon the Buddhist Landscape of Varanasi.

HISTORY OF ARCHAEOLOGICAL DISCOVERIES

SARNATH: THE MRIGADAYA

Sarnath (83°2′ E and 25°23′ N) appears for the first time in the archaeological records during the visit of Cunningham in the latter half of the nineteenth century (Cunningham 1871), who was drawn to the site by the overground structure of the Dhamek stupa (Fig. 3). But planned digging of the buried remains at Sarnath (Fig. 4) was initiated in the year

3. Dhamek Stupa viewed by the earlier explorers.

1905 by F.O. Oertel (*Archaeological Survey of India Annual Report 1904-05*: 59-104). It continued for several years in succession by a number of British officers (*Archaeological Survey of India Annual Report 1906-07, 1907-08* and *1914-15*), and a couple of Indian archaeologists like Daya Ram Sahni and A.K. Sinha (*Archaeological Survey of India Annual Report 1921-22*: 41-45; *Indian Archaeology 1992-93: A Review:* 99), as a result of which the nature and grandeur of this religious establishment came to light (Fig. 4). The chronology of the material remains at this site may be arranged between the time of the Mauryan king Asoka (c. 273-236 BCE) (Mookerji 1968: 89) and Kumaradevi, one of the queens of the Gahadavala king Govindchandra (1114-1154 CE) (Ganguly 1957: 520-54), who have left signatures of their contribution to Sarnath in the form of epigraphs. Sarnath was also identified as Rishipattan-Mrigadaya of *Mahavastu* of the Buddhist text (Horner 1954: 214) by archaeologists. The most recent excavation conducted at the site under the direction of B.R. Mani (ADG) and Ajai Srivastava (SA) (Fig. 5) of the Archaeological Survey of India has

4. Unexcavated mound in front of Dhamek Stupa, Sarnath.

5. Excavation at Sarnath (2014).

pushed back the antiquity of the material remains at the site to about one-and-a-half centuries. Needless to mention that the identification of Sarnath as the place of the First Sermon of Buddha is significant for the history of Buddhist landscape in Varanasi.

Kashi-Rajghat: The City and Ramanagar: the Nigam

The archaeological significance of Kashi-Rajghat was recognised as early as in 1940, when Kashi station was under construction (Fig. 6). The seal bearing the name of Varanasi, the capital of Kashi Janpada, helped in identification of the place with the ancient capital city of the Kashi kingdom. The subsequent excavations carried out at the site during the years 1957-58 and 1966-69 confirmed the initial identification of the ancient city (Narain & Roy 1976: 19). Six chrono-cultural periods were demarcated, indicating that this area was under occupation between c. 800 BCE and 16th century CE. The history of this site is not only pre-Buddhist—it appears to continue even after the decline of Buddhist establishment of Sarnath. This urban settlement has not revealed any Buddhist remain, but the city

6. Excavation at Rajghat (1940).

is mentioned on and off in the Buddhist literature in general and Jataka stories in particular (Cowell 1895-1905). It, thus, becomes an essential part of this monograph and has been incorporated in Chapter 6.

Situated on the right bank of the Ganga river, Ramnagar (83°17′ E & 25° 16′ N) is another small non-Buddhist settlement, near the southern periphery of the Varanasi township (Fig. 7). Ancient settlement here retained 10 m habitation debris divisible into five periods (from top to bottom)—the Gupta, the Kushan, the Post-Northern Black Polished Ware, the Northern Black Polished Ware and the Pre-Northern Black Polished Ware (Jayaswal & Kumar 2006). The highlights of the findings at Ramnagar are the workshop locale of NBPW, and the evidence for the local manufacturing of beads of semi-precious stones. These remains along with their location on the navigation route (by the side of the Ganga

7. Excavation at Ramnagar (2006).

river) and land route suggest it to be a *nigam* or a *mandi.* This trade-based settlement, which was larger than a village but not in true sense a city, was the feeder centre of the cosmopolitan city Varanasi. It might be supplying its produce to other neighbouring settlements, like Agiabir and Jhusi, also.

Ramnagar also is older than the advent of the Lord Buddha in Varanasi, but it was abandoned much earlier than Sarnath. Similar to Kashi-Rajghat, archaeological remains of Ramnagar also are significant for their correspondence with the descriptions in the Jatakas (Jayaswal 2013: 71-89). The summary of its findings, therefore, has been given in Chapter 6.

Aktha: The Rishipattana

After about a century of the initial discovery of Sarnath, intensive archaeological investigations were conducted around Sarnath (between 1994 and 1998). This was to identify supporting settlements of this religious establishment. It was also aimed at identifying the contemporary deposits to the time of Gautama Buddha, which were not revealed by the earlier excavations at Sarnath. Also, the question of why Gautama Buddha chose Sarnath for his First Sermon, remained unanswered. This is because pre-Buddha archaeological picture of the region was unveiled.

The site of Aktha (Fig. 2) was discovered on the confluence of Aktha-*nala* and Narokhar-*nala*, a small tributary water channel of the former, at about a kilometre's distance from the monuments of Sarnath (Jayaswal 1998). Excavation of Aktha (Fig. 8), revealed not only archaeological horizons dating much earlier than the advent of Gautama Buddha (early second millennium BCE), but it has also provided evidence for the identification of Rishipattana of the Buddhist texts. It could be summarised

8. Excavation at Locality-1, Aktha (2002).

that this settlement was located on the mainland route connecting various parts of north India. This route also appears to serve migration of Later Vedic communities (from west to east), as well as sages from Himalayas to plains (north to east), in the second-first millennia BCE (Jayaswal 2009). During the process, Aktha perhaps gained the reputation of the resort/centre for sages, the Rishipattana.

Rishipattana and Mrigadaya, addressed at times together, were two separate entities. For, according to *Divyadana*, King Asoka gives a list of the places to be visited where he wished to construct stupas. In this list Isipatana and Migadava are mentioned separately (Malalasekera 1995: 325). Also, the concept of Rishipattana (Isipatana of the Buddhist literature), as is mentioned in *Mahavastu*, is that, "Isipatana was so called because sages on their way through the air (from the Himalayas), alight here or start from here on their aerial flight" (Jones 1947: 37). Mrigadaya (Migadava of the Buddhist texts) is mentioned to be, "... an open space near Benares where was situated the famous 'Migadava' or Deer Park" (Horner 1954: 214). These references certainly address Isipatana and Migdava as two independent establishments. The very fact that the two are mentioned with a hyphen in the other Buddhist texts, also, is indicative of two separate regions addressed together. Since the discovery of the religious establishment of Sarnath of early twentieth century received all the attention, the area was simply accepted as the Isipatana-Migadava. It continues to be addressed so till today. But, recent archaeological discoveries evidence that it is now possible to identify Rishipattana separately from Sarnath, which was the Mrigadaya. It is only after the area around Sarnath was intensively studied and new sites were discovered and excavated that the incident recorded in *Divyadana* appears to be true. For, on account of the archaeological findings, two ancient settlements—Sarnath (the religious establishment) and Aktha (a hermitage settlement)—may be identified, respectively, as Mrigadaya and Rishipattana.

Recent archaeological findings have revealed that Rishipattana and Mrigadaya were separate entities. The nature and growth of Mrigadaya, the subject matter of Chapter 3, is based on the archaeological findings of Sarnath, while remains of Aktha associated with Rishipattana have been discussed in Chapter 2.

The Craft and Resort Villages

An ancient channel, which was connecting the Ganga river to Sarnath, was traced during our field survey. This dried-up rivulet, Rajapur-*nala*, was dotted with a chain of small rural settlements, where icons and stone blocks for architecture were carved (Fig. 2). The stream was utilised from the Mauryan times to the early medieval period for transportation of large blocks of sandstone as carving medium from the Chunar hills. The carvings were prepared at sites like Kotwa, Rajapur and Asapur and were utilised to adorn the monuments of Sarnath. Excavation at Kotwa (83°03′15" E and 25°20′20" N) was particularly rewarding (Fig. 9), as a small mound here retains evidence for an ancient craft village. Located

9. Excavation at Kotwa (1994).

on the transportation route of sandstone, Kotwa was identified as a chiselling workshop. Its existence is dated between c. 1st/2nd century BCE and 11th /12th century CE (Jayaswal 1998: 184-211).

Another category of rural sites on Rajapur-*nala* was residences or halt places of persons supporting the Buddhist establishment of Sarnath. The small mound at Tilmanpur (83° 02′ 0" E and 25° 21′35") is located on the bank of the channel on one side and on the other, by the side of the Varanasi-Gazipur National Highway (Jayaswal 1998: 119-174). The four cultural periods identified here correspond with the most flourishing early period of Sarnath. These are placed between the Maurya and Gupta periods (Jayaswal 1998: 123).

The above account suggests that it is due to the spade of archaeologists that tangible evidence for the reconstruction of cultural landscapes of Varanasi is available in good proportion today. But, for reliable interpretations of Buddhist landscape, it is necessary to weed out and study such information and indications from non-Buddhist categories, which are distinctively Buddhist. For, in the archaeological records there are remains which bear of Buddhist features, Structures of stupa, vihara, sangharama, and icons of Buddha, Bodhisattva, and Buddhist pantheon may be cited in this category. Along with these, one also notes images belonging to Brahminical and/or Jain faith in archaeological remains. The catalogue of Sarnath museum collection (Sahni 1914: 164-68) is a demonstrative example that Sarnath, at least in early medieval times, was the centre of activities of the followers of all the three religious sects. This category can easily be separated. But, scrutiny of Buddhist remains from the non-Buddhist is particularly complex when daily utility articles of the masses are examined. In other words, in comparison to the pilgrim sites, the exercise is quite challenging on the collections obtained from the city and the rural settlements. As in the discards of dwellers, identification of their religious following and related specific activities are very indistinct. My micro-level scrutiny of archaeological findings of Aktha, however, demonstrated that careful study of material remains may suggest religious format of an archaeological settlement (Jayaswal 2009). Identification of a ritual object, *kapala*, the container utilised at the time of performance of a Vedic *yajna,* and the associating floors retaining traces of ritual performance, is a noteworthy attempt for identification of the main religious following at an ancient settlement. This helped in recognizing Rishipattana.

BUDDHIST MYTHOLOGY AND VARANASI

Another significant source of information for the reconstruction of Buddhist landscape of Varanasi is the Buddhist literature. It may be interesting to note that the place of origin of Buddhism, Varanasi-Sarnath region, fares quite well in the early literature. Even when Buddhism was embraced by large national and international communities, the place of the First Sermon continued to be the nucleus of mythological events, and its dwellers full of divine qualities remembered for centuries. But, surprisingly, not Sarnath but the city of Varanasi was the most sought after background of Jataka stories (Cowell 1895-1905). The stories or the events of the previous births of Buddha in this chronicle are narrated to have happened in Varanasi, the ancient capital of Kashi kingdom. The hero of the stories, the Lord, takes birth in a number of human and animal forms with divine qualities.

The question faced was to which extent can archaeological remains of ancient Varanasi, a good part of which is the Brahmanical habitat, be included in the Buddhist landscape? Or, did the demarcating boundary of two distinct religious landscapes lose grounds so they embraced each other in order to enlarge their respective followings? Correlation of the descriptions of some select Jataka stories with that of archaeological findings of Varanasi, was perused by me earlier (Jayaswal 2013) and has been attempted in this volume also.

The theme of the present monograph also required discussion on the major factors responsible for building sacred landscapes. One finds that the contribution of donors to the making of the Buddhist landscape of

Varanasi was immense. Geographic and geomorphologic features, which invariably shape physical landscape, were equally strong governing factors for the make-up of sacred landscape. The human as well as the natural causes for the origin and growth of Buddhist landscape of Varanasi require attention. Instead of elaborate description of findings and facts collected, in view to maintain spirit of the present series an interpretative approach has been adopted in this book.

2

AKTHA

The Rishipattana

Aktha: The Rishipattana

The first question which comes to one's mind is that why Buddha chose Rishipattana-Mrigadaya to deliver his First Sermon, after he got enlightenment at Bodh Gaya? As was discussed earlier (Chapter 1), both the places were separate entities, up to the time of the Mauryan king Asoka because he is said to have constructed stupas at Mrigadaya and Rishipattana (Malalasekera 1995: 325). If the place of the First Sermon Mrigadaya was Sarnath, then where was Rishipattana? What was the nature of this place when the Lord came here?

Mahavastu, the Sanskrit Buddhist text, mentions that "Once there lived five hundred Pratyeka-Buddhas or Rishis in a big forest at the distance of a *yojana* and a half from Benares" (Majumdar, B. 1947: 5). While explaining the reason for the nomenclature of Rishipattana, in *Mahavastu* the event is said to be of remote past. "Once there lived five hundred Pratyeka-Buddhas or Rishis,"... who... "rose to the sky where they attained *nirvana* and thus their corporeal bodies fell on earth. As the bodies of the Rishis or the Pratyeka-Buddhas fell on the forest, it came to be known as Rishipattana, i.e. where the Rishis fell down" (Majumdar, B. 1947: 5). This description suggests that Rishipattana was established in antiquity. Obliviously the place was there much earlier than the advent of the historical Buddha in this region. Then, the entire region was forested, where *Rishis* lived in considerable number. It is further mentioned that, "Isipatana was so called because sages on their way through the air (from the Himalayas), alight here or start from here on their aerial flight" (Jones 1949: 37). In this statement also there is inference for the occupation of Rishipattana by the roaming sages.

The concept and location of Rishipattana, as is mentioned in the Buddhist scriptures, may be summarised as follows:

1. Rishipattana was located away, but near the city of Varanasi.
2. Rishipattana was a separate and independent entity, like Sarnath and Varanasi city.
3. Rishipattana was the resort of Rishis, who were moving from one place to the other, particularly between the Himalayas and Varanasi. Perhaps their movement was spread throughout the Ganga plain.

The following inferences may be added to the above deductions:

4. The resort of the Rishis would suggest a hermitage-based settlement, where Vedic rituals were being performed regularly.
5. Such a resort would become a reputed centre of wisdom after some time.
6. Rishipattana is said to be of remote antiquity, i.e. much older than the time of the historical Buddha.
7. Mrigadaya was selected for the First Sermon, because it was in the vicinity of Rishipattana, the reputed settlement of learned and wise persons.

The search for Rishipattana was guided by these assumptions. Amidst the ancient settlements of Varanasi, which have come to light through archaeological investigations (Fig. 2), Aktha appears to fulfill all the above criteria. The findings of the site when applied on the proposed interpretative model helped identification of Rishipattana. Its nature too could be ascertained on account of material remains.

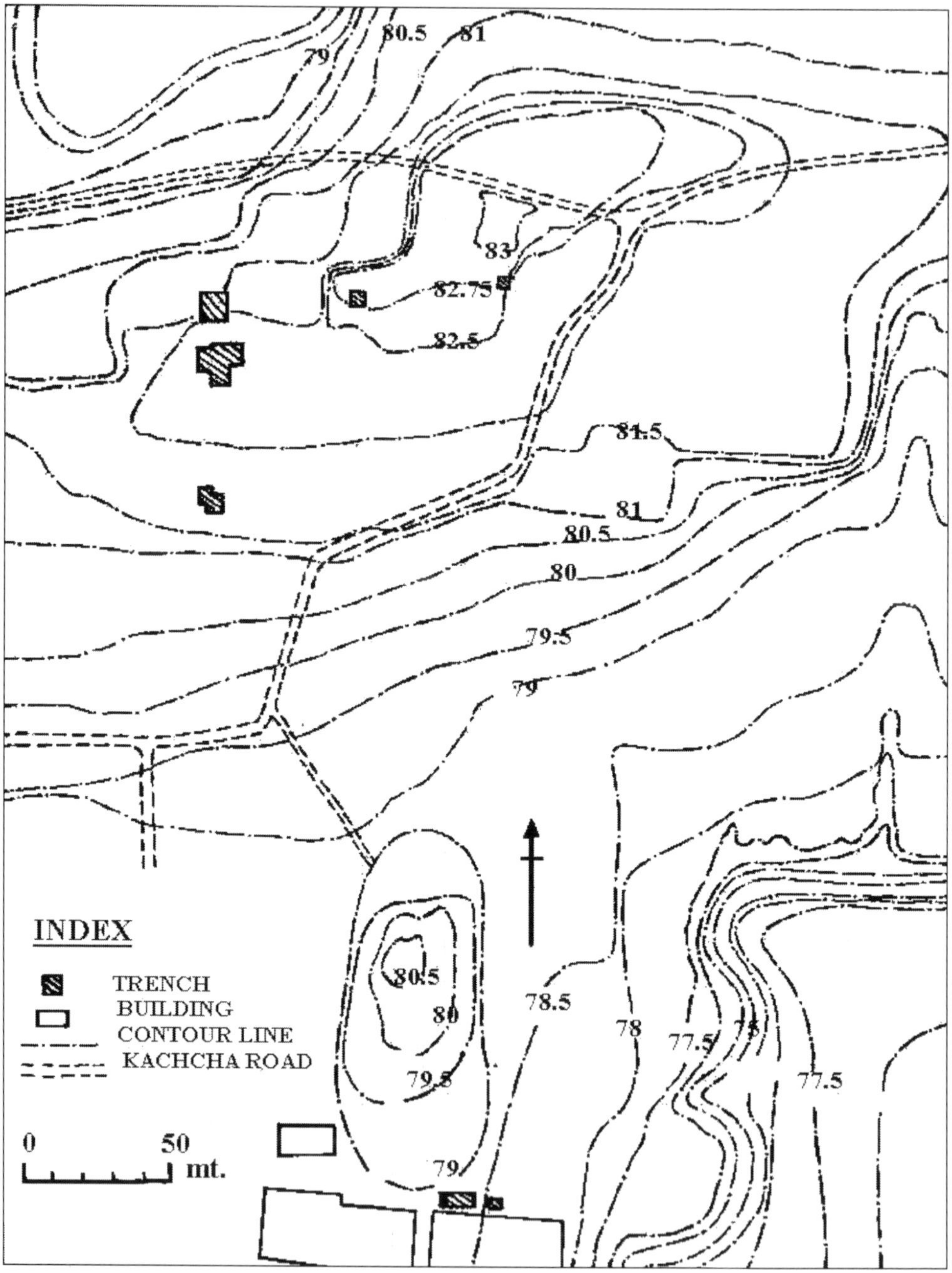

10. Site plan of Aktha.

THE EXPOSED MATERIAL REMAINS OF RISHIPATTANA

The vicinity of Sarnath, particularly the Varuna basin, was explored by me in the year 1994 (Jayaswal 1998). The aim of the investigation was to locate satellite settlements meeting day to day requirements of the famous Buddhist establishment of Sarnath. Two streams, the Aktha-*nala* and Rajapur-*nala*, which originate from Sarang-tal, by the side of which the Buddhist monument complex is located, drain respectively in Varuna and Ganga rivers (Fig. 2). Survey of the banks of the streams, Aktha and Narokhar *nalas*, brought to light an ancient settlement near the modern village Aktha (Jayaswal 1998: 110-11). This site is less than one kilometre (as the crow flies) from the Buddhist establishment of Sarnath. Thus, it was easily approachable from Sarnath. Aktha was excavated in the years 2002 and 2004 with the aim to ascertain its nature and habitation sequence (Jayaswal 2009) and again in 2008-09 (Jayaswal 2009a) to confirm the antiquity of the earliest occupation, through scientific dating.

The site of Aktha is spread in an area of about one square kilometre. The Narokhar-*nala* demarcates the northern boundary of this mound. Flowing from the side of the *Paharia* mound, it passes through the western part of the raised ground. Another stream, Aktha-*nala*, which connects the ancient religious settlement of Sarnath with Aktha, meets a little beyond the north-western boundaries of this site. These channels provide a good natural protection to the flat plateau-like land (Fig. 11). The ancient settlement was located over this stretch of plain land. The surrounding water channels were a good source of water to the inhabitants, and the peripheral region was marked by vast fertile land. The presumed ecology of the locality might have been grassland with patches of tree grooves—an ambience attractive to sages and Rishis to live in serenity and peace.

The ancient settlement at Aktha was in existence between the second quarter of the 2nd millennium BCE and the 3rd century CE, and the archaeological horizon exposed here measured 7.5 metres in thickness. It was divided into 18 layers. The chrono-cultural sequence reconstructed through the findings of these layers is of: the Later Vedic (Period I), the

11. View of Locality-1 with cluster of sculptures, Aktha.

Janapada (Period II), the Maurya-Sunga (Period III), Kushan (Period IV) and Late-Kushan (Period V) times. In this sequence, Period I was pre-Buddhist, while most of Period II could be assigned to the time of Buddha. Remains of the later half of Period III of Aktha are contemporary to the early structures of Sarnath, which are dated to the time of the Mauryan king Asoka. The succeeding periods, IV and V, too were significant, as during this time Sarnath became a reputed religious place, where large offerings of icons and structures were made by the devotees. But, contrary to Sarnath, the significance of Aktha diminished from the Late Kushan period, and it was soon abandoned. The Gupta period, which is unrepresented at Aktha, was the golden period in the history of Sarnath.

The dwelling remains at Aktha were confined to two pockets—the north and the south of the land encircled by streams. At Locality-1 was unearthed remains of later times, while at Locality-2, was the earliest settlement. Locality-1, in the form of a small mound, is situated near the present village. Scattered over its surface were a few early medieval icons, including a Siva-*linga*. Also, at the western periphery of this locality was discovered earlier Yaksha idol, which is now housed in the Sarnath Museum. This image has been dated to the 1st /2nd century BCE (Lin-Bodien 1981). Digging of the site was initiated here, in the year 2002 (Jayaswal 2003), and later in the year 2009 (Jayaswal 2009). As a result, it could be ascertained that this locality was under occupation from the Janapada (Period II) to Late Kushan (Period V) times.

The other occupation of the site was the southern part (Locality-2), which was closer to the Jhaua-jharan mound. The conical mound of Paharia (the modern vegetable *mandi*), located on the confluence of Narokhar-*nala* and the Varuna river, suggests that a large stupa is buried beneath it. An exposed section cut during a non-archaeological operation, which was closely examined by us during 1994, indicated that at least the lower portion of this structure was made of unbaked bricks. This may be accepted as an early feature of stupa architecture. How early, is difficult to ascertain. But, it may be significant to note that the vicinity of this structure retained the earliest habitation debris of the region. It may not be without significance that the remains of hermitage-based earliest settlements at Aktha were exposed from this part. Moreover, the later cultural deposits of Aktha could not be seen at this locality. Remains of this locality and Period I are to be scrutinised for the identification and reconstruction of the nature of Rishipattana.

An accumulation of habitation debris of about three metres, which was unearthed at Locality-2, belonged to single culture, Period I: The Later Vedic Period. On account of the C_{14} dates obtained from the middle floor of this Period it is dated between c. 1800 and 1450 BCE (Jayaswal 2009 a). It may be mentioned that the dates (obtained by C_{14} method) for the succeeding period, the Janapada or the Northern Black Polished Ware, at Ramnagar are countable to 1200 BCE. Period II at Aktha could not be dated by scientific method. But, remains of the Janapada period were overlying the Later Vedic period deposits without any disruption. It is therefore reasonable to assign continuation of the Period I at Aktha also up to 1200 BCE. If this is accepted, then we are dealing with a broad time span of about 600 years (1800-1200 BCE), when the southern locality, which is also closer to the land route, was a residential area.

The remains of Period I, of Aktha and the scientific dates associated with this deposit, bring it close to the Later Vedic period, which is dated to around 1250–800 or 1400–1000 BCE (Pande 2001: 258). This date bracket is stretched by the C_{14} dates (1800–1200 BCE) by more than five hundred years. Even though the dated contexts of archaeology at Aktha are earlier than the proposed date bracket, it may still be logical to label it to Later Vedic because the date proposed for the Rig Samhitas or the early Vedic composition is of very high antiquity (4000-2500-1400 BCE). Besides the dates, culture contents of the period also appear to correspond with descriptions of material remains of the Later Vedic Samhitas. The earliest occupation of Aktha therefore may be accepted to be of the Later Vedic period.

Excavation of the buried remains of the Later Vedic period at Aktha was of very simple nature. It comprised a rich collection of pottery, pottery-disc, utilised bone of animals, and terracotta bead, ball, wheel, and conical object. There was no trace of use of brick and permanent structure. At least four floors were exposed at Locality-2 of Aktha, in succession. The first one came to light during the excavations of 2001-2002. It was a large floor composed of potsherds, iron pallets and compact clay ramming, which was traced in an exposed area of 4.20 m east-west and 4.95 m north-south (Jayaswal 2009: 60). While, the other three floors were exposed in the year 2008-9 (Jayaswal 2009 a: 142-43). That these floors were extensively in use was also indicated from traces of damage, and thick activity debris like burnt clay, bone and pot fragments, oven and pottery-discs covering its surface. Traces of post-holes associated these floors. Also, some mud wall/platform-like structures were attached to at least two of the floors (Jayaswal 2009a: 142). Floor-10 is of particular significance. A 2.50 x 1 m patch of this was covered with charred animal

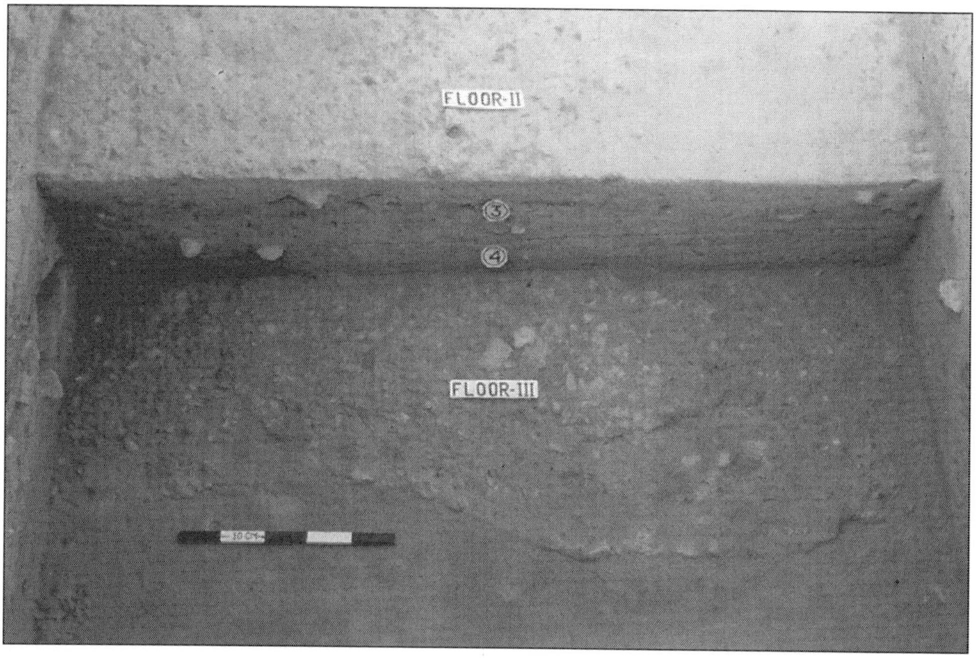

12. View of exposed floor of Later Vedic period, Aktha.

bones and broken pots. Almost in the centre of this floor was placed a circular burnt clay lump (55 cm in diametre and 12 cm high) which had slight depression in the centre. Incidentally, the charcoal samples collected from it were utilised for C_{14} dating, which was mentioned above. A mud wall of 1.85 m length and 0.50 m thickness was at the periphery of this floor and the one lying beneath it (Floor-11). All the findings of Period I of Aktha suggest that the structures of the time were made of perishable material—wood, bamboo, grass (*phusa*) and mud (Fig. 12).

It may not be a coincidence that not only the dates, but even the nature of shelters of Period I of Aktha correspond with the description of the dwellings found in the Later Vedic Samhitas. The texts mention, for instance, that the dwelling houses, *grihas*, were made of wooden posts and beams.

The description available in the Vedic texts further suggest the model which is applicable for the reconstruction of shelters/hutments of the

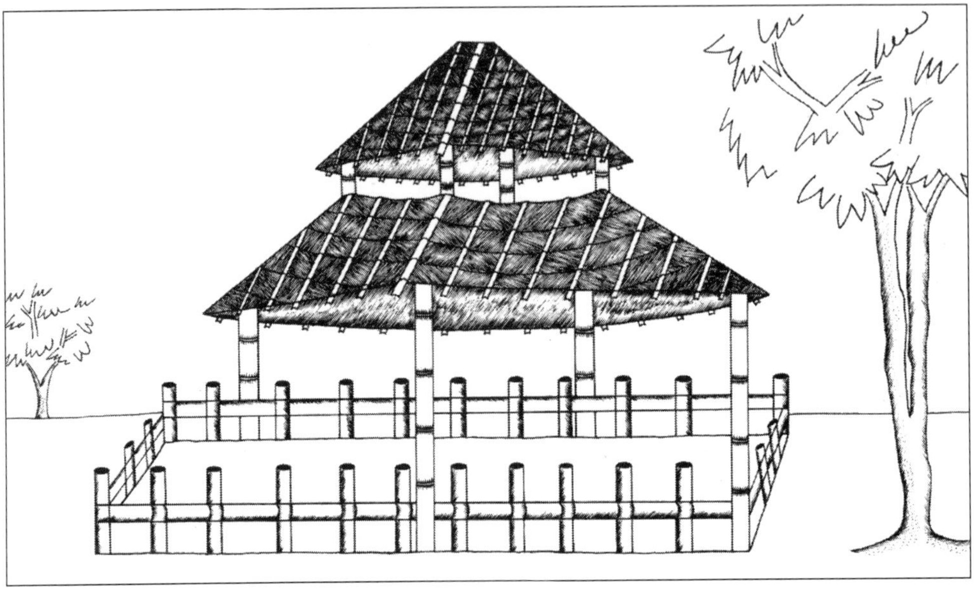

13. Reconstruction of Shala.

Later Vedic times at Aktha. Wooden posts or *upamitas*, for instance, are said to be the upright pillars over which *parimitas* (the horizontal wooden beams) were placed. The latter was to provide support to the superstructure of split bamboo and thatch of the roof (Pande 2001: 268). The *Sala-sukta* of *Atharvaveda* mentions use of *chatai* (mat) and *phusa* (dried grass) for the construction of the superstructure of *salas*. *Sala* provides shelter for rest to the world and wears or is wrapped in chatai, and is covered by *phusa* (Pande 2001: 268-69). Reminiscent of such a structure, which is composed of mats, thatch and wooden posts (Fig. 13), in archaeological context would be the post-holes and the floor, in case it is rammed, like the one which was encountered from the deposits of Period I of Aktha. If this model is accepted, then it may also be held that the nature of the Later Vedic settlement of Aktha was a cluster of *salas*/hutments. This would naturally be in the form of a hermitage-like settlement, presumed residence for sages and rishis.

On the floors and also from the vicinity in the deposit of Period I at Aktha were retrieved pottery-discs, another category closely associated

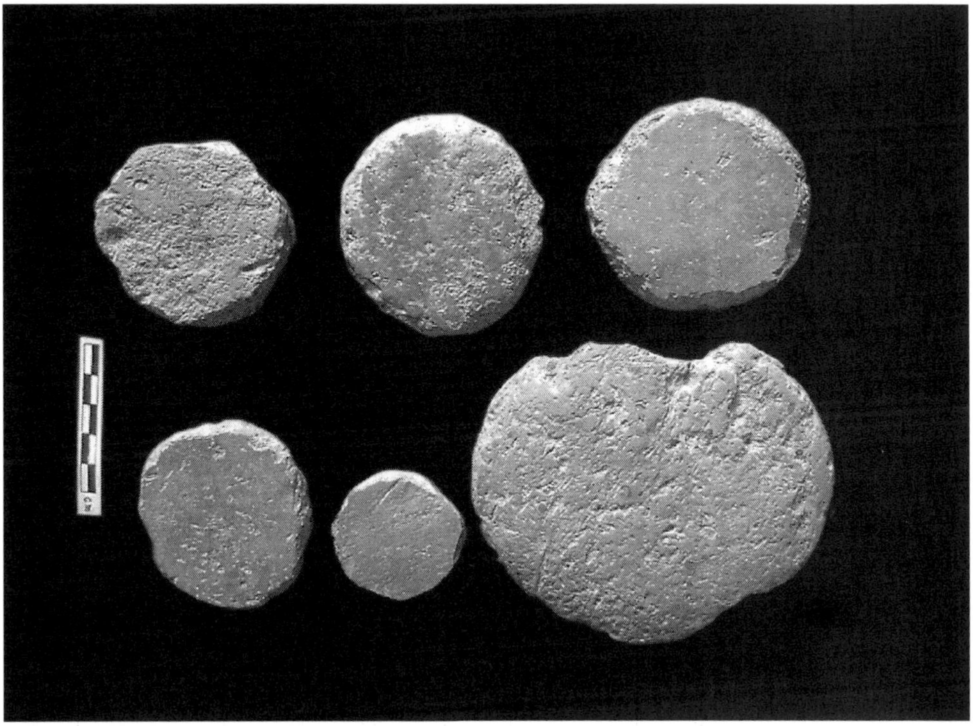

14. Vedic *patra/kapalas* from Aktha.

with Vedic rituals. These are circular potsherds (Jayaswal 2003: 97), which are found in high proportion at proto and early Historic sites of India. Made from the fragment of an earthen pot, this category is often referred to as 'pottery-discs', in archaeological reports. Two types—the perforated and non-perforated pottery-discs—were noted in the antiquity collection of Period I at Aktha (Fig. 14). One is, however, not sure about the ritualistic use of perforated discs. These may be wheels, attached to some figurative clay form, like model of cart, or animal surmounted on wheels, a general presumption. Incidentally, perforated specimens are comparatively restricted in number (19) than the un-perforated discs (102). It is the latter which has been identified by me as kapala, the ritual container in which edible offerings are made to the divinities during the performance of Vedic *yajna* (Jayaswal 2009a: 25-30).

The literal meaning of *kapala* is the broken piece of clay pot or a potsherd, (Dharmadhikari 1989: 20). Mentioned as "pieces broken from a jar" (Kane 1974: 985; 2233), circular or square in shape, these are containers made from shards by grinding their edges. Many a times these were used in group and were placed closer to each other (Eggeling 1882: 34). That this object was utilised individually or collectively, during the performance of Vedic ritual, is apparent from the description of texts. The description for the use of *kapala*s in the *Satapatha-Brahmana* (I.2.I.6), for instance, has been shown through a diagram. The arrangement of eight potsherds or *kapala*s, which is prescribed for use in *Darsapurnamasa-kapalopadhana* sacrifice (Kane 1974: 1031), needs to be arranged in compartments of a circle. The central longitudinal compartment is divided into three, in which from bottom to top are placed three potsherds numbering 1 (*dhurvamasi*), 2 (*dhartramasi*), and 3 (*dharunmasi*). While, in the two blocks of the right longitudinal compartment potsherds number 4 (in upper division, *dharmasi*) and 5 (*marutamsardhah* in the lower division) were to be placed. Similarly, in the left longitudinal compartment, which is divided into three blocks, the remaining three potsherds, viz. 6 (at the bottom, *yantramasi*), 7 (at the top, *vishvabhyah*) and 8 (in the centre, *cidasi*) were kept. It has also been mentioned that the number of *kapala* differs from one to the other sacrifice (Kane 1974: 1031). For example, *Apastamba* mentions placement of *ashta-kapala* for Agni, the *ekadasa-kapala* or *dvadasa-kapala* for Indra-Agni, etc. (Oldenberg & Max Müller 1892: 337. LXXVI). In *Agnishomau,* eleven *kapala*s are to be used for laying offering cake. It is mentioned that ... "after laying down the first four potsherds," (in the centre) "he assigns four of the remaining seven to the southern and three to the northern division" (Eggeling 1882: 34).

Besides arrangements and number of potsherds, one also gets specifications on the shape of *kapala*s in *Satapatha-Brahmana* (Eggeling 1882: 34). For instance, in case of the arrangements of the central compartment of the circle, there is reference for the placement of three square potsherds. "When one potsherd only is required, it is to be of the size of a hand; when two they are to form a circle divided into two equal parts by a line drawn from south to north; when three, the circle is divided into three sections from south to north; when four or five, it is divided into two halves from west to east; and in one case three potsherds are placed in the southern and one (of half-moon shape) in the northern half" (Eggeling 1882: 34). It has been further mentioned that, "The potsherds, though mostly irregular in shape, must always exactly fit one another, so as not to leave any space between. This is effected by rubbing the edges" (Eggeling 1882: 34).

The main characteristic of a *kapala*, which can be summarised from the above description, is that it is one of the main earthen articles utilised during the performance of Vedic rituals. Since these ritualistic offerings are made to the deities in worship through fire, *kapala* are used as a container for these offerings. The numbers to be used may vary, from one to eleven or more, in different rituals. Made from broken part of an earthen vessel, *kapalas* were perhaps made by the devotees by breaking the sides and periphery of the shards. Common shapes of *kapala* were circular, square, semi-circular and irregular. In view to acquire the shape, a part of a jar was acquired. At times the edges of the shaped potsherd were also rubbed.

In archaeological records, shaped potsherds are found in two distinct forms—circular and geometric. Square, triangular, pentagonal, rectangular, semi-circular, pointed and undetermined shapes are the main forms identified in the latter. The circular ones are noted in the archaeological publications under the heads 'Pottery-disc', 'Hopscotch', 'Gamesman', etc. It is the circular-shaped potsherds or the pottery-discs which appear to have wider dispersal both in time and space in the Chalcolithic and Early Iron Age cultures of our subcontinent. The other shaped potsherds are recorded as 'Geometric potsherd', 'Edge ground potsherd', etc., and are not only restricted in number, but have been reported from only a few sites of the Ganga plain. In view to separate these categories I prefer to use terms 'pottery-disc', and 'geometric potsherds'.

Both circular and geometric shapes were prepared from a fragment of an earthen pot. It has been observed that the body of a large vase or base of a pot was suitable for making this circular object (Narain & Roy 1968: 59), which bears all the features of the parent ceramic. For, almost all the types of ceramics of a period, be it Black-and-Red Ware, Northern Black Polished Ware, Black Slipped Ware, Red Ware, Grey Ware, etc., were utilised for the purpose (Gaur 1983: 58-59; Narain & Roy 1968: 59). One also notices all types of fabrics—thin, medium and thick—in the archaeological collections of pottery-discs (Jayaswal 2003: 95-96), suggesting that all kinds of pots which were being used by common men were utilised for making geometric potsherds.

Geometric forms were prepared by two techniques. In one case, the circular or other select shape was acquired by carefully breaking the sides or periphery of the pot fragment. In the other technique, the periphery was also rubbed and ground after the form was made. It may be mentioned that the technique of rubbing the edge was associated mostly with the non-circular shaped potsherds. Both the types—the non-ground edged and the ground edged geometric forms—occur almost side by side in all periods of early historical sites of the Ganga plain. No definite pattern could be noticed in the making technique either in terms of chronology or spatial distribution.

The average size of pottery-discs found from the protohistoric and early historic levels of the Ganga plain have a range of 5-6 cm (diametre). But, one may encounter smaller (about 3 cm) and larger (about 7 cm) discs also, though these are proportionately less. The thickness of these specimens depends on the type of potsherd it has been made from. The pottery-discs on typological considerations may be classified primarily into two categories—un-perforated and the perforated. The perforated category consists of other sub-types as specimen with one hole in the centre; two holes in the centre; and three holes in the centre. Though un-perforated pottery discs preponderate almost all the ancient collections, the perforated ones also occur side by side, in which single perforated discs fare well in comparison to the others.

Pottery-discs of archaeological collections show close parallelism with the description of *kapala* in shape, size and the medium (potsherd). For, as mentioned in the text that *kapala*s are broken pots, the pottery-discs are also made from fragments of an earthen pot. Both of these objects are circular or non-circular geometric in shape. It may be mentioned that the dimension mentioned for *kapala* in the texts is given as one-fourth the size of a palm. If an average size of palm of an adult is divided into four parts, one part of it will be able to accommodate a geometric potsherd of about 5-6 cm diametre or length. It is also noteworthy that an average size, which has been recorded for the archaeological specimens, tallies more or less with this size. But, the height specified for *kapala* in the text, thickness of two fingers, indicating use of thick pots, does not always correspond with the geometric potsherds. For, in archaeological specimens thin potsherds have also been used, as in the case of potsherds made on Painted Grey.

It may be interesting to mention two archaeological contexts which have close correspondence with the recommendation of the use of *kapalas* in rituals. From the Painted Grey Ware levels, at Jakhera, for instance, near a fire pit a heap of pottery-discs were unearthed by M.D.N. Sahi. This context has been mentioned to be indicative of the use of pottery-discs in ritual (Ref. Singh 2004: 362). For, the most promising feature of the above-mentioned context of Jakhera is the heap of pottery-discs near a fire pit, which indicates that in the actual incidence there was a close association of fire altar (*agni-kund*) with that of the pottery-discs. It has been shown earlier that a number of *kapala* are recommended to be used by devotee/devotees while performing the *yajna*, in front of the *agni-kund* or the fire altar. During the performance of *yajna,* after placing a number of *kapala* for offering to various deities, it has further been specified that the remaining ones be piled up (in

Kanvasatapathabrahmanam II.1.4.7- II.1.4.10). The devotee says, "I place you for all the directions (quarters), for the destruction of the enemy." The others (remaining potsherds) (he places) either saying, 'Accumulated above are you' (he places them) (verily silently) (Swaminathan 1997: 29). It appears that the devotee was required to prepare a considerable number of *kapala* for performing a *yajna*. And after arranging a few as per the prescription of the ritual, the remaining ones were to be accumulated. The context unearthed at Jakhera is perhaps reminiscent of one such *yajna* performed during the time of Painted Grey Ware culture. It also would suggest that the pottery discs and geometric shapes found in the archaeological horizons of early historic times are related to the performance of Vedic rituals. Similar conclusions may be drawn in case of unperforated pottery-discs and geometric potsherds of Period I of Aktha, which were objects of Vedic ritual worship.

At Maski, from Megalithic deposits a burial of a child was found containing a pottery-disc. It has been recorded that "a plain un-pierced one from the gravel pit of a child (Period II, Megalithic burial of Class B (iv)", was placed on the chest of the skeleton (Thapar 1957: 110; Pl. XXIX A, 12). This particular specimen has been identified with the play object belonging to the deceased. But, the descriptive account of the Vedic Samhitas, provides clue to its use during the performance of a death ritual. The death ritual as described in the *Asvalayana-grhya-sutra* (Oldenberg 1886: 240; IV.3.5) lists *kapala* as an object of offering on the body of the deceased. "He then should put the following sacrificial implements (on the dead body), viz. in to the right hand the spoon called *Juhu,* in the left hand the spoon *Upabhrt,* ... on his chest head and teeth respectively the *dhruva* (the big sacrificial ladle), the dishes (or the *kapalas*), the pressing stones ..." (Kane 1973: 204-07). It may be deduced that, as per the recommendation of the ancient texts, the practice for both earthen pots and *kapala* as mortuary offering goods may have been in existence during Megalithic times. The pottery-disc in such a context was representative of the earthen pot, an after-death utility item for the deceased, and not an object which was used for play by the child, as has been surmised by the excavator. Whether pottery-discs made on Black-and-Red Ware were associated with mortuary ritual, could only be a guess in the present state of our knowledge. But its possibility is also indicated by the fact that Black-and-Red Ware pottery is usually associated with Megalithic burials. These references further suggest that use of *kapalas* in death rituals too was a Vedic practice.

Made primarily from earthen pots, *kapalas* were composed of all the varieties of ceramic which were used by the common man of the Later Vedic times at Aktha. Made out of Black Slipped and the Red Wares, a total of 102 geometric pottery forms were retrieved from this period, out of which only four were made from the Black Slipped Ware. In the remaining, 44 specimens were made from slipped Red Ware and 54 from un-slipped plain Red Ware. In this collection similar to pots, pottery-discs also are characterised by coarse, medium and fine fabric. Likewise, broken parts of Black Slipped and Red wares, which were catering to the major portion of the need of pots and pans, were used for making pottery-discs at Aktha. Does it not suggest that all the typo-technological types of earthen pots, which were in use by the Later Vedic residents of Aktha, were also the food offering containers for the gods, in worship? Moreover, it was noted that pottery-discs made on Black-and-Red Ware sherd are conspicuously absent at Aktha. Does it not suggest that habitation floors of Aktha were used for daily *yajna* performance, and were completely devoid of mortuary rituals practices?

The earthen pots used by the earliest occupants of Aktha were almost of the same fabric as containers used for offering food to the divinities. Also, the ceramic collection of Period I of this site is the most pronounced category of antiquities. It may be mentioned that this is the most common feature of excavated sites of the middle Ganga Valley in particular and the Indian subcontinent in general. All the needs of edible consumption at the time were catered by earthen pots and pans. Thus, pottery in an archaeological horizon conveys a number of facets of the contemporary society. The colour and texture, for instance, reveal technological attainments while the shape and size convey modelling skills and the requirements of the users. Similarly, the surface treatment of pots in the form of slip, colouring and painting are reflections of socio-religious practices. Together, the techno-morphological features of ceramic collections reveal close interaction between the expertise of pottery production and requirements of its consumers. It is, therefore, not surprising that pottery receives considerable attention of archaeologists who invariably designate a large part of the reports on excavated sites to the earthen pots. This exercise was also followed by me in the detailed report on Aktha (Jayaswal 2009). Instead of reproducing the section on pottery of the report, a concise picture along with interpretation of some main tendencies of ceramic collection of Later Vedic Period of Aktha is mentioned below.

The collection of ceramic from Period I at Aktha comprised three main categories—Black-and-Red Ware, Black Slipped Ware and Red Ware. These are named so because of the colour of the surfaces. For instance, the Black-and-Red Ware is characterised by both red and black surfaces of a single pot. In case of Black Slipped Ware, the entire pot retains a smooth black interior, as well as exterior (Fig. 15). Whereas, a Red Ware pot is red in colour. It may be mentioned that pots of all the three wares were produced from clay acquired from a common source, like pond bed, river bank or fields. Preparation of clay for all the three wares too was the same. That is, in all the cases impurities were to be removed and the clay was kneaded. The finer clay or the clay mixed with coarse grains like sand, husk, etc. does not affect the colour, but it results in determining the texture of the pots which are usually classified as fine, medium and coarse fabric. It is the process of baking which provides colour to baked earthen forms (Jayaswal & Krishna 1986). For giving shape to the vessels, potter's wheel was in use, which can be recognised by the regular circular striation marks on the surface of most of the wheel-made pots. The modelled clay pots, as per the present practice, are dried first in shade.

15. Potsherds obtained from Later Vedic Period, Aktha.

Slip over the surface when applied is prepared by mixing some ingredients like juice of bamboo leaves and mango barb, etc., in very fine grained clay (*kabis)* mixture. Pots are covered with this solution or may be dipped in watery solution in leather hard condition. This practice goes back many hundred years and can easily be pushed back to the Later Vedic period. Traces of this surface treatment are distinct in all the three types of above-quoted wares. The question is then: what makes the three different from one another?

In the traditional process of earthen pottery production, two methods—close kiln and inverted firing techniques—are used for baking. The pots which turn red after baking are fired in close kilns, a practice prevalent from the remote past till today (Fig. 16). Pots are arranged individually usually within a shallow circular pit (Jayaswal & Krishna 1986: 57). Fuel, straws, hay (*pual*), dry leaves, cow dung, etc. are arranged along with the clay models. The entire heap of models in such a kiln is

16. Kiln for baking red pots.

covered with a layer of fuel, which is then plastered with a thick coat of clay, with a hole at the lower part/bottom. The kiln is lit for six to eight hours. As a result of this firing, the baked models turn red.

However, in black pottery, which is baked by inverted firing, smoke is generated periodically during the process in the lit kiln, which in this case may be a large earthen pot, or a small composition which can be opened while the process of baking is in progress (Fig. 17). Fuel, mostly in the form of goat dung or cow dung, is added to generate smoke throughout the process of baking. This inverted firing technique converts the entire pot, grey and/or black, after the baking process in complete. The thick slip provided on the pots at the pre-firing stage, if rubbed with oil, results in shiny black surfaces, as one notices in the case of Black Slipped Ware.

Production of Black-and-Red pottery involves principals of both the techniques—the close kiln with constant inflow of oxygen—and at the same time disruption of oxygen in such a way that parts of the pot are

17. Kiln for baking black pots.

kept hidden and protected from receiving it. This is done by arranging the clay models in a special way. In case of baking a Black-and-Red Ware, the pots are placed in the kiln fixing one over the other, and are not placed individually, as is the case of producing a red pot. This is done so that half or a little portion of the pot is covered by the other. When placed in a kiln, only the open portion of the pot receives oxygen and turns red after baking. The hidden portion which is deprived of oxygen flow during the baking process turns black. The well-baked pot in this case generally retains a black interior, while its upper half of exterior turns red, leaving the lower exterior also black. A blotchy line of demarcation between the twin colours may be seen, suggestive of filtration of oxygen in the covered place, making it distinct from the bi-colouring of the surface. The line of separation of red and black surfaces, if it is so painted, is distinctly marked. Black and red pottery, thus, represents special skills and deliberate efforts of baking earthen models. The above-mentioned three categories of pottery of Period I of Aktha, thus, are the result of two firing techniques, which result in black (Black Slipped Ware) or red (Red Ware). While, the third one—Black-and-Red Ware—is a combination of the two.

The Black-and-Red Ware in the Later Vedic Period at Aktha was in use in very restricted proportion (Jayaswal 2009: 61). This ware is important for two reasons. One, that it is made of a special firing technique, and the other, that it occurs in quite early context (early 2nd millennium BCE) in the Ganga plain. The pre-iron using archaeological horizons of the region, for instance, Period II (dated to 1450-1200 BCE) of Atranjikhera (Gaur 1983), and Period I (1200-700 BCE) of Narhan (Singh 1994: 63-64) are characterised by this ceramic. The C_{14} dates of Period I of Aktha (1800-1200 BCE) also align with the above date bracket. It may be mentioned that occurrence of Black-and-Red Ware in various culture contexts, like Megalithic, Chalcolithic, Early Iron Age, etc., too, is an issue to be debated in detail at some point of time.

Black-and-Red Ware pots used during the Later Vedic times at Aktha were mostly small and large bowls with restricted number of dishes (Fig. 18). These shapes also have been reported from other contemporary sites of the Ganga plain. The glaring similarity may be noticed in the bowls of Period I of Aktha and Narnah (Singh 1994: 63-64). At both sites, use of very large bowl-shaped pots, with comparatively thin sides, was common. A range of forms in the shape of rim sides along with some such special types as lipped bowl/basin were also found at both the sites. Similarly, dishes which are not recorded in Black-and-Red Ware, at Narhan, and found at Aktha resembled some forms associated with Period II at Atranjikhera (Gaur 1983: Fig. 33; D-1b). Black-and-Red Ware of Later Vedic Period of Aktha, like other contemporary sites, are characterised by table ware shapes, for serving

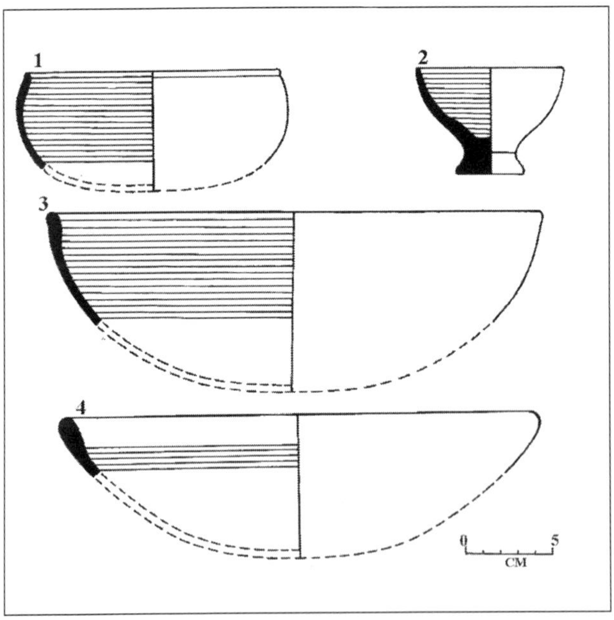

18. Main shapes of Black-and-Red Ware pots, Aktha.

and consuming food. But, their archaeological context, placement in the Megaliths (post-cremation burials) and unearthed burial at Maski does indicate utilisation of Black-and-Red Ware in mortuary rituals.

Occurrence of Black Slipped Ware was comparatively higher than the Black-and-Red Ware. It may be recalled that occurrence of this ceramic from early dated context in Period II of Atranjikhera, Period I of Narhan and Period IA at Rajghat, further confirms the early date for Period I of Aktha. Made of medium to fine fabric, this ceramic tradition was constituted primarily by bowls and dishes (Fig. 19). Deep bowls and beakers, with and without pedestal, were the main forms. The pot fragments of the Aktha collection in most of the cases are weathered as a result of which the black slipping is peeled off and traces are available in patches. A series of range in colour of the core of the pots was noticed, which were of white, steel grey and smoky grey. Black slipping, whenever found, was thick, uniform and of good quality. Though there were basin or large bowls (diameter more than 25 cm), the main size and forms of

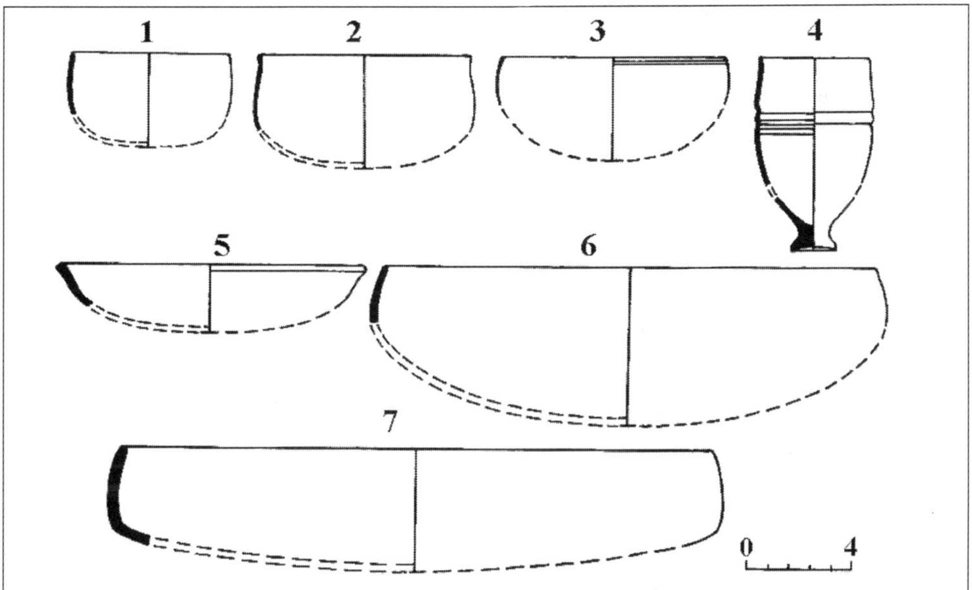

19. Bowls and dishes in Black Slipped Ware, Aktha.

this pottery were bowls and dishes, representing the table ware set. The worn-out surface condition (removal of black slip) of Black Slipped Ware shards from Period I of Aktha, may suggest long duration use of this pottery.

Red Wares formed the major bulk of pottery retrieved from Period I at Aktha. It was characterised by all the three fabrics—coarse, medium and fine—and also untreated and slipped surfaces. In most cases, the core of the pots was of light or pale red shades, but was covered with thick deep red or chocolate slip. No painted pot was noted at this site. Besides a wide range of bowls and dishes, *ghata*-shaped vases, basin, *handi,* etc. were common (Fig. 20). In the collection of Aktha, the characteristic shape in bowls was marked by narrow mouth and wider bases.

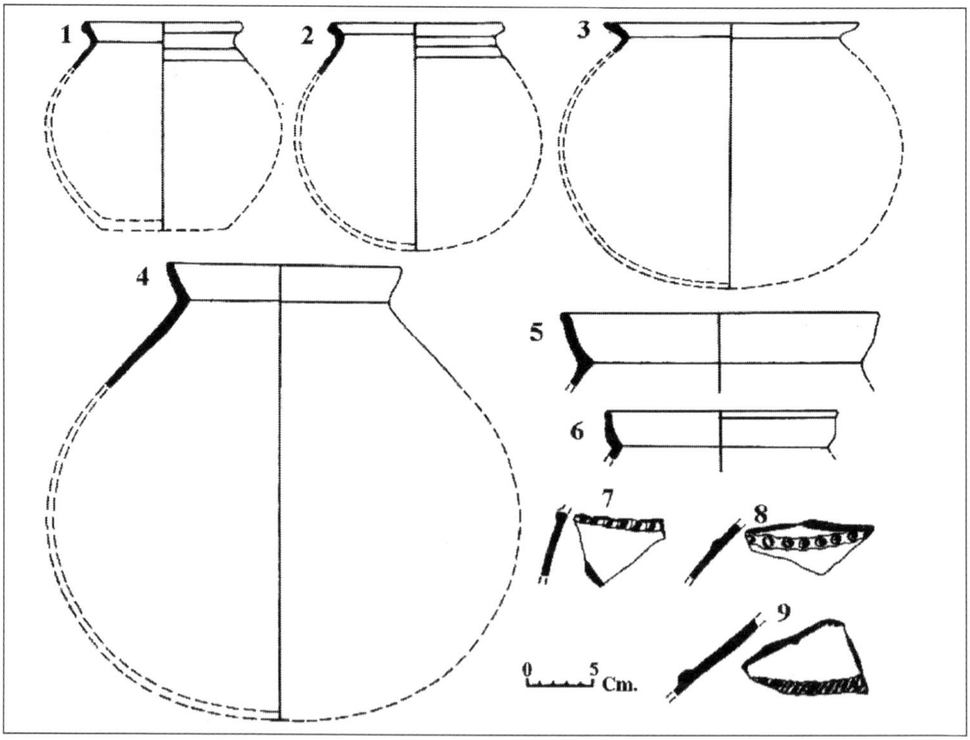

20. *Ghata* and storage pots in Red Ware, Aktha.

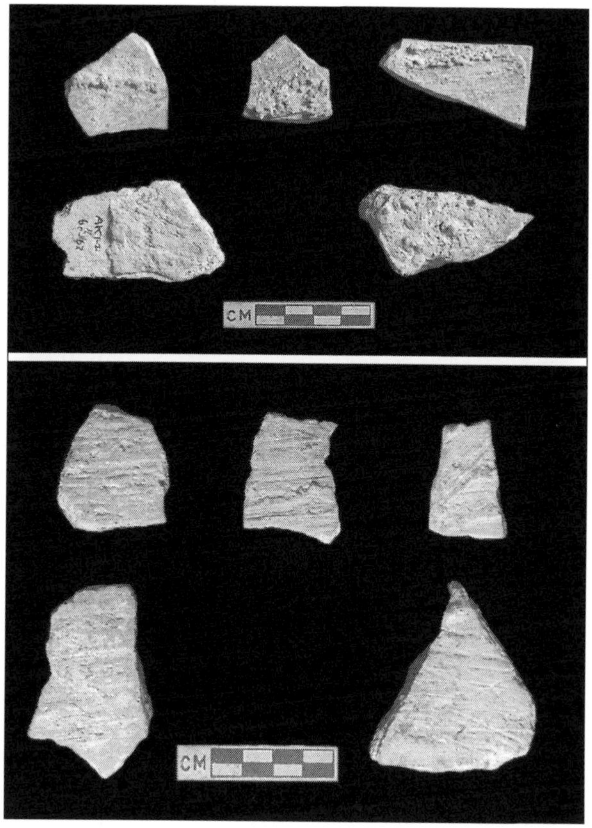

21. Hay impressed gritty ware pottery, Aktha.

A distinct type in the collection of Red Wares of Period I at Aktha was Pale-Red-Gritty Ware (Jayaswal 2009 a: 144). Its core is rough due to the presence of small hematite granules, which were mixed in the clay prior to the modelling of the pots. But, the smooth upper surface of the pots suggests that the modelling of the shapes was done on fast wheel. A good proportion of this category was treated with applying thick paste like slip on the upper, inner or both the surfaces, in leather hard condition (Fig. 21). A good number of these retained hay impression. Horizontal, slanting and zigzag striation marks, pressed with a bunch of hay *(pual),* over the thick slip coated surface of the pots in leather hard condition, is a distinct feature of this pottery. As a result, the slip sticks to the body of pots as an applied layer of gritty paste with crude thin, broad and uneven striation marks. The purpose for such a surface treatment is not known. But, the tradition appears to continue for centuries at this site. For, in an oven of Late Kushan times (Period V) at Aktha, deep red wheel-made pottery with similar thick coat was found in large quantities. The context suggested use of such pottery with fire altar/ritual.

The most striking feature of earthen pots utilised by the Akthians of the Later Vedic times was the simplicity of the unpainted surfaces. Existence

22. Painted Black-and-Red Ware bowl, Narhan.

of painted potsherds was conspicuously absent in the ceramic collection of Period I at Aktha. This tendency particularly becomes pronounced when one finds that use of painted pots in some of the other contemporary sites of the Ganga plain was quite frequent (Fig. 22). Take for example, Narhan, where in an almost contemporary context, painted pots are present in a large proportion (Singh 1994: 63-64). But, similar to Aktha, there are some other sites, like Atranjikhera (Period II), where the use of undecorated or unpainted pots was prevalent. Whether these two diverse tendencies are indicative of existence of different communities or class of users, is a question which rises naturally in one's mind. Does it not suggest that users of pottery of the earliest period here were indifferent to decorated pots and pans? In other words, is not this tendency characteristic of the presumed lifestyle of saints and rishis ? If yes, then the later Vedic inhabitants of Aktha may be identified as sages or rishis.

Another noteworthy feature of the Aktha finding is that the number of antiquities, or the daily utility items, besides pottery and *kapala*s, is very restricted. Made on terracotta (baked clay), metal (iron and copper) and bone, the objects comprise simple domestic articles. Take for example, the total number of terracotta beads found from Period I at Aktha was eleven. Made mostly by wheel, and kiln-fired, these beads are primarily *ghata* and areca-nut shapes. The type identified as springle-whorl (*takli)* has a wide historical coverage, both in terms of time and space, in the Ganga plain. This

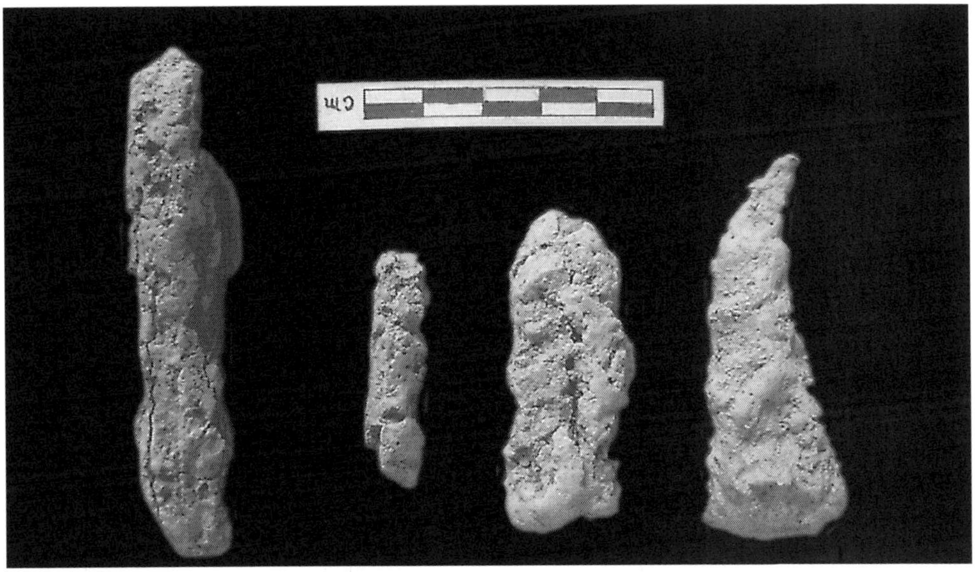

23. Iron objects of Later Vedic times, Aktha.

is testified from the reporting of the sites Rajghat (Narain & Roy 1977), Prahladpur (Narain & Roy 1968), Sravasti (Sinha 1967), Hastinapur (Lal 1985), Tilmanpur (Jayaswal 1998: Fig.7; 1-6), Atranjikhera (Gaur 1983), and Bhitari (Jayaswal 2001: Fig. 50; 1-7) etc. Occurrence of springle-whorl at all the early historical settlements suggest cloth weaving on large scale by a large number of inhabitants. Whether it was done by individual families or by a particular section of the society is difficult to ascertain. But, weaving cloth was in vogue at Rishipattana is evident by the findings of springle-whorl in Period I at Aktha.

Besides beads, only one terracotta ball (d.1.75 cm) and disc (d. 5 cm) were found from Period I of Aktha. Both of these were made of well-levigated clay and were kiln fired.

The Akthians of the Later Vedic period were well versed in iron technology. In the category of iron implements, sickle and chisel were identified (Fig. 23). Due to imperfect technology, most of the specimen received heavy corrosion. Though both of the above objects were discovered from the upper horizons, it may be mentioned that disintegrated iron lumps were noted throughout the deposit of Period I, at Aktha, with the tendency of increase in number in the upper levels. Later Vedic Samhitas mention both copper and iron. The words used for these are *Loha-ayas* (copper) and *Krishna-ayas* (iron). It may be interesting to recall, in Rig Samhitas the word used for metal is *ayas*, which is listed along with gold and silver metals.

Animal bones, food refuge were utilised for various day to day activities in the Later Vedic period at Aktha. Two types of tools associate this Period. One, the finished tools and the other, pointed and edged refuge. The tool-kit of finished implements comprised points and arrow-heads, which together total eight, out of the total of 16 bone artifacts (Fig. 24). The other category, which is marked by cut and broken pieces, was also of equal proportion and appeared to have been domestic utility implements for piercing and scraping. Some of the bone tools bore marks of roasting. Besides food for this could also be deliberate efforts to provide durability to the working edge. Use of bone tools is a common feature of a number of protohistoric and early historic sites, while the utilisation of broken bone fragments as tools has been reported from the Neolithic-Chalcolithic levels (dated to around 1200 BCE) of Senuwar (Thakur & Jayaswal 1991).

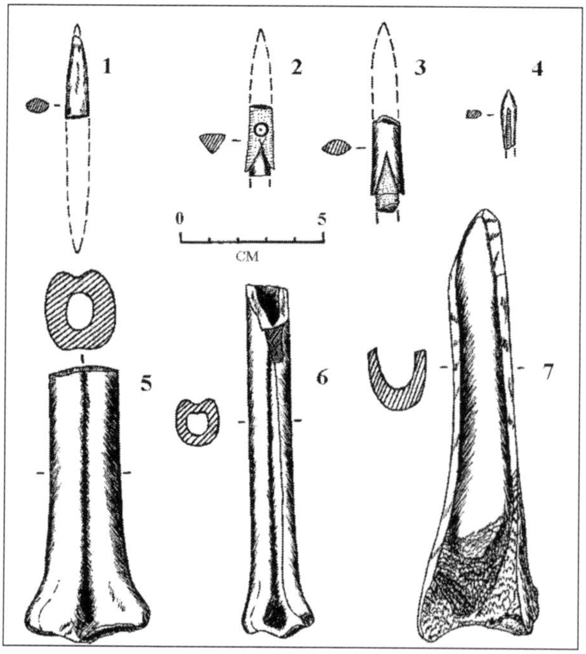

24. Bone tools of Later Vedic times, Aktha.

A highly restricted use of lithic and iron media was in use for daily utility items. This is testified from the above description of the antiquities of Period I of Aktha. Bone appears to be a comparatively common medium, and was perhaps exploited to its capacity for finished products and also in natural/little modified forms. Use of bone, stone and iron though was common in the Later Vedic period, according to literary accounts; the distinct craft of the period was *dorn silpa* or carpentry, with a list of articles in use (Pande 2001: 264-65). The chisel made of iron, found from Period I at Aktha, was one of the essential components of the carpenters' tool-kit. This implies that a number of wooden articles must have been used during this period. The restricted number of daily utility articles found in association with the deposit of the period appears to be result of two factors: the most common medium used during the period was wood, which has perishable quality, and also perhaps the nature of settlement was such that only limited amount of articles were used, as would be in the case of a hermitage or an *ashram*. Both these factors were perhaps applicable for Period I at Aktha.

The reason for Aktha becoming a resort (*pattana*) for sages (*rishi*s) was its special geographical advantages. This settlement was situated at the junction of such major routes which connected various regions passing through Kashi Janpada. There was "the old Grand Trunk Road from Rajgriha through Banaras, Saketa and Sravasti towards Taxila and frontiers, linking India with Central and Western Asia" (Mookerji 1980: 606). The modern land route connecting north and south Bihar and various parts of Uttar Pradesh touches Aktha. The city of Varanasi is a little away (about 5-6 km south). Aktha marks the junction of the highways connecting Gorakhpur-Allahabad, Ballia-Lucknow, Lucknow-Buxar, Ayodhya-Vaisali, Ayodhya-Patna, etc. Of course, all these routes are much later in date. But their proto-types might have served the moving populations of the second millennium BCE.

The hypothesis that settlements located on junctions of important trade routes soon develop into cities is not applicable to Aktha. For, in spite of the geographical advantage, this settlement did not become an urban centre. On the contrary, it appears to continue as a hermitage-

25. Terracotta model of a *Rishi*, Aktha.

based settlement. That the hermitage bias of the place continued in subsequent centuries too is testified from the findings of Periods II-V. For, reminiscent of fire rituals, related pottery and antiquities were found in the deposits of Janapada to Kushan times. A supporting clue for the above assumption—that Aktha was the resort of *rishis* and sages—may be had from a terracotta human figurine (Jayaswal 2009. Pl. XXV) which was retrieved from the upper level of Period III (Fig. 25). Though later in date, it is noteworthy for its peculiar features. On account of high conical hair dress like *Jata-Juta*, this figure can be identified as a hermit or might be a clay effigy of a Vedic rishi who lived at Rishipattana.

Akthians were adapted to the Varuna valley ecology for more than about two thousand years, the earlier half (1200 years) of which was pre-Buddha. Testified by the thickness of the earliest horizon (about 3 m thick), the Period I at Aktha suggests hermitage-habitat marked by simplicity in artefacts. The main reason for the establishment of Aktha in the Later Vedic period appears to be movements of saints from north to south-east on the northern land route, or the route of migration of communities from the west (Saraswati Valley) to the east (banks of Sadanira in north Bihar). Located by the side of this route, this small settlement appears to

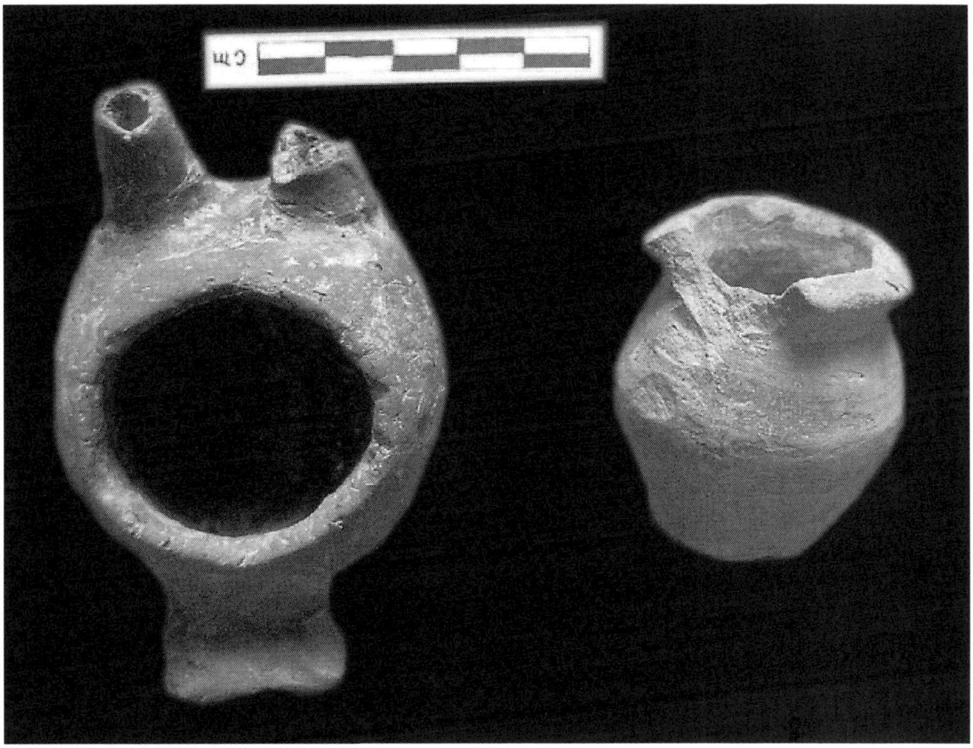

26. Miniature ritual pots, Aktha.

take form of a resort for rishis and sages, who were frequently going up and down between Himalayan region and various parts of the middle Ganga plain. Soon it might have earned fame as the port of the sages, or Rishipattana. That these visitors were followers of Vedic religion is testified by the nature of exposed habitation floors and associated antiquities discussed above. The floors with the use of fire and *kapalas* (the containers of the Vedic sacrifice) are indicative of performance of Vedic ritual at a large scale at Aktha. The hermitage format appears to continue throughout its life span (between 18th century BCE and 3rd/4th century CE) at this settlement (Jayaswal 2009 a).

It may be held that the visit and stay of the sages and the learned ones helped Aktha to gain the reputation of being a centre of wisdom. To Gautama Buddha, who was eager to preach his wisdom and learning to mankind, such a place of reputation would certainly have attracted him. Also, since Aktha was located en route a major connective system of the Indian subcontinent, it was also suitable for the spread of his teachings to distant places. Remains of Period II at Aktha, which is of the Northern Black Polished Ware complex, was of the time when the Lord came to the Rishipattana-Mrigadaya.

Findings of Aktha are significant for the history of Varanasi. Besides pushing back the antiquity of habitation of Varanasi, it has added a significant chapter to the pre-and early Buddhist history of the Ganga plain. Identification of a hermitage-based settlement with profound ritual performance in this area corroborates the place to be a resort of the saints and sages, as described by the scriptures. The categories of daily utility items from the earliest horizon and from all the upper levels also testify to this hypothesis.

3

SARNATH

The Mrigadaya

Sarnath: The Mrigadaya

NOMENCLATURE

It may be interesting to note that the most famous and vibrant Buddhist pilgrimage sites of today, Sarnath, is named after the Brahmanical deity Siva. Cunningham writes, "Sarnath means simply the 'best of Lord', which title is here applied to the god Mahadeva, whose symbol—the *lingam*—is enshrined in the small temple on the bank of the lake (*Sarang-tal*). It is an abbreviation of Saragganatha, or the 'Lord of Deer', appropriate address of Mahadeva, who holds a deer in his left hand" (Cunningham 1871a: 105). But, this certainly is a later address to this holy place. Since, association of the place with the deer is also mentioned in the Buddhist scriptures. It is said that Gautama Buddha, in one of his previous births, roamed here as king of the deer. Impressed by his commitment to save a fellow deer, to be offered to the king of Banaras for his meals, the king not only stopped the practice to accept deer for his kitchen, but, "... made over the park, for the perpetual use of the deer, on which account it was called the 'Deer Park' (*Mrigadava*)" (Cunningham 1871a: 106). In the epigraphic records, Sarnath is addressed as *Saddharmachakra.* Discussed later (Chapter 4), one is not sure if this name of Gupta and medieval times was used widely. But, Mrigadaya appears to be a popular nomenclature for Sarnath in the ancient texts. As has been mentioned earlier, Mrigadava or Mrigadaya is said to be the place where the Lord turned the Wheel of

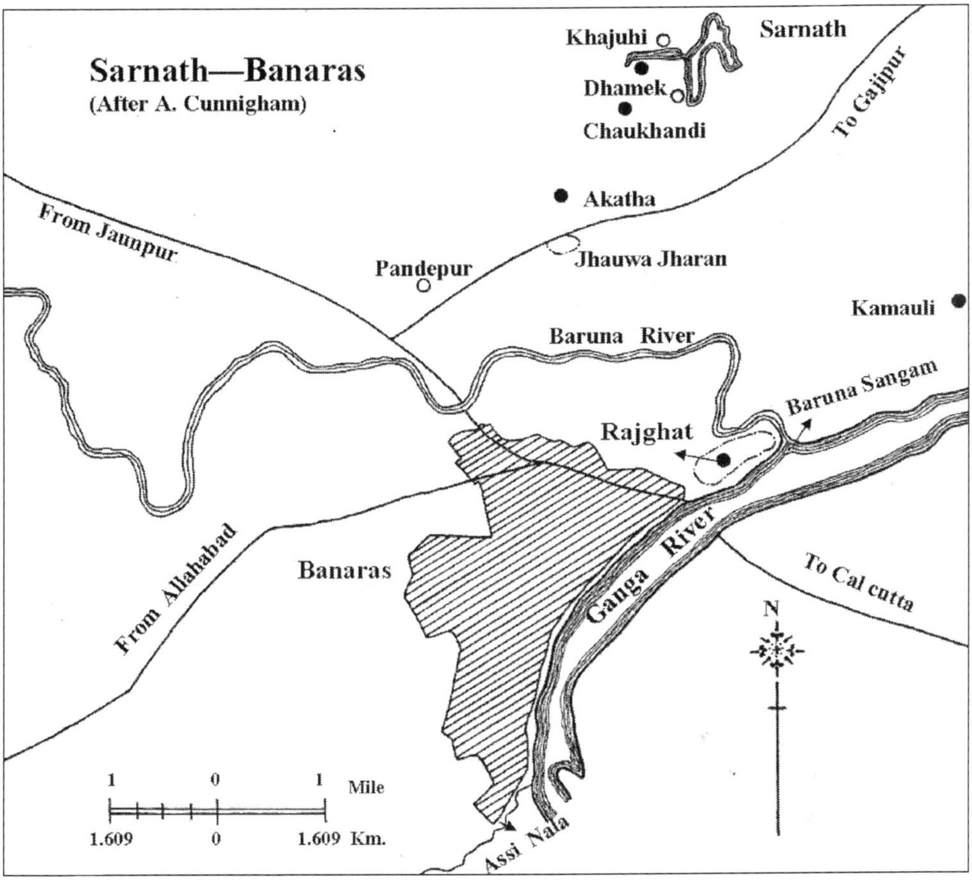

27. Sarnath and other sites of Varanasi.

Law. The archaeological findings of modern Sarnath testify that this place was the ancient Mrigadaya (Fig. 27). Its location, as described in the Buddhist texts, was, "...an open space near Benares where was situated the famous Migadava or Deer Park" (Horner 1951: 214). This also confirms the identification of Sarnath with Mrigadaya.

GEOMORPOLOGY AND ENVIRONMENT

The life span of the Buddhist establishment of Sarnath has been ascertained between 3rd century BCE and 12th century CE. It was abandoned after the later period. Once deserted it was also erased from the memory of the people.

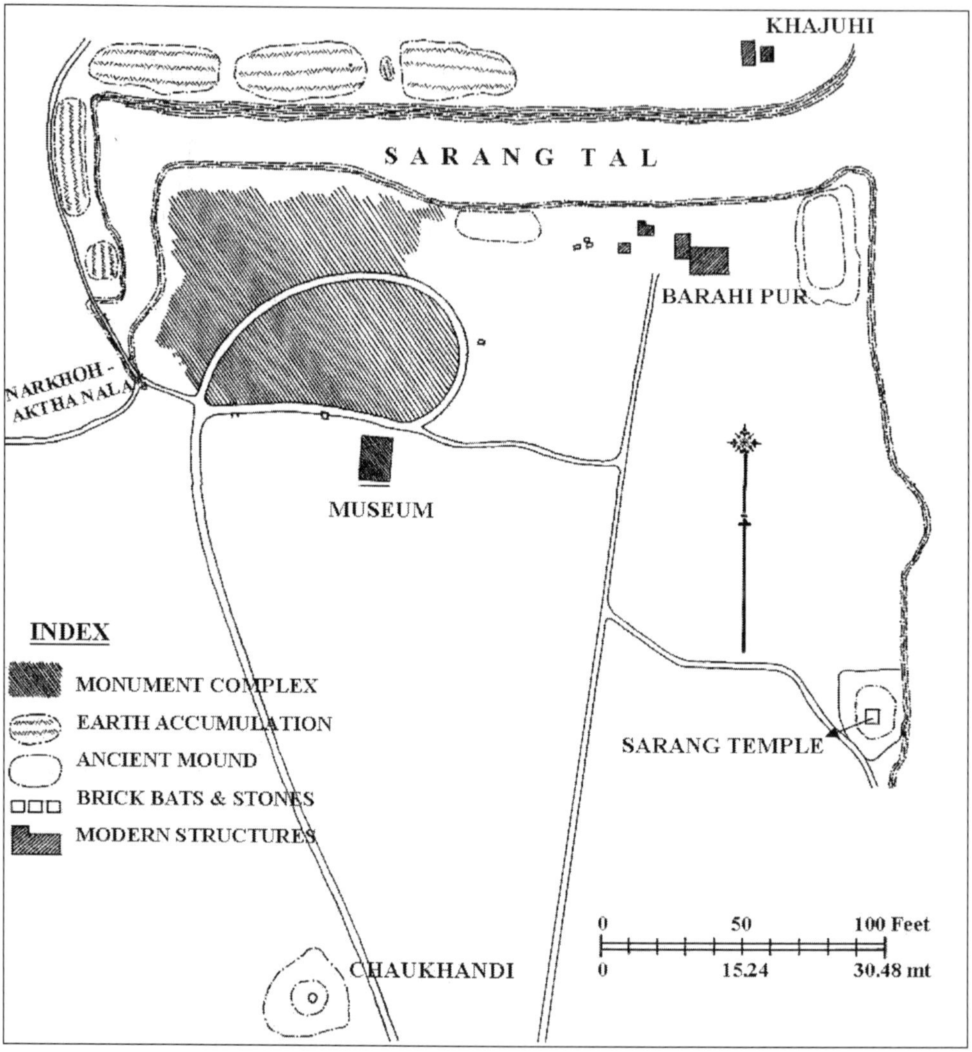

28. Site plan of Sarnath monuments.

After about eight centuries, the site came to light because of a scavenging operation to obtain material from the ruins. The details of this event and other discoveries of eighteenth and early nineteenth centuries are briefed by Cunningham (Cunningham 1871a: 103-30). When he visited Sarnath in 1862, he noticed a mound and five monuments—Dhamek, Chaukhandi, Jagat Singh stupa and two monasteries (Fig. 28). He records that, "With the exception of

Chaukhandi, the whole of these remains are situated on an extensive mound of brick and stone ruins about half a mile long and nearly a quarter of mile broad".

Cunningham also mentions that the mound at Sarnath was surrounded on three sides by water pools. "On the north and east there are three large sheets of water which communicate with one another. To the east lies the Norakar or Sarang-tal, which is 3000 feet long and 1000 feet broad. On the north-east this communicates with the Chandodar or Chandra-tal, which is of the same size but of less irregular shape (Fig. 29).

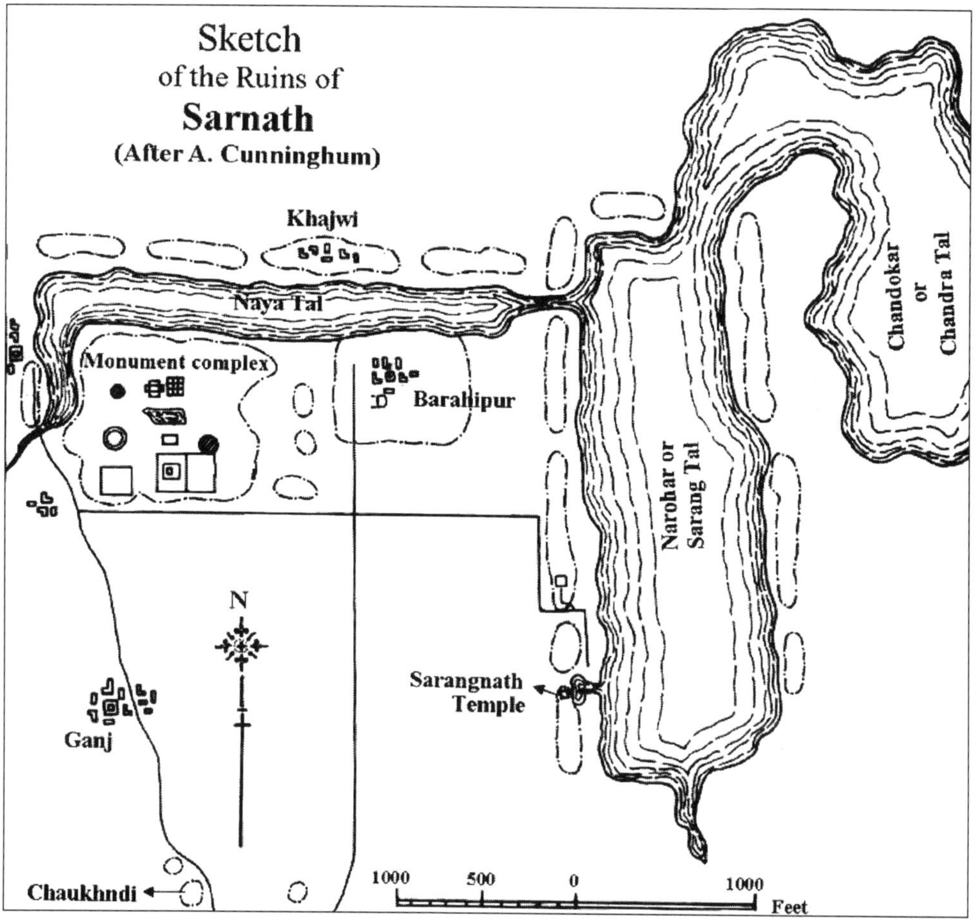

29. Geo-physical map of Sarnath.

On the north lies the Naya Tal or 'New Tank', which is upwards of half a mile in length, but little more than 300 feet in width" (Cunningham 1871a: 106). Prior to Cunningham, travel accounts of the Chinese monk, Xuanzang, too have recorded existence of these water bodies at Mrigadaya. "To the east of the Sangharama enclosure is a clear lake of water 200 paces in circuit: here Tathagata occasionally bathed himself. To the west of it is a great tank about 180 paces round: here Tathagata used to wash his begging-dish. To the north of this is a lake about 150 paces round. Here Tathagata used to wash his robes... In each the water is deep and the taste sweet, it is pure and resplendent in appearance, and neither increases nor decreases" (Beal 1884. Book VII: 48-49).

The above descriptions may be accepted to reflect the palaeo-environment of Mrigadaya. The sacred space here is bounded at three sides by a chain of water bodies. The southern end of it was a wide stretch of land, which was an open space for communication and expansion (Fig. 29). But, leaving the exception of Chaukhandi stupa, which is located at some distance from the cluster of monuments, the southern area was occupied only up to a little more than one kilometre from the southern bank of Naya Tal. Thus, it may be held that the establishment of Mrigdaya was confined within the boundaries formed by the three lakes. It was this restricted sacred space which experienced human endeavour in terms of built and rebuilt structures for about fifteen centuries.

Cuningham's recording of the environment is also significant. "The Mrigdava, or the 'Deer Park', is represented by a fine wood, which still covers an open area of about half a mile, and extends from the great tower of Dhamek on the north to the Chaukhandi mound on the south" (Cunningham 1871a: 107). It may be interesting to note that if a forest cover can grow in seven to eight centuries at Sarnath, its existence can well be comprehended during pre-human occupation in the region. Existence of forest in Rishipattana-Mrigadaya area is also suggested by a mythological narration of *Mahavastu*, which was discussed earlier (Chapter 2). The ancient bio-diversity of Sarnath can be drawn as having a deciduous forest patch/

patches, surrounded by rich water bodies. It was this eco-zone which was selected by the Lord and his followers, the earliest inhabitants of Mrigadaya.

ARCHAEOLOGICAL FINDINGS

The history of the discovery of Sarnath is embedded in a non-archaeological operation. It was in 1794 that the forgotten monuments of one of the most pious landscapes were pulled down. Cunningham writes that, "The earliest excavations of which we possess any record were those by Baba Jagat Singh in 1793-94" (Cunningham 1871a: 118). Dharmarajika stupa was first to be hammered down for the purpose, while marks of damage on the Dhamek stupa also are of the same time. This ghastly act was performed at the instance of the Diwan (Jagat Singh) of Raja Cheta Singh, who consumed the precious debris of the holy Buddhist pilgrimage as building material of Chetganj bazaar of the modern city. An important in situ object, which was displaced and lost in this venture, was the relic casket. Cunningham's efforts in collecting information regarding this precious antiquity are of archival value. He identified the scooped out reminiscent of the Dharmarajika stupa, also known as Jagat Singh stupa, which at the time of his visit, in 1835, was in the form of a 520′ wide circular pit. Located to the west of Dhamek stupa, the centre of this pit was re-excavated by employing an old labour named Sangkar, who had previously participated in the scavenging operations conducted by Jagat Singh. Cunningham could retrieve a circular sandstone box at the depth of 12 feet below the ground, which was left in situ by Jagat Singh. Cunningham writes, "The box was a large circular block of common Chunar sandstone, pierced with a rough cylindrical chamber in the centre, and covered with a flat slab as a lid" (Cunningham 1871a: 1115). In this box was placed "a cylindrical box of green marble about 15 inches in height and 5 or 6 inches in diameter. The contents of the inner box (as was informed by labour Sangkar) were 40 to 46 pearls, 14 rubies, 8 silver and 9 gold earrings (*karn phul*), and three pieces of human arm bones" (Cunningham 1871a: 11-15). The marble casket was handed over to Duncan and the sandstone box was handed over to the Bengal Asiatic Society. Was this the relic casket kept in Dharmarajika stupa during the time of Asoka? This important question will be discussed later.

This devastating act of Jagat Singh, though a black event in the history of Varanasi, is remembered also for drawing attention of archaeologists and Indologists to the Buddhist heritage of the area, as a result of which a series of archaeological operations were conducted at Sarnath. A summary of these, based on Majumdar, is given below (Majumdar, B. 1947: 23-25).

Colonel C. Mackenzie was the first to explore and collect icons from this site (now placed in Indian Museum, Kolkata). This was followed by the visit of A. Cunningham (1835-36). He is recorded to have examined Chaukhandi mound, opened Dhamek stupa (Fig. 30), identified a monastery and a temple located north of Dharamrajika stupa. A large

30. Excavation of 20th century with Dhamek stupa at the background.

collection of sculptures and carved stones which was obtained was shifted partly to Kolkata (now housed in the Indian Museum). But, a considerable part was also used in construction of bridge over the Varuna river. Sherring has written that, "In the erection of one of the bridges over the Barna (Ducan Bridge), forty-eight statues and many other sculptured stones were removed from Sarnath and thrown into the river...and that in the erection of the second bridge, the iron one, from fifty to sixty carloads of stones from the Sarnath buildings were employed" (Sherring 1868: 280).

Major Markham Kittoe, too, conducted excavations at Sarnath in the year 1851-52. He exposed a number of stupas around Dhamek, and a quadrangular structure which he identified as 'hospital' (Fig. 31). He undertook cleaning of another monastery, west of the Jain temple, but could not complete it due to his sad demise. His work was followed by E. Thomas and Fitz-Edward Hall, respectively. After a gap of about a decade, in 1865, C. Horn also was involved in the exposure of structures, which

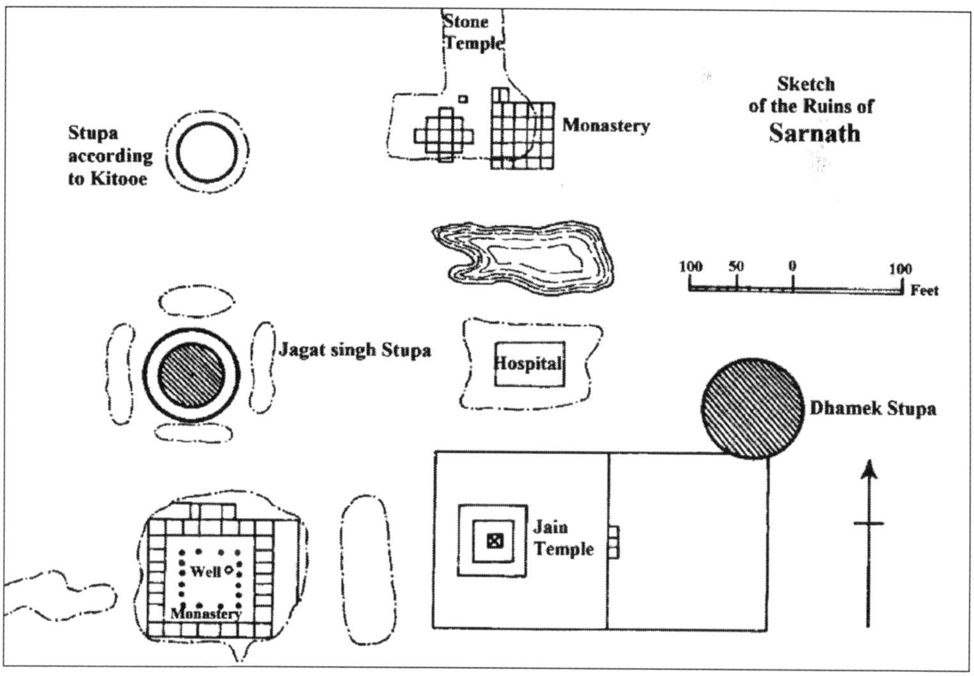

31. Plan of structures exposed by Kittoe.

32. Fragments of Asokan pillar and other structures from excavation of the western side of the temple area.

was subsequently undertaken by Rivett-Carnac in 1877. The latter discovered a Buddha image, while the findings of Horn were also sent to Kolkata (Indian Museum).

The first spade of planned excavation which fell at Sarnath was in the year 1905, by F.O. Oertel, who took approval from the Archaeological Department for digging the site. He exposed the main shrine, found the Asoka pillar and its lion capital (Fig. 32), and examined Chaukhandi mound. During this operation he discovered 476 icons and 41 inscriptions. He is also credited with publishing the result of his excavation in the *Archaeological Survey of India Annual Report* (1904-05: 59-104). This practice of scientific excavation was carried on by John Marshall and Sten Konow, subsequently, in the year 1907 (*Archaeological Survey of India Annual Report 1906-07*: 43-80). In the discoveries, an inscribed statue of Buddha, part of an inscribed

33. View of monuments of main shrine area from the top of Dhamek stupa.

umbrella and stone inscriptions of 11th century CE and that of Kumaradevi are noteworthy. About a decade later (1914-15), excavation was resumed by H. Hargreaves, who probed north, east and west of the main shrine (*Archaeological Survey of India Annual Report 1914-15*: 97-131). Discovery of the inscriptions of Kumargupta II and Buddhagupta, along with the remains dating between Mauryan and medieval periods, are reported by him. This was followed by excavations conducted by Rai Bahadur Daya Ram Sahni, for two consecutive years (1921-22). Sahni exposed most parts of the area lying between the Dhamek stupa and the main shrine, and Monastery II (*Archaeological Survey of India Annual Report 1921-22*: 42-45), and made available the ancient format of Mrigadaya.

In 1992-93, a limited area of Sarnath was excavated by the Archaeological Survey of India (*Indian Archaeology 1992-93: A Review*: 98-99). Two trenches of 5 x 5 m dimension were laid at the place near the lion pillar capital. An apsidal structure at this place was subject to the probing, which was ascertained to be of late Mauryan period (*Indian Archaeology 1992-93: A Review*: 99).

As a result of these field investigations, and later cleaning operations by the Archaeological Survey of India, material remains of this Buddhist pilgrimage of Sarnath have come to light (Fig. 33). The premises of this establishment, which is situated on the southern shore of Sarang-tal, is strewn with structures and icons. The focal point of this complex is the high rising overground stupa, Dhamek (Fig. 30). Most of the structures and carvings cluster in the low-lying area in all the four cardinal directions of the complex. On account of the style of carvings, epigraphs and context, multi-cultural growth of the nucleus of this Buddhist landscape has been ascertained. This lies between the time of the Mauryan king Asoka (c. 273-236 BCE) (Mookerji 1968: 89) and Kumaradevi, one of the queens of the Gahadavala king Govindchandra (1114-1154 CE) (Ganguly 1957: 52-54). That these remains are material expression of the faith of the devotees in the *Dhamma*, and were donations at the place of the First Sermon by the Lord, goes without saying. Construction of monuments, installation of icons and carved architectural forms, during Maurya, Sunga, Kushan, Gupta and post-Gupta periods successively enriched and expanded territories of this Buddhist pilgrimage, century after century.

Excavations conducted at Sarnath so far have not revealed a distinct pre-Asokan horizon. But there is no doubt that this pilgrim site was in existence right from the time of the First Sermon delivered by Buddha. The details on the possibilities and nature of Mrigadaya between 6th and 3rd centuries BCE have been discussed later in Chapter 4.

MRIGADAYA OF THE ASOKAN TIMES

The first group of archaeological remains of Sarnath date to the time of Mauryan king Asoka. It comprises three monuments—The Dharmarajika/ Jagat Singh stupa, the apsidal temple/monastery and the inscribed pillar with lion capital (Fig. 34).

The Dharmarajika stupa, as it is known after the 10th-century inscription giving name to a group of monuments, was constructed at the instance of King Asoka. It is referred to in the texts that after dividing the ashes of the Lord obtained from reopening seven of the earlier stupas, Asoka got

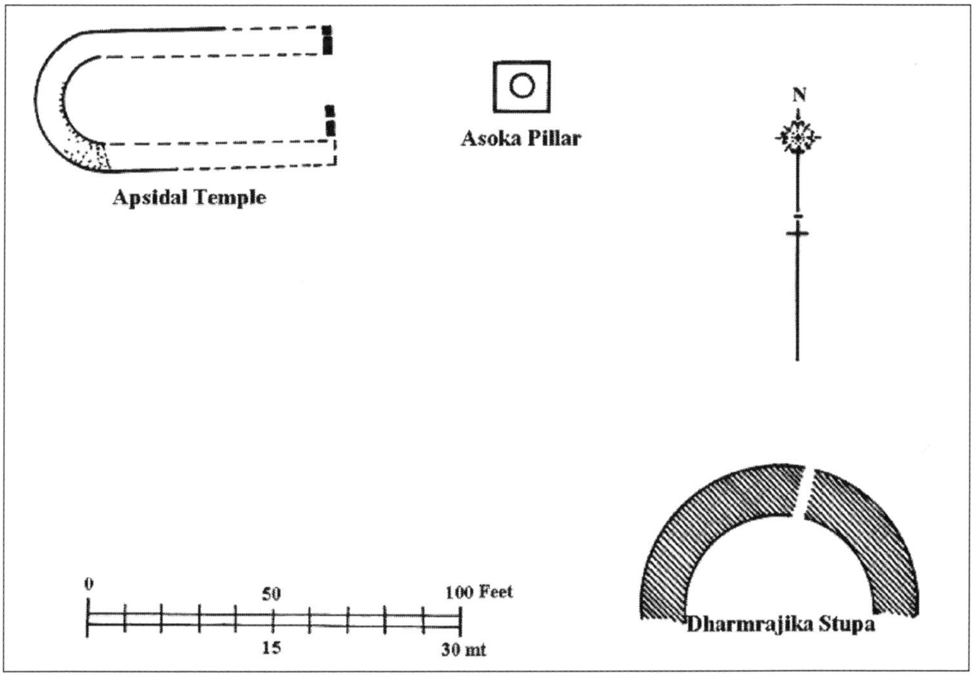

34. Location and Plan of the structures of Mauryan times.

many stupas constructed at Buddhist sites with the same name—Dharmarajika (Vogel 1906: 223). That he also had constructed a stupa at Mrigadaya is recorded in the Buddhist texts (*Divyavadana*. 389-94). Xuanzang further confirms this by stating that, "To the south-west of the *vihara* is a stone *stupa* built by Asoka-raja. Although the foundations have given way, there are still 100 feet or more of the wall remaining" (Beal 1884: Book VII: 45-46). Xuanzang's statement, when scrutinised with the archaeological findings, suggests that initially Dharmarajika stupa was constructed by Asoka. But, the one which was seen by him was not the original stupa of the Mauryan times. The spade of Marshall and Konow revealed a number of stages of construction, dating from 3rd century BCE to the 9th/10th century CE of this stupa (*Archaeological Survey of India Annual Report 1907-08*: 65). He might have seen the stupa after the additions of the 5th/6th century CE, since his date of visit to the place was in the 7th century CE.

The Dharmarajika stupa of Sarnath is said to have had five constructional phases, dating between Mauryan and the early medieval periods. The original stupa, according to Marshall and Konow, date back to the time of Asoka. The *anda* or the dome of this stupa, a loosely constructed masonry, measured 44′ 3" (approximately 18 m) (Majumdar, B. 1947: 26), and was composed of bricks (measuring 19½"x 14½" x 2½" and 16½"x 12½" x 3½"), mostly wedge-shaped,... "the smaller end being laid nearer the centre of the *stupa*; but no effort made to bond the courses together" (*Archaeological Survey of India Annual Report 1907-08*: 65). The stupa was also covered with a thick layer of concrete. The cylindrical green marble relic casket containing a circular stone box, which was recovered from this structure during the eighteenth century, was found at a depth of 18 cubit below the surface (Majumdar, B. 1947: 30), perhaps kept in the centre of the dome constructed during the time of Asoka. Along its circumference was 4.5-4.8 metre (15′-16′) wide ambulatory floor, which was also a brick construction. Remains of this *pradakshina patha* was recorded beneath the concrete flooring of the main shrine, north of the stupa, at a distance of 60′ from its centre. The width of this passage was 15′-16′, and it was encircled by a brick wall (4′5" high and 3′4" thick), with four openings at four cardinal points. The excavators state that this: "is the first example that we have in India of a *pradakshina* closed in with a solid wall; instead of an open railing" (Marshall and Konow, *Archaeological Survey of India Annual Report 1907-08*: 645). It may be significant to note that the unusual feature of this stupa was the brick wall surrounding the passage, instead of a railing.

Though Majumdar has identified the *hermika* of this stupa with the monolithic railing and shaft (Fig. 35), which were found enshrined in the main shrine complex by Oertel (*Archaeological Survey of India Annual Report 1904-05*: 68), and Marshall and Konow (*Archaeological Survey of India Annual Report 1906-07*: 89), the excavators do not say so. Instead, it has been mentioned in the excavation report that the earliest epigraphic records on this composition are of 1st–2nd centuries BCE, which would

35. Sandstone *hermika* with Mauryan polish, Sarnath.

post-date Asokan times. The question whether the Dharmarajika stupa in its first stage was adorned with a stone *hermika* and *chhatravali* is difficult to ascertain, but its possibility is strong.

36. Fragments of Asokan pillar, under the canopy, Sarnath.

The second monument of the earliest group of Buddhist remains at Sarnath is the inscribed Asokan column, which was surmounted by four seated lions. Parts of the shaft are kept under a canopy at the place of its recovery (west of the main shrine) (Fig. 36), while the lion capital is housed in Sarnath Museum (Fig. 37). Excavation of the western side of the main shrine area first by Oertel and then by Marshall has brought to light fragments and in situ base of this column.

Xuanzang's description of the pillar erected by *Asoka-raja* may be significant to note (Beal 1884: Book VII: 45).

> In front of the building, ..(*the stupa*),... is a stone pillar about 70 feet high. The stone is altogether as bright as jade. It is glittering, and sparkles like light; and all those who pray fervently before it see from time to time, according to their petitions, figures with good or bad signs. It was here that Tathagata (*ju-lai*), having arrived at enlightenment, began to turn the wheel of the law (*to preach*).

But, whether the Chinese traveller had seen the pillar with lion capital and inscribed shaft is a question of debate (Jayaswal 2012: 235-236). There are two striking omissions in his description. One, that the shaft was inscribed, and the other, that the crowning member of this column was the four-lion capital. Interestingly, these omissions were also noted by Marshall as early as 1907 (Sahni 1914: 31). The omission with regard to the animal capital at Sarnath becomes particularly glaring when it is compared to the description of the pillar at Vaisali. For, the same travel account mentions the lion capital on the top of the pillar, at Vaisali, which is said to be standing by the side of the stupa constructed by Asoka raja (Beal 1884: *Book VII*: 67). Similarly, ignoring the inscription on the Sarnath pillar, which elaborates the norms to be followed by the Buddhists monks and the nuns, also appears to be surprising. For, an edict in which directives for religious establishments are issued would be crucial for a Buddhist traveller like Xuanzang, who was visiting the country for a proper comprehension of the religion of his faith. The question with which one is confronted under the circumstances

37. Lion capital of Asokan pillar, Sarnath.

38. Railing post found in association with Asokan pillar.

is, whether the famous Asokan pillar with lion capital and the inscribed shaft was seen by Xuanzang at all. And also, if he was not describing the pillar under consideration, was there another pillar which was erected at Sarnath during Mauryan period, seen by him? The history of discovery of Sarnath pillar, particularly the details of digging around the Asokan column, is significant for finding plausible explanations to these inquiries.

The excavations conducted at Sarnath during the years 1904-05 and 1906-07 resulted in obtaining most of the members of the Asokan column. In view of the importance of the discovery, Marshall's words have been reproduced here (*Archaeological Survey of India Annual Report 1904-05*: 68):

> At the short distance to the west of the shrine were found the stump and fragments of a large round column. First the lion capital was exhumed close to the western wall of the shrine, next some fragments of the shaft, and lastly, the stump of the column in situ, protruding slightly above the concrete terrace. On clearing the débris from above the stump, I noticed a few letters in early characters. The concrete was broken through and a long inscription exposed to view, which on later examination proved to be an Aśoka edict. The fracture of the column had taken place immediately above the concrete terrace: with it, unfortunately, the first two lines were broken up into tiny fragments and nearly all lost.

The above account ascertains that the famous lion capital of Sarnath was attached to the inscribed shaft. This column was located to the west of the shrine. And, in this case it was not standing close to nor was it standing right in front of the Jagat Singh stupa, which was constructed initially by Asoka. That this pillar was standing as an independent monument is also attested by the fact that it had an enclosure of stone railing (Fig. 38). For, Oertel has noted that the floor on which the inscribed pillar stands "... was found, embedded in their original positions, parts of six stone railing posts and two cross rails ornamented with rosettes. The fragments bear no inscription..." (*Archaeological Survey of India Annual Report 1904-05*: 69).

The other noteworthy feature is that the inscribed part of the shaft was buried beneath the debris and floors of earlier times and just a small portion of it was in view, after the concrete floor was laid in this locality (Fig. 39). The date of the concrete cover is therefore important to ascertain.

39. View of inscribed shaft of Asokan column in the process of exposure.

40. Kushan and Gupta inscriptions on Asokan column.

During the excavations of 1906-07, Marshall and Konow record the details of the concrete floor and the deposits underlying it (*Archaeological Survey of India Annual Report 1906-07*: 68).

> The concrete floor around the *main shrine* marks a relatively late epoch in the history of Sarnath, and one of the initial objects of last season's excavations was to examine the ground below it, particularly in the neighbourhood of the Aśoka pillar. The floor was accordingly removed in front of the western porch, leaving a strip of concrete, approximately 3'10" wide, parallel to the shrine... At this place the concrete is about one foot thick, consisting of several (at least five) distinct layers, superimposed one above the other at different epochs. Underneath the floor, at a distance of

> 12′ from the shrine, three stone steps were laid bare, the topmost of which was found about 1′1" below the upper surface of the concrete, while the lowest was some 3′ below. These steps do not appear to bear any relation to the *main shrine,* as neither do they run parallel to it nor does their centre line coincide with the centre of the west façade. The stairs lead down to a stone pavement which surrounds the Aśoka pillar, and measures 18′10″ from north to south and 16′9″ from east to west. This pavement (No. I in the site plan), which was broken on the south side, was to a great extent composed of stones taken from older structures, among which were found bases of images, carved stones, rail-bars and other architectural fragments. Among them may be noticed, particularly, sculpture shown in Plate XIX, 1. It belongs to the Gupta period and is the latest of all.

Marshall categorically states (*Archaeological Survey of India Annual Report 1906-07*: 35):

> In a short article regarding these and other excavations, which I contributed to the Royal Asiatic Society's Journal, I stated that nothing of a later date than the Kushana period had been found beneath the concrete floor, but this statement must now be modified, as one of the blocks of the stone pavement around the Aśoka column proves to have been taken from an early Gupta building, and the lowest layer of the concrete floor above it can, therefore, hardly be earlier than the later Gupta epoch.

It is thus apparent that the inscribed portion of the shaft of the Asokan pillar, which was covered by the concrete floor, appears to have been laid sometime during the late Gupta period. Besides, the latest and the third inscription which is of one line and was engraved on the Asokan column, is also dated to the early Gupta period (Sahni 1914: 30). The exposure of the inscribed block for view, thus, could be assumed by the time of the Gupta period, while its disuse and cover by the late Gupta period. It may therefore be held that at the time of the visit of the Chinese traveller Xuanzang in the early 7th century CE, the inscribed shaft of the Asokan column was covered beneath the concrete floor. If this is accepted, then the question is: which was the Asokan pillar of Sarnath described by the traveller?

Xuanzang mentions that the pillar was standing in front of a stupa constructed by Asoka. But the inscribed column with lion capital of Sarnath was erected in front of the apsidal monastery (Fig. 34). This is apparent if one pieces together the history of discoveries of the pillar and the structures of the western side of the main shrine or the Asokan pillar area. The noted details on the base of the pillar by Marshall (*Archaeological Survey of India Annual Report 1906-07*: 70) read as follows:

> From the section of the pillar and its surroundings, it will be observed that the lower part of the shaft to a height of 7′5" was left undressed. This portion was, of course, left buried in the ground from the outset, and we may assume that the dividing line between the rough and polished surfaces marks the ground level when the column was first erected. We shall see later on that bases of various buildings have come to light approximately at this level and we can hardly be wrong in assigning them to the Mauryan period. The polished part of the pillar, it should be added, begins at a depth of 6′9½″ below the stone pavement, and 8′ below the bottom of the inscription, while the distance from the top of the innermost brick wall to the stone paving is 2′8½″, and up to the base of the inscription 3′11.

In the description of Marshall there is reference for the recovery of "a fine alms-bowl, of black clay with glossy surface", logically accepted to be the occurrence of Northern Black Polished Ware bowl from the level 3′ below the stone pavement (*Archaeological Survey of India Annual Report 1906-07*: 70). As per the findings of the antiquities and also the archaeological accumulation at the base of the Asokan pillar, the lower level between the foundation (the stone slab) and the corresponding thickness of deposits to the undressed portion of the pillar (7′5") could be assigned to Mauryan times (Fig. 41). An apsidal structure, which was unearthed near the Asokan pillar, needs special mention here (*Archaeological Survey of India Annual Report 1914-15*: 109).

> Due west to the Aśokan column and at a distance of 54′4″ were discovered the foundations of an apsidal building 82′6″ in length, 38′10″ in width, the apse towards the west, the entrance presumably facing the Aśokan column.

In the light of all these observations, it appears that the inscribed pillar was erected in front of the apsidal structure, which was the monastery of the Mauryan period. This assumption also has a logical base that the verdict which has been engraved on the pillar is related to the upkeep of monks and monastic organisation. This is well reflected in the contents of the epigraph of the Sarnath pillar edict, in which entitlement for dwelling by monks and nuns has been clearly mentioned. The translated version of the edict reads: "His sacred Majesty King Piyadasi....The Church is [not] by anyone to be divided. But whosoever, monk or nun break up the Church, shall be made to don white robes and made to dwell in another dwelling" (Sahni 1914: 30). The position of the epigraph on the pillar also is significant to note (Fig. 36). As the inscribed side of the pillar faced the monastery and not the Dharmarajika stupa, it may, therefore, be held that the Asokan pillar with inscription was standing in front of the entrance of the apsidal structure, where monks and nuns were residing, for whom the verdict was engraved by the emperor.

41. Exposed view of base of Asokan pillar (early 20th century).

The above account makes it apparent that it was not the lion capital pillar of Asoka, which is being recorded by the traveller. It appears there was another pillar with typical Mauryan polish, which was in situ when Xuanzang visited Sarnath.

The collection of six blocks, stored presently under the canopy to the western side of temple (Fig. 36), is important to note. There are distinctively two groups of blocks used as part of the shaft of the pillars. All of these have polished surface.

A: *Inscribed block and its counterpart* (2 in number):

1. Inscribed block: It is 2.04 m long (with a possibility for its continuity below the present ground). It is polished and has been painted in ochre colour, traces of which are distinct at the lower portion. It measures 71.65 cm at the diameter and 2.25 m at the circumference. The weathered surface of the block indicates peeling off the upper surface along the circumference.
2. Almost similar in composition, this block is 1.82 m long with 1.97 m circumference and 62.73 cm diameter. It is uninscribed. In texture, however, it appears similar to the above block.

B: *Narrow and well-finished pink sandstone blocks* (4 in number):

3. Composed of fine grain and pinkish sandstone, it is 2.14 m long and measures 1.76 m at circumference and 56.05 at the diameter.
4. Similar in composition to the above, it is 1.85 m long, and measures 1.85 at the circumference and 58.91 cm in diameter.
5. Similar in composition to above, it is 0.86 m long, measures 1.90 at the circumference and 60.50 cm in diameter.
6. Similar in composition to above, it is 0.35 m long block with damaged sides.

Close examination of the above-mentioned six blocks indicates that these formed part of two separate pillars. The first, group-A, which is composed of buff-coloured sandstone, is of coarse texture in comparison to the other category. The total length of these is countable to 3.86 m, and the range of diameter between 71.65 cm and 62.73 cm, which indicates a tapering tendency of about 10 cm for a length less than four metres (from the base of the inscribed block to the top of the uninscribed block). The second, group-B is, constituted by the remaining four blocks, which are made of finer textured pink sandstone with hematite palettes.

42. Mauryan pillar inset in a brick structure, southern chapel of main shrine.

The surface treatment of this group is also of better quality. The total length countable for this group comes to about 4.43 m. The general diameter range in this case falls between 60.50 cm and 56.05 cm, indicating a gentle tapering tendency of a little more than 5 cm. It may be mentioned that the smallest broken piece of 38-20 cm is the narrowest block, which is quite different from all the others. It may also be mentioned that the part of the pillar which stands erected through the middle of the south chapel of the main shrine also appears to be comparable in texture and finish with the later group of blocks.

While going through the photo albums of old excavations (1906-07), in the photo-archives of the Archaeological Survey of India, Delhi, this author could find a photograph of a pillar standing in the southern chapel of the temple (Fig. 42). Incidentally, this pillar has been identified as the shaft of some *chhatravali*, presumed to be attached to a stupa. The stupa in turn is surrounded by a railing of Mauryan times.

> The plan and the cross section of the shrine show the position of this little stupa which is built up in the foundation and wall of the south chapel, and therefore of earlier date than the main shrine (*Archaeological Survey of India Annual Report 1904-05*: 68).

It has been further noted that, "the *stupas* inside are not set in the middle of the railing but are pushed somewhat to one side." (*Archaeological Survey of India Annual Report 1906-07*: 89).

The above-mentioned illustration clearly demonstrates that the pillar was embedded almost in the centre of a brick stupa, covering almost the entire height of it. Also, the portion of the standing pillar seen in the chapel has striking compositional similarities with the Mauryan pillars. The two pieces of architecture—the stone pillar and the brick stupa of the south chapel—together appear very illogical composition. For the pillar is very large for being the shaft of an umbrella crowning the small stupa. And since this stupa was of later construction than the Mauryan railing, it appears that the south chapel was perhaps the original place where these members were installed before the main shrine complex was constructed. This situation, shaft-pillar and railing of the time of Asoka, was the same when the Chinese traveller visited the place. One wonders if Xuanzang is referring to this. Most likely this unit was part of the Dharmarajika stupa complex which was dismantled some time during post-Mauryan time. The possibility for another pillar standing infront of the stupa is likely, which was seen by the visitor. It may, however, be difficult to reconstruct the full appearance of the pillar since, neither the travel account mentions the crowning member, nor have fragments of imposing animal composition of Mauryan times been reported. But, it may be held that the original size of this pillar was perhaps as long as the lion capital pillar. And the second group of blocks stored under the canopy appears to he fragments of the same.

The third structure of Asokan times is the apsidal *chaitya*-hall/ monastery, facing the west. The Asokan column with lion capital was standing at a distance of 16.30 metres from its entrance. It has also been recorded, by the excavator, H. Hargreaves for instance, that, "Due west to the Aśokan column and at a distance of 54'4" were discovered the foundations of an apsidal building 82'6" in length, 38'10" in width, the apse towards the west, the entrance presumably facing the Aśokan column" (*Archaeological Survey of India Annual Report 1914-15*: 109). It is difficult to ascertain whether the structure was a *chaitya-griha* or vihara. Majumdar, for instance, states that, "The earliest construction shows the layout of an epsidal temple *(chaitya*-hall)." He further adds: "The skeletal remains of the foundation of the apsidal temple leave no doubt that this type was also, like the *vihara*, necessitated by the exigencies of monastic life" (Majumdar, B. 1947: 34).

Since this is the earliest *chaitya*/monastery of Mrigadaya, excavators' recordings of its exposure may be interesting to note. Hargreaves states: "Of this structure only the foundation now exist and this in a complete state only on the west. In the centre of the apse the width of the foundations is 8'6" but 64' from the eastern end. These almost completely disappear being marked only by a line of brick on edge sometimes with two lines of bricks laid endwise on the inner side." Composed of bricks corresponding with the Mauryan structures of the middle Ganga plain, in size: "the bricks forming the base of this structure are large and thick, varying from 20½" x 9" x 3" to 20" x 11" x 4"" (Jayaswal 2009: 107), the outer façade of the structure was decorated with stucco. The excavator remarks that: "In all places the outer face of the remains is covered with stucco even where only a single brick remains" (*Archaeological Survey of India Annual Report 1914-15*: 109). This structure appears to have fallen in disuse sometime before the Kushan period. The area lying north-east of the Dharmarajika stupa, where the apsidal structure was constructed, was not only hidden by the superimposition of such structures as the enclosure wall and other later masonry, but was also erased from the memory of people by the time Xuanzang visited this site.

The apsidal structure may be dated to Asokan times. The excavators have assigned a Late Mauryan date, and also confirmed that there was no trace of pre-Mauryan or the replacement of the wooden parts to masonry. Hargreaves notes that "... as the foundations are only 1'9" above the Mauryan level and no earlier remains exist beneath, the structure may fairly be ascribed to the late Mauryan period" (*Archaeological Survey of*

India Annual Report 1914-15: 109). In a much later investigation, A.K. Sinha also arrives at the same conclusion as he has noted: "The recent work could also confirm that the apsidal structure was built sometime in late-Mauryan period, i.e. c. third-second century BC" (*Indian Archaeology 1992-93: A Review:* 99). This assumption and the other fact which was noted by Marshall—that the floor level of the Asokan column and that of the structure in consideration was same—would confirm the date of the apsidal structure to the Mauryan period.

Indications for the existence of a large monastery at Mrigadaya, prior to the time of Asoka, are present in the content of the epigraph on the Asokan column. That the Sangha is not to be divided by any monk and nun was the dictate for maintaining discipline in the Sangha (Sahni 1914: 30) This would mean that a good number of monks and nuns were already residing here when Asoka was addressing them. It may be logical to deduce, therefore, that the monastery was of pre-Asokan date. It was discussed earlier that the common media used for structures, prior to Asokan times, were perishable in nature. Whether the same pre-Asokan monastery of Sarnath was transcribed in bricks, during the time of Asoka, is difficult to establish due to the fragmentary nature of the Asokan epigraph and lack of proper exposure and recording of the basal deposits of the monastery, is very likely.

That all the architectural marvels of the Mauryan period discovered at Mrigadaya were donations by king Asoka will go unquestioned. Being royal in nature, these donations are confined to large building constructions complying imperial dictate. It may be significant to note that the structural offerings at the Buddhist sites initiated by King Asoka laid the foundation for the construction of large monuments, which was subsequently followed at a large scale by kings and affluent devotees.

The available archaeological remains of the time of Asoka at Sarnath, discussed above, direct one to draw a line from the Mulagandhakuti Vihara, to the south and western periphery. This small area would have included the Dharmarajika stupa and an uninscribed pillar in its front, and the apsidal monastery and the inscribed pillar in its front, as two groups of monuments. Occupying the south-western part of the Mulagandhakuti Vihara, this cluster appears to be the nucleus of the First Stage (datable to the 3rd century BCE) of the Buddhist landscape of Mrigadaya. The water bodies in the vicinity of this nucleus and the soundings might have been the extended part of this landscape.

MRIGADAYA OF POST-ASOKAN TO PRE-KANISHKAN TIMES

In the publications on Sarnath by earlier archaeologists, the post-Asokan remains are variously addressed as 'Late Mauryan', 'Sunga', 'Kanava', and '2nd and 1st centuries BCE', etc. The last was preferred by the excavators, who relied mostly on the paleographic characteristics of the epigraphs to date the exposed monuments. Under the circumstances it appears logical to classify the remains of the period under a broad historical frame—'the Post-Asokan–Pre-Kushan'. The suggested period lies between two distinct categories of material remains—the Asokan (3rd century BCE) and Kanishka-Kushan (1st century CE), which are not only distinct, but are dated by epigraphs. While, the ones lying in between the two are not very pronounced.

The period under consideration was politically as well as culturally dominated by Sunga. Pushyamitra Sunga ascended the throne after overpowering the last Maurya king, Brihadratha, in 187 BCE (Mookerji 1968a: 95). More than a century's governing the Sunga dynasty was taken over by the Kanavas in the second and third quarters of the 1st century BCE (75-30 BCE) (Mookerji 1968a: 99-100). In this chronological succession, Late Maurya, Sunga and Kanava, it is the Sunga dynasty which contributed most. Its patronage to the pilgrimages is significant. It has been established, for instance, that, "The Sunga period saw the revival of the Brahminical influence" (Mookerji 1968a: 98). In spite of this, it was during this period that the stupa of Bharhut and railing and gateways of the Asokan stupa at Sanchi were built. The carvings of the Sunga period are classical examples of transformation of ingenious carving styles on wood and ivory to stone. Moreover, plastic art took a turn from the royal dictate to the patronage and expression of the indigenous masses.

The count and nature of monuments of the period under consideration are indistinct at Sarnath. Majumdar, for instance, states that, "No trace of any structure erected during the Sunga dynasty has yet been brought to light at Sarnath" (Majumdar, B. 1947: 15). But, in the same breadth he states that exposure of the area near the Asokan column and the main shrine has yielded the two fragments of a head carved in the round and a stone railing, which may be assigned to the 2nd century BC (Majumdar, B. 1947: 15). He also mentions 12 railing posts belonging to Kanava period, which were discovered from the north-west of the main shrine (Majumdar, B. 1947: 16). Besides, the remains of a railing comprising 74 uprights and 108 cross-bars are reported from the main shrine (*Archaeological Survey of India Annual Report 1906-7*: 95-6). On account of the available information, addition of railing to structures and sacred spots may be accepted as the major contribution of the post-Asokan pre-Kushan period at Mrigadaya.

Railings enclosing a sacred spot, be it a tree, structure or monument, were a common practice during Late Maurya-Sunga period. The depictions in the Sanchi and Bharhut panels testify this practice. Its antiquity may go further back. It may be recalled that tree in railing is depicted on coins of 3rd century BCE (Jayaswal 2009: 217). It may be argued that a similar practice was also in vogue at Sarnath, where two sets of railings, the monolithic railing, and the fragments of a large enclosure could be identified.

The earliest railing of Sarnath was found inside the southern chapel of the main shrine (Fig. 35). This railing is carved out of one block of pink sandstone, and bears Mauryan polish. "The railing consists of 16 uprights, 5 along each side, with a massive plinth beneath, a beveled coping above and three lozenge-shaped horizontal bars between. In the corners are the quarters—circle brackets pierced with stanchion holes, intended, perhaps, to receive supports for an overhead copy or for flags"

(*Archaeological Survey of India Annual Report 1906-07*: 89). The possibility that this was fixed here after transfer from its in situ position, and that it was the *hermika* of Dharmarajika stupa, is suggested by Marshall and Konow, as well as Majumdar, who also dates it to the Mauryan period (Majumdar, B. 1947: 30).

But, there is a possibility that the monolithic railing did not serve as the *hermika* to the Dharmarajika stupa since the date of this railing appears to be a little later than the Stage I of construction of the Dharmarajika stupa of the time of Asoka. The older one of the two epigraphs on this railing is said to bear characteristics of 1st/2nd century BCE (*Archaeological Survey of India Annual Report 1906-07*: 96). If this is to be accepted then the epigraph was engraved much after (about a century or more) the *hermika* was placed on top of the dome. This obviously is not a logical assumption. It is also difficult to find a logical explanation as to why the *hermika* was pulled down after some decades of the completion of the stupa. It is therefore a possibility that the railing was providing fencing to an auspicious spot, say where the Lord sat and delivered his First Sermon at Mrigadaya. This spot, besides being demarcated, had also the provision of coverage, which is suggested by the holes carved out at its four corners. Both the options—that the monolithic railing formed part of *hermika,* or it was meant to demarcate an auspicious space—remain an open issue for debate.

The Sunga period, though credited with donative additions of beautifully carved railings and gateways to stupas, appears absent in Sarnath. Dharmarajika stupa perhaps was never encircled with a stone railing. However, the parts of railing, upright pillars and cross-bars, which were found by Oertel in the vicinity of the Asokan pillar and the main shrine (*Archaeological Survey of India Annual Report 1904-05*: 66), are assumed to be parts of a stupa railing, which bears donative inscriptions in Late Mauryan character (2nd /1st centuries BCE). The probability that the railing under consideration was meant for demarcating the stupa area does not stand when the constructional history of Dharmarajika is

43. Railing posts discovered from Mulagandhakuti Vihara.

taken into consideration. It was noted above that the stupa constructed during the Asokan period was devoid of a railing. It may also be noted that, as the excavators record, the Stage II of construction of this stupa was Kushan/early Gupta times. If this is true, then the possibility of addition of railing to the Dharmarajika stupa during Late Mauryan/Sunga times is to be ruled out. The question remains: where was this railing erected? And, what was its function?

The second railing (Fig. 43) was erected at the Mulagandhakuti Vihara. It has been recorded by Marshall and Konow that the "south, east and north walls of the building were furnished on the outside with a stone railing comprising 74 uprights and 108 cross-bars" (*Archaeological Survey of India Annual Report 1906-07*: 79). The upright posts of this structure were 8¾" deep, 10½" broad and 5' high, while the cross-bars were of 2'2" dimension. The coping-stone measured 6'6" long, 11" broad and 14" high. To strengthen this railing, the interstices between the upright and cross-bars were filled with masonry. The structure can be dated to 2nd century BCE, on account of the donation epigraph written in Brahmi script (*Archaeological Survey of India Annual Report 1906-07*: 95-96). Besides, the carving on the rail pillars also are of Sunga-Kanava style (Fig. 44).

44. Close-up view of railing post bearing Sunga-Kushan motifs.

The Mulagandhakuti Vihara or the main shrine was such an auspicious spot, which was built and rebuilt successively. As the archaeological indications are and also the legend points, it was this spot where the Lord delivered his First Sermon, or it was the chamber of the Lord which was called *Gandha-kuti* or the Mulagandhakuti Vihara. If this was true, then structures were in existence at this spot right from the time of Gautama, the Buddha. It may be significant to note the excavator's observations: "...a large court measuring 47' from north to south and 27" broad internally is said to have 2'5" thick wooden posts. It has been further noted that the west wall ...seems to have originally formed part of a somewhat earlier building, now presumably buried under the main shrine" (Marshall & Konow in *Archaeological Survey of India Annual Report 1906-07*: 97-98 & 78).

The format of the landscape in the post-Asoka pre-Kushan period was more or less the same as during Asokan times. It may be held that the Dharmarajika stupa, Asokan pillars and the apsidal monastery were more or less in their original form in this period also. But, the constructional activities might have changed the appearance of Mulagandhakuti Vihara, by replacing the wooden railing of the earlier times with carved railing of stone, around 2nd/1st century BCE. Whether some other structures of the premises also were transcribed from wood to stone, or were freshly built, is difficult to ascertain. Similarly, though plausible, it is difficult to demonstrate whether some parts of Mulagandhakuti Vihara were renovated by durable medium at the time of emperor Asoka also.

IV

MRIGADAYA OF KUSHAN AND EARLY GUPTA TIMES

The Kushan/early Gupta period remains at Sarnath have been mostly clubbed together in excavation reports and earlier publications. Accordingly, the remains of 1st to 5th centuries CE of Sarnath form the subject matter of this part of the book. Two major dynasties—the Kushan and the Gupta imperial powers—ruled during the period. Though Varanasi formed part of Gupta kingdom, it was not an integral part of the territory ruled by the Kushan. But, the cultural landscape of the Kushan was extended much beyond their kingdom including the entire Ganga plain. Varanasi is said to be an administrative unit during the time. Contribution in the form of construction of structures and offering of images during Kushan period is well documented at Sarnath. But the inscriptions and nature of artefacts suggest that there was a break in the donative activities at this Buddhist site for about one-and-a-half centuries. Inscriptions of the Kushan-early Gupta period of Sarnath, for instance, record that donations at Sarnath were made during the reign of Kanishka (3rd Regnal year = 81 CE), and Asvagosha (ruling in the 41 Kushan Era = 119 CE), say in the last quarter of the first and first quarter of the 2nd centuries CE. The following group of epigraphs dates mostly to the Imperial Gupta rule—4th to 5th century CE. Thus, a gap of about one-and-a-half centuries (first quarter of 2nd and second quarter of 4th centuries CE), Later Kushan to pre-Gupta period is distinct in the archaeological remains of Sarnath being devoid of donation records.

This hiatus coincides with the change in the political and religious scenario of north India. The Kushan power declined shortly after the reign of Vasudeva (AD 145-176) (Sircar 1968: 151). Vasudeva is said to have been a devotee of Siva. It is also well established that the decline of the rule of the imperial Kushans gave rise to several republican and monarchical states in north India. "The prevalence of Naga rule over considerable portions of northern India in the third and fourth centuries AD" (Sircar 1968: 169) was the result of breaking of the Kushan empire. However, the change in the governance of the late/post Kushan time is significant for the history of Varanasi. As, one of the ruling dynasties of Naga, the Bharsivas, who are recorded to have performed the 'ten horses sacrifice' at Dashashvamedha locality of Varanasi city (Sircar 1968: 169), paved stone for Saivism in Varanasi. Being staunch Siva devotees, it may be held that it was due to their patronage that the seeds of Saivism in this holy city (Jayaswal 2011: 130-32), were sown. Desertion of such sites, like Aktha (identified as Rishipattana earlier), around the same time (2nd–3rd centuries CE), may indicate that the small Buddhist settlements also lost their identity around the same time in Varanasi region. It was, therefore, found logical to deal with the 'Kushan' and the 'Early Gupta' remains of Sarnath in two separate sub-sections—A. Imperial Kushan and B. Imperial Gupta.

A. Imperial Kushan

Rulers of the first two centuries of the Common Era, the Kushans, a branch of the Uchi tribe of Central Asia, not only embraced the indigenous religions of the Indian subcontinent, but added substantially to its material expression. The most dynamic patron of religious institutions, philosophy and arts was Kanishka (78-102 CE). His commitment to Dhamma in his later reign enriched Buddhist pilgrimages by donative constructions—the stupas and monasteries (Sircar 1968: 147). Initiation for carving of the Buddha image during his regime was a milestone for both Budhhism and plastic art of India. At Sarnath, the practice of offering to a Buddha idol had begun during his reign, which added a new chapter to the history of this site. The Bodhisattva image donated by Bala Bhikhu, during the regnal year of Kanishka (countable as 81 CE), is a landmark in the history of Buddhist art in general and the Sarnath school of sculptures in particular. Not all the successors of Kanishka were patrons of Buddhism (Sircar 1968: 151). In the last quarter of the 2nd century CE, during the reign of Vasudeva (145-76 CE), the royal patronage appears to have shifted from Buddhism to Saivism.

In view to highlight the contribution of the Kushans in the growth of Mrigdaya, the remains of this period have been divided into two parts—the structures and idols. The monuments constructed during the Kushan period at Sarnath are difficult to identify. In excavation reports and earlier publications, two categories are mentioned—renovation or addition of earlier structures and possible new constructions. The Dharmarajika stupa was renovated and a couple of monasteries were perhaps renovated and some new ones built (Majumdar, B. 1947: 16) at Sarnath in the period under consideration.

It has been recorded, for instance, that the first addition to the original form of the Dharmarajika stupa, the Asokan monument, was made during Kushan or early Gupta times by Marshall and Konow (*Archaeological Survey of India Annual Report 1907-8:* 65). According to Majumdar, this addition was done during the Kushan period (Majumdar, B. 1947: 16). The present author intends to agree with the later assumption. The history of religious patronage mentioned above also reflects so. Further, it may be recalled that Kanishka is said to have opened many stupas built by Asoka. After taking out relic caskets, he redeposited these in the same stupa (Majumdar, B. 1947: 16). This act was performed at Mathura, not very far from Varanasi. Is it not therefore possible that the same exercise was performed during his regime at Mrigadaya, which was one of the most holy pilgrimages of Buddhism? If this act was also repeated at Mrigadaya, the possibility of which is strong, then in the process of opening and redepositing of the relic casket the entire structure of dome of the stupa would first need to be dismantled and thereafter it would be reconstructed.

Two facts regarding the Dharmarajika stupa are relevant to this discussion. One, that the relic casket of Dharmarajika stupa of Sarnath was intact till the structure was pulled down in the 18th century. This fact testifies literary account suggesting that the Kanishka replaced the relic caskets of the stupas, which he opened. The other, that the crowning members—the *hermika* and the *chhatravali* of the Mauryan construction were displaced. Displacement of these two members would be an obvious act in such an operation. This too is suggestive in the field reports of Sarnath.

The monolithic *hermika,* which was discovered in the southern chapel of the main shrine, for instance, is said to be surmounting the Dharmarajika stupa, and was assumed to have been shifted from its original place. The excavator notes that:

> The railing is unfortunately badly fractured, and must have been so from an early age, as there are large breakages on the north and west sides, which had been made good with brick-work long before the main shrine, as it now stands, was built. It is quite possible, therefore, that the railing originally stood elsewhere and was transferred to this spot in sections, after it had been broken (Marshall and Konow in *Archaeological Survey of India Annual Report 1906-07*: 89).

The *hermika* and shaft of *chhatravali* thus appear to have been brought down when the dome of the Dharmarajika stupa was opened, most probably at the instance of emperor Kanishka. The relic casket was replaced thereafter and the dome reconstructed. This rebuilding of Dharmarajika may be identified as the first addition or Stage II of construction. The shaft of *chhatravali,* bearing Muaryan polish, might have been placed in erect position with the help of a brick masonry, stupa, in the southern chapel of the main shrine (Fig. 42). Later, when the relic casket was replaced in the stupa, it was not possible to place the earlier *hermika-chhatravali* composition on the top. Since both of the surmounting compositions were of sacred nature, these were preserved as part of worship architecture in the shrine complex, where the two are situated now.

During constructional Stage II of Dharamarajika, the *anda* (dome) of the stupa was enlarged. From its earlier diameter of 44′3", it was enlarged to 51′. Composed of bricks, both full (17" x 10½" x 2¾") and half, this masonry was found preserved in the southern part of the stupa. Enlargement of the dome in this stage covered the *pradakshina patha* of Stage I (*Archaeological Survey of India Annual Report 1907-08*: 65; Pl. XVIII). The core was filled with rubble and clay, and was covered by well-laid bricks and concrete, respectively. The dome was encircled perhaps by a *pradakshina patha,* which is not distinct due to overlap of the later constructional phases.

A few monasteries at Sarnath were constructed and perhaps also renovated during the Kushan period. Remains of a monastery of the Mauryan period suggest that location and perhaps demarcation of the monastery area was towards west of Mulagandhakuti Vihara. Besides building a monastery in the western area, monasteries were also constructed during the period north of the main shrine. Though it is not certain that the northern monastic area was occupied in pre-Kushan times, in the exposed structures the earliest levels appear to be of the Kushan period. If this is accepted, then it may be held that the expansion of residential area of monks and nuns was a new feature of the Kushan landscape (Fig. 45) of Sarnath.

The pre-Kushan monastery area lying west of the Mulagandhakuti Vihara appears to have three constructional phases. The first one, discussed earlier, was of the Mauryan period. The excavators record that after the disuse of the apsidal structure, the Mauryan monastery was superimposed with walls and a platform. The nature of these structures, which appear to date between post-Asokan and pre-Kushan, could not be ascertained (*Archaeological Survey of India Annual Report 1914-15*: 109-110). A long wall lying between the monastic structures and the Asokan column was also constructed during this stage. In the third constructional phase, a monastery was constructed at this place. This Kushan-early Gupta composition was found superimposing the northern side of the apsidal structure. A structure of unusual plan, it is reported to comprise a row of four cells (of the average size of 8′4" x 7′10") and a 5′4" wide corridor. To

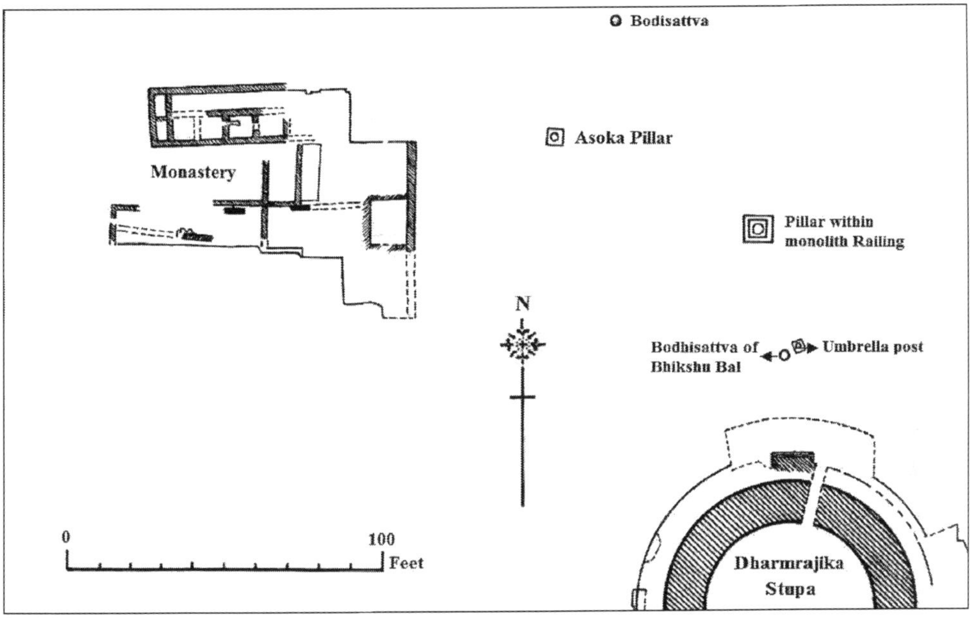

45. Location of plan of structures of Kushan times.

its western axis was a room (4′ wide), covering the entire length of the side. The total length of this burnt brick (16½″ x 10½″ x 2½″) structure measured 52′. The row of cells and the verandah leave no doubt that this was a monastery. It may be recalled that the Asokan column standing in front of the apsidal structure was meant to record the royal dictate of conduct for the monks and nuns, who were residing in it. This residential area appears to be in disuse. The monastery in consideration was constructed at the same spot during Kushan times. The inscribed column of Asoka was still intact. A short inscription, not complete, was also engraved on the Asokan pillar during the Kushan period. Thus, the structures and the inscriptions testify that the pillar and the monastery of the western side continued to form one complex in Kushan times, as was the case in Mauryan times.

Similarly, the Monasteries II, III and IV of Sarnath have been assessed to be of Kushan/early Gupta in date (Majumdar, B. 1947: 38040). The peripheral region of the Mulagandhakuti Vihara, particularly the north, was the dwelling area of monks and nuns during the Kushan to the medieval times. This complex of Sarnath is built and rebuilt superimposing one after the other a number of monasteries. As a result, the earlier constructions, which may have been constructed during the Kushan period, are restricted. The demonstrative example of it are the remains of Monasteries I and II.

Monastery II, which was buried beneath Monastery I, also known as Dharmachakra-Jina Vihara, is recorded to be superimposing a Kushan structure. It has been noted that beneath the upper structure, of early Gupta period, rested another earlier monastery. "Trenches sunk below the level of this monastery (*early Gupta*) revealed another and much earlier monastery" (Majumdar, B. 1947: 38). It is further noted that, "The wall of the earlier edifices was found standing in parts, to a height of 3 feet and had been used as foundation of the later wall" (Majumdar, B. 1947: 38). The antiquities, limited in number, which were found from the plinth date, to c. 1st century CE, and may only suggest an early date of buried structure (Marshall & Konow in *Archaeological Survey of India Annual Report 1907-08*: 56). The true nature of the Kushan monastery cannot be determined. The other monastery of Kushan/Gupta period is Monastery III. It is said that the level of this was low and was similar to Monastery II. Though Majumdar dates this structure to Late Kushan times (Majumdar, B. 1947: 39), the excavators assign this complex to the Gupta period (*Archaeological Survey of India Annual Report 1914-15*: 56). Similar is the case with Monastery IV, which too has been dated to the Gupta period by the excavators.

On account of the above, it may be summarised that the donation constructions of the Kushans at Sarnath presumably have been identified. The ones which are recorded are so fragmentary that their nature is difficult to ascertain. However, the vihara superimposing the apsidal structure of the Mauryan period, if taken to represent the period, may show that the monasteries of the pre-Gupta times were perhaps not fully developed and as elaborate as those of the Gupta and the post-Gupta periods. The renovation and enlargement of the Dharmarajika stupa, carried out during this period, also does not seem to add much to the architectural quality of this monument.

46. Bodhisattva image donated by Bala Bhikhu, Sarnath.

Contrary to structures, icons of the Kushan period at Sarnath are an important source for historical reconstruction of religious practices vis-à-vis image carving themes and executive skills of Buddhism of the beginning of Common Era. A new tradition which was initiated during the period was offering of idols to this pilgrimage. Initiation and prevalence of this practice on one hand gave impetus for carving of Buddha images, and on the other establishment and growth of local production centre/ centres, which may be addressed as the 'Sarnath School of Sculpture'. Three colossal Bodhisattva/ Buddha images, which were recovered from the vicinity of the Mulagandhakuti Vihara, are illustrative examples and need special mention.

The oldest inscribed image discovered at Sarnath is the large image of Bodhisattva, which was donated by Bala Bhikhu during the 3rd regnal year of Kushan king Kanishka (Fig. 46). F.O. Oertel records that it ... "was discovered mid way between the main shrine and Jagat Singh *stupa*"... (*Archaeological Survey of India Annual Report 1904-05*: 78). In its vicinity were lying broken parts of a large umbrella and the stump of an octagonal column (Fig. Nos. 5 & 7 of excavators' plan). The twin composition—the idol and the shaft mounted umbrella—is composed of deep red sandstone. This medium was obtained as per Oertel... "from the Paharpur quarries in Bharatpur State, between thirty and forty miles from Agra and Mathura"

(Oertel in *Archaeological Survey of India Annual Report 1904-05*: 97). Sarnath in particular and Varanasi region in general was utilising sandstone of the Chunar hills for local carvings throughout the ancient and medieval periods (Jayaswal 1998). The Bodhisattva image is an exception, and perhaps suggests that this composition was not locally produced, but was imported to Mrigadaya from Mathura, which was an established centre for carving images during the Kushan period. The iconographic features of this image also are similar to the Buddha idols at Mathura.

The image in consideration was recovered in three pieces: the body, the feet and the head. Together it measured 9½"high. Housed presently in the main hall of the site museum of Sarnath, this image has been described by the excavator thus:

> The figure wears a lower garment tied with a band to the waist, while the shawl or cloak worn over it is thrown lightly by over the shoulder, and the end is held up by the left arm. The right shoulder and arm are bare and, to judge from the broken fragments of the right arm, the right hand must have been raised in the *abhaya mudra.* Between the feet, facing the spectator, is standing an animal apparently intended for a lion. This may be placed there to help in identifying the statue ... (Oertel in *Archaeological Survey of India Annual Report 1904-05*: 79).

The image also bears traces of red and yellow paint.

On the other side of the Mulagandhakuti Vihara, towards the north, was found another colossal Bodhisattva image, which faced east (Fig. No. 9 of excavators' plan). Though this composition was a little smaller (6' high and 2'5" broad at the shoulder)—the idol and the umbrella shaft have striking similarity with the Bodhisattva image donated by Bala Bhikhu—it is uninscribed. The animal between the feet of the image is also not perhaps the lion. But, its identification is difficult due to the eroded surface. Sahni, however, has identified it as a crouching dwarf or Yaksha (Sahni 1914: 37). The head and the right hand, which was perhaps in *abhaya mudra*, were broken. The left hand is placed on the hip and clenched into a fist. The girdle and its loop also are depicted similar to the Bala Bhikhu image. The nature of garment too is similar to the above statue, but the folds of the

47. Carved *chhatravali* found with Bala Bhikhu Boddisatva image, Sarnath.

drapery are shown by shallow incised irregular lines over the flat surface (Sahni 1914: 37), suggesting the infusion of the Gupta style in an otherwise Mathura style of carving of Buddha images. The other striking feature of the composition in hand was that it was carved from buff sandstone of Chunar hills, thus suggesting a local production. Sahni writes, "I conclude that this image was prepared by a sculptor of Benares in imitation of the Mathura image referred to" (Sahni 1914: 37).

The third image too is of Bodhisattva (or could be of Buddha, before his enlightenment). Discovered towards the south-east of the Mulagandhakuti Vihara, this headless image (7'6½" high) was fractured

48. Locally carved Boddhisttava image of Kushan period, Sarnath Museum.

at the knee. Though the position of right hand is similar to the other two, raised up to the shoulder in *abhaya mudra,* the position of left is slightly changed. Instead of the hip, it has been placed on the thigh. Also the carving of drapery in this image is slightly improved. Sahni notes that, "In dress and style the image is similar to B(a)2 (the second image described above), but the drapery which in the preceding image had deteriorated into irregular shallow lines, is totally absent on the front of this image except over the left hand. In this respect, therefore, this image clearly marks a transition to the Gupta period when in the Sarnath sculptures drapery well-nigh disappears" (Sahni 1914: 37). Similar to the above two, this image too was attached to a stone umbrella, which could not be retrieved by Oertel, the excavator. The 11′ high octagonal shaft of the umbrella, however, was found lying near the image, which was placed on a medieval stupa (Sahni 1914: 38). Made of buff-coloured Chunar sandstone, this image was also painted in red, traces of which were found on the feet and above the ankle.

Besides the above three statues, which are products of Mathura and Varanasi, there are some other broken parts of images of the Kushan period, which on account of stone and style fall in one or the other. For example, Oertel's finding of a fragment of halo was made of Sikari sandstone. The plain reverse of this carving is adorned with scalloped ornament on the margins. While, the obverse depicts a foliage of the *pipal* tree, which suggests that it formed part of a Buddha image depicting the Lord either before or after enlightenment (Sahni 1914: 38). Presumably a counterpart of the halo is a fragment of seated Buddha/Bodhisattva, carved out of Sikri sandstone in Kushan style of Mathura. On the feet of this cross-legged figure are carved *triratna* and *chakra.* This image was unearthed from the north of the Mulagandhakuti Vihara in 1907-08. Likewise, Sahni has reported four other broken parts of Buddha/Bodhisattva images, which are made of Chunar sandstone, and were local productions. A Buddha head is particularly interesting to note, since it is carved out of Chunar sandstone (Sahni 1914: 39), but in Kushan style of Mathura. Unearthed by Oertel (*Archaeological Survey of India Annual Report 1904-5: 92),* the head is marked with a number of peculiar features—an *ushnisha* (the hump in the middle of the scalp) and an *urna,* a hollow mark between the eyebrows. The latter is not found in any of the Gupta images of Sarnath or Mathura. The nose, lips, chin and earlobes of this square cut face are damaged. But the eyebrows are delicately marked by a raised curved line (Sahni 1914: 39). The other head of the Kushan collection was discovered by Marshall and Konow from the south of Structure No. 37, about 6' (*Archaeological Survey of India Annual Report 1906-7: 80).* The absence of *urna, ushnisha* and fold on the neck of this composition, along with depiction of schematic curls on the scalp, makes it different from the other head. Though this is also carved in the Kushan style of Mathura, its medium is red Chunar sandstone (Sahni 1914: 39).

The nine carvings of Buddha/Bodhisattva of the Kushan period in the Sarnath collection throw significant light on the process of origin and development of the Sarnath School of sculpture. Though flourishing during the Gupta period, its foundation was laid during the time of Kanishka. The import of the colossal Bodhisattva image, the masterpiece of Mathura

49. An exposed stair case of Dharmarajika Stupa, Sarnath 2014.

to Sarnath for donation by Bala Bhikhu, not only initiated the practice of donation of idols at this site, but it gave a model to the local stone carvers. Copy of the style in Chunar sandstone by local artists reveals both to improve and experiment of chiselling, while maintaining the main stylistic features of the Mathura School. Besides, a shift from the Mathura style to the Sarnath style is well represented in the depiction of drapery of the colossal images of Bodhisattva.

Sarnath during the Kushan period was more or less similar to the Mauryan and Sunga periods. The main identified monuments of the period are Dharmarajika stupa, the inscribed column of Asoka, and the monastery facing the pillar. The marked change in this was a comparatively larger Dharmarajika stupa, from which the Asokan *hermika* and *chhatravali* composition was dismounted. The possibility that an alternative was provided to it, though not available, is likely. Similarly, the view of the monastic area also had a fresh look, with construction of a square/rectangle planned monastery, which covered the apsidal structure of the earlier phases. The northern monastic area, which also has monasteries of Kushan period, was perhaps a fresh addition, since no traces of pre-Kushan structure have so far been exposed from this locality. What was the look of the Mulagandhakuti Vihara, during Kushan times could be anyone's guess. The railing/railings of the Sunga times, which might have enclosed the Sacred Space, must be in existence. But, whether the masonry to protect it and some other parts of this nucleus area were constructed during the Kushan period is difficult to ascertain at present.

B. Imperial Gupta

The coming of the Gupta dynasty to power was a milestone for both the political and cultural history of India. It reinstated political stability, after the imperial power of the Kushan faded out. Chandragupta, a local chief of Patliputra, established Gupta rule in 319 CE, when he ascended the throne of Magadha with the support of the Lichhavis of Vaisali. Samudragupta is credited with unifying, expanding and consolidating the territory ruled by the Guptas. The illustrious son of Chandragupta and Kumaradevi (the Lichhavi princess), Samudragupta succeeded in carving a large and stable empire which was extended in the north up to the foothills of the Himalayas, in the south up to the Narmada, the Brahmaputra in the east and Jamuna and Chambal in the west. Though he was a follower of Vedic practices and had performed the *Ashvamedha-jnana,* he was also a patron of Buddhism (Majumdar, B. 1947: 18). Besides being a successful warrior, he was a creative writer and a musician. At the time of Chandragupta II, who succeeded Samudragupta in CE 376/380, the Gupta power was at its peak. He also led successful campaigns against Sakas and others, and was also a patron of art and literature. Majumdar has stated "...it is necessary to remember that this age (Gupta) was largely the creation of Samudragupta and Chandragupta II. Their conquests brought that imperial peace which rendered possible progress of culture and civilisation, which has rightly earned the epithet 'Golden Age' or 'Classical Age' for the period of Gupta rule in India" (Majumdar, R.C. 1954: 23). It was now that the Chinese pilgrim Fa Hien visited the 'Deer Park'. The Gupta legacy after Chandragupta II passed on to Kumargupta I, who ruled for more than 40 years after ascending the throne (414 CE).

His reign was also peaceful and prosperous and culturally very creative. But, during the end of his reign, invasion by the Hunas appears to have disrupted the peace and prosperity of the imperial power. Skandhagupta, his son who had returned after winning the war against the Hunas in 455-5 CE, is recorded to have narrated the event to his mother, implying that his father was not alive. After some conflict regarding succession, Skandhagupta ascended the throne and upheld the prestige and sovereignty of the imperial Guptas till 467 CE. History and genealogy of the Guptas after Skandhagupta is vague.

The age of the imperial Guptas, besides there political attainments, is remembered for developing various facets of Indian culture. The plastic art, painting, minor arts and crafts were patronised and mastered. A vast literature of normative texts, guiding arts, crafts and architecture, religion and sociological issues were penned down. Image worship, which had started a couple of centuries ago, had to be formalised. For this individual deities were personified in a way that these were recognised by the devotees. Iconography of various gods and goddesses, thus, had to be crystallised and written. The deities in worship were then thought to be enshrined for the sake of their protection. Building of temples was inevitable. The origin and development of temple architecture was one of the major contributions of the Guptas. All this happened in the 5th century CE.

It may not be a coincidence that a gap of about one-and-a-half centuries from the fall of imperial power of Kushan to the rule of the Guptas is distinctly marked in the archaeological remains of Mrigadaya. The most creative, prosperous and peaceful reigns of Chandragupta II and Kumargupta I (between last quarter of 4th and the second quarter of the 5th century CE) appear to coincide with the images and structures dated to early Gupta period at Sarnath. It was during the 5th and 6th centuries CE that Sarnath appears to be strewn with monasteries, stupas and shrines. Side by side, idols of the Lord in large quantities were donated here. The niches of the monuments, like Dhamek stupa, were adorned with images. Also, the earlier practice of offering independent images of Buddha to the auspicious spots continued. Some of the Buddha images of Gupta period in Sarnath are masterpieces of Indian plastic art. The monuments identified of the period at Sarnath are Monasteries II, III and IV, the shrine of the Mulagandhakuti Vihara, Dharmarajika, Chaukhandi and Dhamek stupas.

Incidentally, this list does not fully correspond with the list of structures mentioned by Fa Hien, who had visited Sarnath during the reign of Chandragupta II. The traveller mentions four large stupas and two viharas (Majumdar, B. 1947: 18). The fourth imposing stupa of the area was perhaps the one on which the modern temple of Sarangnath (Siva) is located. It may be assumed so because the mound beneath this temple is steep conical, and its eroded surface reveals patches of masonry. However, this mound awaits exposure for confirmation of its existence and details.

All the three monasteries of early Gupta times are situated in the north of the Mulagandhakuti Vihara (Fig. 50). At the western side of

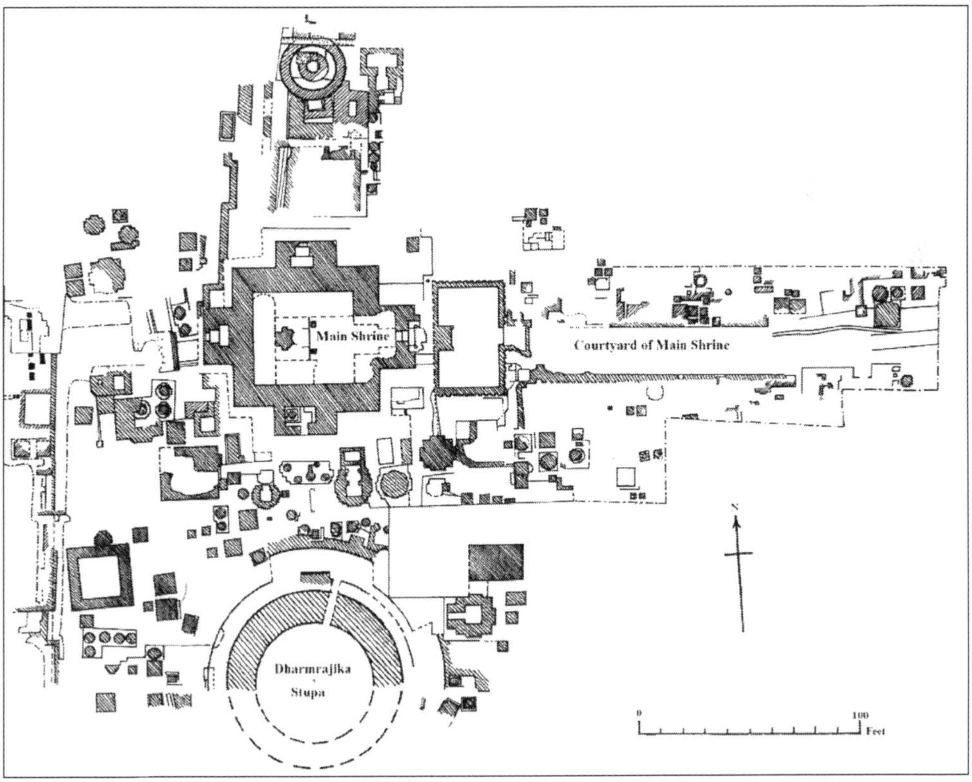

50. Plan of monuments of Gupta and early medieval times.

Dharmachakra-Jina Vihara (Monastery I), the outer wall of Monastery II demarcated the western limits of the monastery area. The square inner court (90'10") was encircled by a low wall (3'3" high and 1'8" thick). This wall was supporting the pillars of the verandah, which was built between the courtyard and the dwelling cells. Remains of the verandah, which were traced on the southern and western parts, were 9'8" wide. A row of nine cells unearthed on the western side was composed of 4'10" thick brick wall in front and 3'8" partition-walls at the sides. The outer wall of the western side of this structure was 10'1" thick. This was traced up to the length of 165'2" (*Archaeological Survey of India Annual Report 1914-15*: 54-56). The average size of bricks used in this masonry measured 15" x 9½" x 2¾". This structure has been dated to the period under consideration. Though some antiquities found from the plinth of this structure are assigned to c. 1st century BCE, the exposed part is dated to the Gupta period (*Archaeological Survey of India Annual Report 1914-15*: 56).

Exposure of Monastery III has brought to light a somewhat similar plan of a vihara, like the earlier one. A courtyard paved with flat bricks was surrounded by dwelling cells. The exposed area revealed seven cells in a row, which opened in a pillared verandah; this was attached to the inner courtyard. The passage was provided with niches (1'3" x 1'4½"), which were noted on the northern wall (*Archaeological Survey of India Annual Report 1907-08*: 57). "The verandah pillars, intercalated by a wall, are approximately 1'3" square at the base. The square base of the columns is octagonal in the middle, above which the corners are cut to form a hexadecagon with a necking of inverted lotus petals and again reverts below the cap to the square." On account of style of carving on the pillars, the structure is dated to the late Kushan period (Majumdar, B. 1947: 39). However, the architectural features of this structure take it closer to the Gupta period, as these compare well with Cave No. XI of Ajanta and Monastery II of Sarnath. The doorways of the cells (6'7" high and 4'2' wide) were adorned with carved bricks, as is testified by the top part of the lintel of Cell No. 3 (southern side), and the doorjambs and lintels were of wood (*Archaeological Survey of India Annual Report 1907-*

08: 58). The inner walls of the cells were perhaps plastered. The average height of the wall was 10 feet. The thickness of the wall suggests that the monastery had at least two storeys (Majumdar, B. 1947: 39). Pillars attached to the verandah of the upper storey were also identified. The windows were fixed perhaps with pierced stone slabs. The entrance to this structure was through the cell east of Cell No. 3, while the entrance to the first floor was from the chamber, which was located at the back of Cell No. 3. The courtyard had a provision for draining refuse water. This underground drain (10" deep and 7" wide) passed through the verandah and the passage at the southwest corner of the monastery.

Monastery IV also followed the architectural tradition of the Gupta viharas. Organised in three parts—the rows of cells, a pillared verandah in front and a courtyard in the middle, this structure was also built of brick and stone. Traces of three cells each of the north and the south axis, and the 7'6"–7'10" verandah and the brick-paved courtyard which were recovered in the north-east corner, at the "depth of 14'6" below the level of ground" (Majumdar, B. 1947: 39) testifies to the plan of this monastery. The pillars of verandah were set in a low wall (2'2" high and 3'3" broad). The stone pillars were 8' high. The other architectural details noted by the excavators are: "The front wall of the cells is 3'6½" wide, the party walls 2'4", and the back wall of the monastery 6'1" (Marshall & Konow 1911 in *Archaeological Survey of India Annual Report 1907-08*: 59). A drain to the north-eastern corner and the slope of the courtyard level towards the drain were other features similar to Monastery II. Lessening of the thickness of walls is characteristic of later constructions of the Gupta times. It was noted at Bhitari that the width of walls of the structures of the time of Kumargupta I were reduced considerably in the masonry of the time of Skandhagupta (Jayaswal 2001). If this tendency is taken to be an indication for determining the chronology of the Gupta structures, then Monastery IV was constructed later than Monastery III.

This monastery fell in disuse at some point of time, which is evident from a colossal image of Siva (12 x 1½' high 3'11" broad and 1'10" thick) found placed over the top of the wall of the eastern row of cells.

Placement of this post-Gupta statue obviously post-dates use of the monastery. "They plainly belong to a much later date, and could not have been put where they were found until the monastery we are describing was in ruins and covered over with debris" (Marshall & Konow in *Archaeological Survey of India Annual Report 1907-08*: 59). The image has been assessed to be of late medieval time (Majumdar, B. 1947: 66). However, a good number of iron implements were found on the floor of this complex, which were contemporary to the monastery. These were daily utility implements like vegetable cutter, sickle, knife blade, chisel, and rings. The other metal objects were a brass ring and a small chain (*Archaeological Survey of India Annual Report 1907-08*: 59).

The combination of twin media, the brick and the stone, used for the construction of monasteries at Sarnath goes hand in hand with the Gupta monuments of the middle Ganga plain. Close to the Buddhist pilgrimage site are located the temples of the time of Kumargupta I and Skandhagupta at Bhitari (Jayaswal 2001: 205). This group of buildings too is built of bricks and stone. Though decorated bricks prepared by moulds were used in both the groups of monuments—the temples and the monasteries—chunar sandstone blocks were utilised for the pillars, doorways, etc. (Figs. 51 & 53). Use of wood in monuments of the Gupta period has come to light. At Bhitari, the large post-holes exposed on brick floors of its locality BTR-2 are indication of the use of wooden posts (Jayaswal 2001: 150. Fig. 44). In

51. Doorjambs, Post Gupta period, Sarnath.

Monastry III at Sarnath, the excavators have also noted use of wood for the doorjambs and lintels (Marshall and Konow in *Archaeological Survey of India Annual Report 1907-08*: 58).

The unearthed masonry of the early Gupta times is noteworthy for the construction of unusually thick walls. The outer walls of these monuments, be it a temple as in the case of Bhitari (Jayaswal 2001), or a monastery of Sarnath, are very wide. At Bhitari, the average width of it was 1.80-2 m, while in case of Monastery II at Sarnath, it measured 10′ (about 3 m).

52. Carved architectural fragment, early medieval period, Sarnath Museum.

Contrary to the outer wall, the inner partitions were made either by 4′10"–2′7" (1.47 m–0.80 m at Sarnath and 1.6 m Bhitari) wide or 3′8" broad walls. The composition of thick walls utilised both complete (15" x 9½" x 2¾ = 38.10 x 24 x 6 cm Sarnath - 40 x 25 x 6 cm Bhitari) and broken bricks (22 x 20 x 5- 29 x 24 x 6 cm, noted at Bhitari) (Jayaswal 2001: 84). "Outlines were arranged by complete bricks, which were moulded in large quantities and wide variety, as per the requirements, while the filling, ... was accomplished by broken bricks. These bricks fragments were inset in thick coat of clay" (Jayaswal 2001: 205). It was also observed that the use of broken brick was not due to economic constraint, as is assumed at times, but was a deliberate attempt to give stability to thick masonry. The same technique of construction is also envisaged in the Gupta monasteries of

Sarnath. Façade of the walls were also decorated by designed bricks at both of these sites.

The tradition to build viharas appears to be well established by the Gupta period. Western India, which has rich concentration of Buddhist caves, evidenced development of chaitya-griha and vihara, besides worship and dwelling monuments. Here the monasteries of early phase are represented by Cave No. XI of Ajanta. Being the oldest cave of Ajanta, it is dated to c. 400 CE, almost early contemporary to the Gupta monasteries at Sarnath. Saraswati notes that the "*Vihara* was naturally planned in the form of a row of cells round a central court, which in excavated example took the shape of a central hall" (Saraswati 1954: 474). "Cells of irregular shape encircle three sides with pillared verandah in front forming a façade" (Saraswati 1954: 475). The axis opposite the entrance to this cave had three cells, in the centre of which was installed an image in a later period. This cave is recorded to be the earliest example of a pillared courtyard/hall (Saraswati 1954: 475).

The three monasteries of the Gupta period of Sarnath discussed above appear to follow the general architectural features of vihara. The plan consists of a square court in the centre, which is respectively enclosed on at least three sides by a pillared varandah and the row of cells or dwelling chambers. Since these are constructed by bricks, they differ marginally from the rock-cut viharas of western India. Besides the central courtyard, the façade of the rock-cut vihara was elaborately carved. At Sarnath, the carvings are confined mostly on the stone lintels, doorjambs and pillars. However, use of decorated bricks on the façade of the walls too was to give the structure a decorated look. But, the main plan of the rock-cut cave and the brick-made monasteries was alike.

Dhamek stupa, situated on the south-eastern part of the monument area of Sarnath, is a solid cylindrical structure. The dome of this stupa is 93′ in diameter. Cunningham gives the height of this stupa as 110′ above the surrounding ruins. But Oertel, who had exposed a terrace in front of the Jain temple, fixed the point of measurement of this monument from an exposed terrace 12′ above the road level. According to him, the height of the top of the dome was 104′, while the foundation level goes down to 39′ below the terrace (Oertel in *Archaeological Survey of India Annual Report 1904-05*: 72). The lower part of the structure (up to the height of 36′9") is composed of stone, while the upper part is a brick masonry. The upper part of the dome is composed of bricks (14′ x 8′ x 2″), and was encased by stone. A shift from the solid stone construction to the brick masonry was perhaps due to constraints of time and finances. The eight projections on the drum of the stupa are 21′6" wide and were placed 15′ apart from one another. These projections have provision for installation of images in niche. The projections and the lower part of the drum of Dhamek were adorned with geometric pattern carved in relief in typical Gupta style.

Cunningham in search of relic casket bore holes from the top to the bottom and across the dome. He sank three shafts in 1835—one vertical in the centre of the dome, while the two horizontal ones were placed above and below the stone constructed portion. He found an inscribed slab in 6th/7th century character, at a depth of 3′ from the top (Majumdar, B. 1947: 41). He also noticed evidence for an earlier structure made of bricks lying below the stone construction, at a depth of 110′. Oertel is of the opinion that the earliest construction of this stupa may be of Mauryan times (Oertel in *Archaeological Survey of India Annual Report 1907-08*: 74). But, the relics of the Lord could not be located by Cunningham, who records to have missed it due to certain unavoidable negligence. But Oertel is of the opinion that Dhamek was a memorial stupa "erected on the spot, where Maitreya received an assurance from Sakyamuni that he would be the next Buddha". If one takes note of the chronology of the events and also topography of the area of the Sarnath monuments, it may be held that the Dhamek stupa located on the south-eastern expansion of the sacred landscape had its foundations sunk deep through Kushan and Mauryan horizons. It was perhaps coeval with the base of the Asokan column. Constructed during the Gupta period, the floor of this structure occupies the highest contour of the unexposed area. The stone constructed part of the lower dome is certainly of Gupta period. The possibility of an earlier structure of Mauryan period expressed by Oertel, if means true, the working level of it must be almost on the same contour on which the floor of apsidal structure and Asokan pillar rested, which is difficult to establish in the present state of our knowledge. For, the given explanation by Oertel, that this stupa was constructed at the place where Maitreya received assurance from the Lord, has to be examined from multiple angles.

Construction of Stage III, or the second addition of Dharmarajika stupa, ascertained by the excavators, coincides with the period under consideration. The alteration of this stupa after the Kushans is dated to 5th/6th century CE, "when a *pradakshina patha* or circumambulatory passage of nearly 16′ across enriched the stupa and was encompassed by a solid outer wall of 4′5" high pierced by four doorways at each of the cardinal points" (Majumdar, B. 1947: 23). The dome was also enlarged, as per the diagram, showing history of construction of Dharmarajika stupa (Pl. XVIII in *Archaeological Survey of India Annual Report 1907-08*). Marshall and Konow note that the material used was "anything but lasting" (*Archaeological Survey of India Annual Report 1907-08:* 65). Thus, the structure needed strengthening in the succeeding century.

The brick structure Chaukhandi is also identified as a stupa built during the Gupta period. This is the first monument while approaching Sarnath from the Ganga and Varuna banks. Situated at a distance of about 2km from the nucleus, the Mulagandhakuti Vihara, this imposing structure marks the southern boundary of the Buddhist site under discussion. Locally known as Chaukhandi, or the square mound, this monument is accepted to be a memorial stupa, erected on the spot where Gautama Buddha on his way to Mrigadaya first met his five disciples (*Archaeological Survey of India Annual Report 1904-05:* 76). Cunningham sank a shaft in the centre of this large masonry in 1836, but could not find the relic casket. Excavations conducted by Oertel brought to light a concrete passage around the stupa, the lower part of which was composed of three square terraces each about 12′ high and 12′ broad. The octagonal stupa line was traced on the highest terrace (*Archaeological Survey of India Annual Report 1904-05:* 75). The octagonal plan of the stupa had starlike points at the angles. Oertel noted that, "Each terrace was supported by outer and inner walls with a number of cross walls to strengthen them" (*Archaeological Survey of India Annual Report 1904-05:* 75).

The Chaukhandi stupa measures from the ground to the top of the octagonal chamber 84′ (Majumdar, B. 1947: 25-26). It may be interesting to note that Xuanzang mentions the height of this stupa to be 300′, while according to Oretel's estimation it was 200′ high. Buddhist images of Gupta and early medieval times were discovered from this area. It is, however, difficult to demarcate the constructions of the Gupta and medieval periods separately. But, the octagonal tower which surmounts this stupa was constructed by Akbar to commemorate the visit of his father Humayun in 1588 CE, as per the inscription on the northern doorway engraved in AH 996 (*Archaeological Survey of India Annual Report 1904-05:* 75).

Mulagandhakuti Vihara is mostly addressed as the 'main shrine' in the excavation reports and the early publications on Sarnath. As has been mentioned earlier, this was the sacred area where the Lord stayed. The initial constructions (of Buddha to the pre-Asokan times) in this part appear to be of wood. The enclosure and the structures were transcribed in stone and masonry during successively periods. Mulagandhakuti Vihara perhaps acquired the status of a temple, the Shrine, during Gupta period. This is suggestive from the history of origin and development of structural temples of north India.

Mulagandhakuti Vihara, which was renovated and reconstructed a number of times, appears to have been built as a temple for the first time during the Gupta period when architecture of a structure enshrining a deity was crystallised (Saraswati 1954: 503-5). The other significant fact to be noted is that the origin of structural temples lies in the Buddhist rock-cut caves. At Udayagiri, two compartments—the sanctum and the pavilion—essential parts of a shrine, can be seen for the first time. The temples at Sanchi (Temple No. 17) and Tigwa were the next stage of the development of temple architecture. The square sanctum attached with an opening in the pillared portico became purely structural. Incidentally, Temple No. XVII of Sanchi is regarded as a Buddhist structure, suggesting construction of temples also by the Buddhist followers in Gupta times.

It may further be noted that the two cave temples of the Udayagiri hills were constructed during the reign of Chandragupta II. Temple of Cave No. 6 at Udayagiri, which was a combination of rock-cut and structural architecture, is significant. For, it marks the beginning of structural temples. It also records the name of the king and the date of 82 Gupta Era (402 CE), when this experiment was performed (Meister et al. 1988).

Nearer home, temples were constructed at Bhitari during the time of Kumargupta I (414-455 CE) and Skandhagupta (455-467 CE) (Jayaswal 2001: 75 & 127). These examples testify that by the 5th century CE, temples of Brahmanical and Buddhist following were being constructed in north India. On account of this, it may be held that the Mulagandhakuti Vihara was also transformed from a simple enclosed sacred place to a planned temple-complex during the 5th century CE. It may be possible to assume a more precise date for the initial construction of this shrine on account of the inscribed images found from the premises. The dated image of the standing Buddha unearthed from the south approachway (at the depth of 3′8" below the surface) is recorded to be the gift by monk Abhayamitra in the 154 Gupta Era, which will fall within the reign of Kumargupta I. There were also other images found from the same locality, which on stylistic grounds appear to be contemporary to this image (*Archaeological Survey of India Annual Report 1914-15:* 99). These images suggest that donation activities had concentrated in the premises of the main shrine area, particularly during the reign of Kumargupta I.

The main shrine complex is a 18′ high brick masonry, surrounded by a concrete floor which extends 40′ in all the directions. Facing east, the plan of the shrine resembles the Christian cross. The central chamber, or the *garbhagriha,* which was square in plan (60′ x 60′), was attached with projecting chapels at south, west and north and a portico to the east. These chapels enshrined Buddha images, traces of which were recorded in the southern chapel. The exterior of the structure was marked by projection as may be viewed in the exposed parts. The temple had thick walls suggesting an imposing superstructure (Majumdar, B. 1947: 29). Xuanzang records that the 'Chief fane (Mulaghandhakuti)' was about 200 feet high and surmounted by a golden amra fruit. This description does suggest the existence of a lofty *shikhar* of this shrine during the 6th century CE. That the shrine had a tower from the beginning, though difficult to demonstrate, is possible because it is evident from the other existing examples that the temples of 5th century CE were adorned by developed *shikhar* in this part of the country (Jayaswal 2001), as is testified by the Gupta temple of Bhitargaon. The original construction of the main shrine of Sarnath had undergone many changes, and it is difficult to mark the successive phases of this building. For instance, a brick wall was constructed in the main chamber at a later date, which reduced the size of the inner chamber considerably (25'6" on each side). Similarly, the use of earlier architectural members in haphazard manner to the later masonry further shrouds the original composition of this monument. But, the concrete floor surrounding this structure may be accepted as the horizon which demarcates the early Gupta from the Later and Post-Gupta phases. It was noted earlier that below this concrete cover was found buried ruins of early Gupta and remains of Pre-Gupta times.

Donation of images by Buddhist devotees, which was initiated during the Kushan period, geared up during the Gupta times. The centre of the offerings was the main shrine area. A cluster of images, both dated and uninscribed, for instance, was discovered from the eastern side of the main shrine. Unearthed from the south of the approachway, the inscribed images are dated to Gupta Era 154 and 157, of the reign of Kumargupta I and Buddhagupta (*Archaeological Survey of India Annual Report 1913-14: 99*). The name of the donors on these are monks and nuns. That this pilgrim site was adorned with a large number of masterpieces of the

53. Preaching Buddha image of Gupta period, Sarnath.

Gupta period is testified by the rich collection of Buddha images housed in the site museum of Sarnath (Figs. 53 & 54).

The nature of landscape of Deer Park (Sarnath) described by Fa Hien (4th century CE), who had visited Sarnath during the reign of Chandragupta II, was marked by four large stupas and two viharas (Beal 1869: 134-36). He records that "On Buddha's arrival the five men rose and saluted him and here they have erected a tower ... also on the following spots, on a site sixty paces to the north of the former place where Buddha, seated with his face to the east, began to turn the wheel ... also on a spot twenty paces to the north of this, where Buddha delivered his prediction concerning Maitreya, also on a spot fifty paces to the south of this... in all these places towers have been erected which still exist". He further notes that, "In the midst (of the park) there are two sangharamas which still have priests dwelling in them" (Beal 1869: 136-137).

54. Standing Budha image in *abhaya mudra*, Gupta period, Sarnath.

The four stupas of this description could be identified as Dharmarajika, Dhamek, Chaukhandi and the unexposed mound on top of which the modern temple of Sarangnath is located (south-east of the main group of monuments. But, instead of two, three monasteries have been identified as of Gupta period in the excavation report. If the description of the Chinese traveller is relied upon, then it may be held that at least one monastery and the Mulagandhakuti Vihara post-date his visit.

The omission of the main shrine in the description of the travel account is significant, as it may suggest that the temple was constructed here post-date the visit of Fa Hien. Another fact important to recall is that beneath the concrete floor were buried early Gupta to Mauryan remains, which is indicative of a hiatus in the growth of this pilgrimage. Perhaps this religious establishment received considerable damage, in which imposing monuments like the Asokan column was also damaged. Oertel also records that, "I cannot help thinking that Sarnath must have experienced a period of neglect or desertion before the shrine was constructed" (*Archaeological Survey of India Annual Report 1904-05*: 69). This was the time when most of the earlier ruins were covered and large monasteries and shrines were built. Incidentally, Fa Hien's account does not record any devastation at this site. The major event which post-date Fa Hien's visit and pre-date Skandhagupta's reign is invasion of the Hunas, who by historical estimations reached this part of the Ganga plain. If this is accepted then it may be held that after the destruction caused by the Huna invasion, Skandhagupta and his successors contributed to restoring and reviving Mrigadaya. Evidence for repair of images during the early Gupta period has been recorded from Sarnath. Hargreaves, for instance, has reported discovery of an image of Buddha close to the one found from the east of the main shrine. The later one is dated to 154 CE (of the time of Kumargupta I). The other image which is of the standing Buddha (4' 10½" high) is similar in style. "Nose and drapery on right show iron dowel and matrices", which are indicative of its repair in ancient period (*Archaeological Survey of India Annual Report 1913-14*: 99). There were other examples of ancient repair of idols. The one which is inscribed of 157 CE (of the time of Buddhagupta) was also repaired by insetting iron dowels. It may be recalled that Skandhagupta, after restoring imperial Gupta power by defeating the Hunas, reconstructed the temple at Bhitari. The main temple, in the premises of inscribed pillar, was dedicated to Lord Vishnu, which was constructed over the foundations of an earlier temple made by his father Kumargupta I (Jayaswal 2001). This would imply that not only the original construction of the main shrine, Mulagandhakuti, at Sarnath took place during the reign of Skandhagupta, but, the broken icons were also caused to be repaired during his time.

V

LATE GUPTA AND EARLY MEDIEVAL

The time span between the later Gupta and the early medieval periods was the final stage of expansion of the Buddhist landscape of Sarnath.

Many older monuments had existed during this period. Some of these were repaired and also perhaps enlarged. Only a few new monasteries were constructed. The general view of monuments with an input of chronology is available in the description of Xuanzang, who visited this pilgrimage in 7th century CE. The following parts of his description are particularly significant:

> To the north-east of the river Varuna about 10 li or so, we come to the *sangharama* of *Lu-ye (Stag desert).* Its precincts are divided into eight portions (*section)* connected by a surrounding wall. The storeyed towers with projecting eaves and balconies are of very superior work (Beal 1884: 45).

In this description, Mrigadaya is said to be located at some distance from the Varuna river and the nucleus of the pilgrim site is said to be enclosed by a wall. The inner space was perhaps divided into eight sections. Traces of enclosure wall, though, were found in the northern area of the monument complex, and this wall appears to demarcate the monastery area located in the west and north of the main shrine (Fig. 50).

"In the great enclosure is a *Vihara* about 200 feet high, above the roof is a golden covered figure of the Amra (*An-mo-lo*-mango*)* fruit. The foundations of the building are of stone, and the stairs also, but the towers and niches are of brick. The niches are arranged on the four sides in a hundred successive lines, and in each such niche is a golden figure of Buddha" (Beal 1884: 45).

This description of the main Mulagandhakuti Vihara in fact is the existing view of the main shrine. It may further be added that composed of stone and bricks, this structure had a large tower, *shikhar*, and a decorated façade, with niches embodying Buddha figures.

The travel account further mentions that "South-west of *Vihara,* is a stone stupa built by Asoka-raja. Although foundations have given way, there are still 100 feet or more of the wall remaining. In front of the building is a stone pillar about 70 feet high." It was here that Tathagata (*ju-lal*), having arrived at enlightenment, began to turn the wheel of law (*to preach*) (Beal 1884: 45). It may be interesting to note that donative offerings made by Mauryan king Asoka in 3rd century BCE remained in the memory of the people for about a thousand years, up till 7th century CE.

The Dharmarajika stupa mentioned by Xuanzang was not in good condition. It may be mentioned that the stupa which the visitor was looking at was the one after its repair in 5th /6th century CE (Stage III). This would imply that the structure was repaired more than a century ago from the time of its recording. It is interesting to note that Xuanzang found the stupa in depleted condition, and Marshall and Konow explain the quality of construction of Stage III. The excavators note, "That material used were, as just stated, anything but lasting; and it was probably not very long before the buttress (IV) on the north side had to be inserted, in order to prevent the shell falling away. No doubt it was for the same reason, also, that the *pradakshina* was finally filled in altogether, as being the easiest method of buttressing up the whole of the base of the *stupa*." (*Archaeological Survey of India Annual Report 1907-08:* 65).

Dharmarajika stupa was repaired and renovated at least three times during the later Gupta and early medieval times. The excavators have dated the Stage IV of repair of Dharmarajika to 7th century CE. "The few finds made in the debris filling appear to indicate that this took place about the 7th century AD. The next two additions (VI and VII) we assign to 9th or 10th century AD, and the last (VIII) to the final building epoch at Sarnath, when the great monastery on the northern side of the site was erected. The brickwork is of precisely the same description, as we find there" (*Archaeological Survey of India Annual Report 1907-08:* 65). The final stage, according to this description, would date to 12th century CE.

Xuanzang records that, "By the side ... (three *stupas* where there are traces of the sitting and walking of the three former Buddhas), is a *stupa*. This is the spot where Maitreya Bodhisattva received assurance of his becoming a Buddha" (Beal 1884: 46).

This stupa has been identified as Dhamek. It has been mentioned earlier that the main structure of this monument was composed of stone and brick, which was the workmanship of Gupta period. On account of the floral designs on the stone encasing of this stupa, it could be assigned a period of 4th/5th century CE. If this is so and also the account of the pilgrim is taken note of, then up till the 7th century CE this monument had maintained its grandeur.

He describes the stupa at Chaukhandi as: "Leaving this place, and going 2 or 3 li to the southwest of the *sangharama,* there is a stupa about 300 feet high. The foundations are broad and the building high, and adorned with all sorts of carved work and with precious substances... There are no successive stages (*to this building)* with niches: and though there is a standing pole erected above the cupola (*fau poh),* yet it has no encircling bells (Beal 1884: 45).

This stupa may be identified as the terraced stupa of Chaukhandi. It was noted earlier from the accounts of the excavator that this monument was perhaps constructed during the Gupta period, but was also in use up to the early medieval times, which is suggested by the findings of images. It may be held that when the Chinese traveller came to Sarnath, this monument was in use and in good condition.

The two structures, which were new additions to the group of monuments at Sarnath during early medieval times, need special mention. These are Monasteries I and VI.

Known as Dharmachakra-Jina Vihara, Monastery I is located to the north of the Mulagandhakuti Vihara. The excavators, Marshall and Konow, record that, "In 1907 we discovered, in the monastery area, a singularly imposing structure dating approximately from the 12th century AD." (*Archaeological Survey of India Annual Report 1907-8:* 43). A precise date for this complex could be ascertained later due to the epigraph found from the vicinity. Kumaradevi, queen of the Gahadawala king Govinda Chandra (1114-54 CE) of Kanauj, is said to have constructed this monastery (Majumdar, B. 1947: 36).

Monastery I was found in badly damaged condition (*Archaeological Survey of India* Annual *Report 1907-08:* 43-46). However, the south-western part of this masonry complex, which is comparatively intact, when excavated revealed a surrounding wall of the quadrangle ... "around which the monastery is built," ... this wall... "returns towards the north, but after a space of 6 feet breaks off abruptly..." (*Archaeological Survey of India Annual Report 1907-8:* 43).

The total area occupied by Dharmachakra-Jina Vihara at its ground measured 760' m in east-west direction. The monastery complex was also enclosed by a wall, which was intercepted by carved bastions. A long wall stretching from the second gateway (west) to the western limit of the site was traced in the excavations (Majumdar, B. 1947: 36). The main entrance to the monastery was from the east, which opened into a 114' long (east-west axis) courtyard. The entrance was "flanked on the outsides with richly carved bastions with a neatly constructed gate-keepers lodge within" (*Archaeological Survey of India* Annual *Report 1907-8:* 45-46). The boundary wall of the eastern side, which embodies the gate and encircles the courtyard, is composed of 4'4" thick masonry. The boundary wall is composed of brick-bats, which fills the inner part, while its façade is constructed of complete and chiselled bricks placed neatly. The monastery had a second gateway, which was not in full alignment with the earlier one. Attached to a spacious courtyard, this gateway was located on its eastern axis. The second gateway, a larger composition than the previous one, was also decorated and attached to it was a gatekeepers' chamber. "But, between the bastions and the lodge, instead of a mere wall, there was a large gatehouse, measuring 61' x 28' and containing several chambers" (*Archaeological Survey of India Annual Report 1907-08:* 45). Excavators presume this gateway to look like a *gopuram* of the South Indian temples, since the foundation of it is massive. The medium used for the gateways, the chiselled brick and stone, and the nature of composition was same as the main building of the monastery. Some pilasters were also recovered from the area, but the elevation of the structure could not be ascertained due to its ruined condition.

The main courtyard was attached to two smaller courts in the south and perhaps in the north. The floor of the courtyard was covered by 4′ x 2′3" x 1′ sandstone slabs, and was also covered by a concrete floor, corresponding with the concrete flooring of the eastern part of the main shrine. Exposed near the western boundary wall, the courtyard at three sides was encircled by dwelling cells. Near the north-western corner of the court was exposed a well, surrounded by a low parapet. A great drain was exposed, which was draining all the refuge water from the monastery. Exposed up to the length of 52′, its side walls were 6′ high and about 2′6" thick. Its floor was covered with sandstone slabs and the drain too was covered by sandstone slabs (average size 5′3" x 1′6" x 8"). The drain was about 6′ deep and 3′4" wide.

The basement of this monastery was made of chiselled bricks decorated on the outer and the inner façades by insetting moulded bricks up to the height of 8′. This structure was found in a badly damaged condition. The stone carved lintels and doorjambs were found lying in basement and over the courtyard. Existence of another storey of this monastery can be presumed from the debris. The images recovered from this complex date between late Gupta and early medieval, suggesting that the Dharmachakra-Jina Vihara superimposes some earlier structures.

Monastery VI, which is also known as 'a Hospital', as per Major Kittoe's identification, has two constructional phases—the earlier phase belonged to the early Gupta period, and the later to the 8th or 9th century CE (*Archaeological Survey of India Annual Report 1907-8:* 62). The floor level of the earlier building was exposed at 4′9" below the later one, and in plan and medium, it is quite different from the later masonry.

The later monastery could be dated on account of a sealing, which was obtained from a cell and was inscribed in a script of 9th century CE (Majumdar, B. 1947: 41). Built of smooth chiselled bricks, this structure also had a quadrangle in the centre. As per Cunningham's estimation, it measured 60′ (east-west) and 42′ (north-south). The parapet wall on the south side of this courtyard measured 1′2½″ high and 3′2" wide. Composed of thick rubble brick, it was coated with lime plaster. In this were set stone columns, which were to support the verandah. Four pillar bases were found in situ during excavations (*Archaeological Survey of India Annual Report 1907-8:* 63). The dwelling cells which opened in the verandah had stone thresholds and doorjambs. Use of earlier material could also be noticed in this monastery. The entrance to this complex was from the west, and through twin chambers. With regard to architectural features, this structure may be classified with monasteries. But, since Major Kittoe discovered a number of pestles and mortars inside it, he named it 'Hospital' (*Archaeological Survey of India Annual Report 1907-8:* 63). Marshall and Konow have identified it as a monastery.

Besides the listing of the above-discussed monuments, Xuanzang mentions that, "Within the precincts of the enclosure (of the *sangharama*) there are many sacred vestiges, with *viharas* and *stupa,* several hundred in number. We have only named two or three of these" (Beal 1884: 48). The excavated remains around the main shrine have brought to light a number of votive stupas, small structures (shrines), and of course idols of Buddha and Bodhisattva, corroborating the travel account and also providing evidence that numerous offerings of small structures and images were being made at Sarnath during the post-Gupta and early medieval periods. The nucleus of the Buddhist landscape had a dense concentration of material offerings, before it was deserted.

4

DONORS AND DONATIONS

Donors and Donations

The statement that, "Mrigadaya could attain status of one of the most significant and well established pilgrimage of Buddhism was due to the generous patronage of the donors", would not appear an overstatement if one glances through the structures and sculptures found at Sarnath. The earliest group of structures and sculptures—monastery, Dharmarajika stupa and the lion pillar of the time of Mauryan king Asoka, for instance, to the Dharmachakra-Jina Vihara of the early medieval period which was constructed by queen Kumaradevi—are donation to the place where the Lord turned the Wheel of Law. Similarly, the offerings of icons at this site between Kushan and early medieval times, too, were significant acts of donation. Donors or patrons, one of the main carvers of this Buddhist landscape, thus form an integral part of this theme.

It was narrated in the previous chapter that Sarnath or Mrigadaya, as has come to us, is composed of a number of small and large monuments, many of which were adorned with icons and carved stone panels (Chapter 3). One gets a glimpse of donation practices in the ancient texts, and recordings engraved on the offerings. The epigraphs or the engravings on the images or on architectural slabs are an authentic source for determining the name, status and date of individual donations. At Mrigadaya, the epigraphs date between Mauryan and early medieval times, which coincides with the structural history of the site. On account of these, it is possible to reconstruct the chronology, as well as list the status of individual donors, which is attempted below.

BUDDHA TO PRE-ASOKAN TIMES

When Shakya Muni came to Mrigadaya, it was a natural habitat with access-pools and forest patches where deer resided. It has been discussed earlier in this book (Chapter 2) that the area of Rishipattana and Mrigadaya was characterised by a wide stretch of grasslands inset with streams and ponds of sweet water, which was particularly suitable habitat for quadric-pedal fauna like deer. It was also conjectured that Rishipattana, though said to be occupied by hermitage-based settlements going far in antiquity, human habitation at Mrigadaya does not go beyond the advent of the Lord and his followers. This implies that the pre-*Dharmachakra-pravartana* stage of this pilgrimage, therefore, was completely devoid of constructions and human settlement.

The advent of Tathagat at Mrigadaya initiated dwelling in this natural habitat. After the event, delivery of the First Sermon, there was certainly a large following of the Lord. The process of offering by his devotees to sustain him and his *sangha* would have been imperative. This initial stage must have been offering of consumable articles like food and clothes. The common items of daily utility such as pots and pans, and of course shelters for dwelling, might as well would have been arranged by the devotees. But, the evidence for this presumption is meagre. For, the nature of Sarnath between the First Sermon (6th century BCE) and the donation made by Mauryan king Asoka (3rd century BCE) is not represented in the archaeological remains. It has been mentioned by the excavators (*Archaeological Survey of India Annual Report 1914-15:* 106; *Indian Archaeology 1992-93: A Review*: 99), for instance, that no pre-Mauryan level could be traced during the digging of the site. Not even in the western part of the main shrine where Mauryan remains are located. Nor does one find clear reference to donation of this period at Mrigadaya in Buddhist literature. Take for example, the list of the eight stupas (8+2 if Piplivan and Drona are included), constructed on the ashes of the Lord just after his *Mahaparinirvana*, does not include Isipatana-Mrigadaya (Kashyap 1958: 9). This implies that Sarnath was perhaps deprived of such monuments, which were constructed under royal patronage soon after the *Mahaparinirvana* of Buddha. Also, it is difficult to speculate whether the place continued as the natural habitat of deer, referred to as 'Deer Park', or had developed into a flourishing religious settlement. Perhaps a combination of both was the scenario.

In spite of the paucity of the material remains, it may be held that donation at Sarnath might have started right from the time of the *Dharmachakra-pravartana* incident. Since life of a Buddhist monk or nun depends primarily on the offerings made to them by the followers of the Dhamma. It is hard to comprehend that offerings by devotees were not made at Mrigadaya, where not only the Lord performed the pious act of turning the Wheel of Law, but Sangha was formed immediately thereafter. In *Vinaya-Pitaka,* it is said, for instance, that a merchant, Yasa, went to the Deer Park (Rishipattana?) and was accepted as a lay disciple by the Lord. At the time *Sangharama* was already formed by the induction of the five disciples to whom the First Sermon was delivered by the Lord (Horner 1951: 23-24). Glimpse of offering by lay devotees to the monks too can be had from the Buddhists texts. According to *Vimanvatthu*, for instance, a resident near Fisherman Gate of Varanasi saw monks passing through the gate and took them to her house and offered them food, etc. She also constructed a pavilion to house them and listen to Dhamma (Horner 1954: 43), suggesting that even common citizens of Varanasi city were making offerings to the monks. Indications of structure building too are found in such literary descriptions. These instances are suggestive of donation of food and structures, in city, as well as at Mrigadaya during the 6th century BCE and thereafter.

The paucity of material remains of pre-Mauryan period at Sarnath may be due to the use of perishable material for the construction of buildings, as was the case during the Northern Black Polished Ware period in the Middle Ganga plain. Closer home, the findings of Period IB of

Kashi-Rajghat, the capital city of the Kashi Janpada, throws significant light on this issue. The date for Period IB, on account of the C_{14} date of 490 ± 100 BCE, is countable to c. 6th/5th to 4th centuries BCE (Narain & Roy 1976: 24), which makes it contemporary to Buddha. Though remains of dwelling structures of the period could not be unearthed, their existence in the form of reed-walled huts with mud plastering has been assumed by the excavators (Narain & Roy 1976: 24). That perishable material was being used both for small and large structures is also attested by the traces of a large wooden platform (34 m long and 5 cm thick) and a clay embankment along the bank of the river, and traces of clay-rammed floors and post-holes, reminiscent of wooden posts, from the settlement.

Evidence of religious and dwelling structures in the form of donations in pre-Buddha period at Sarnath is not available, yet their possibility is strong. The recent excavations conducted in 2014, at Sarnath by the Archaeological Survey of India, has given a pre-Asokan date (4th century BCE) of the charcoal samples, which are dated by MS dating (personal communication with Dr. B.R. Mani and Dr. Ajai Srivastava). Though a distinct pre-Mauryan horizon has not yet been ascertained by the excavations, the possibility of its existence cannot be ruled out.

DONATIONS BY ASOKA AND HIS SUCCESSORS

The very first record for the visit and donation at Mrigadaya is of the time of Mauryan emperor Asoka. In Rock Edict VIII, the king addressed as 'Piyadarshi' is claimed to have initiated in his tenth regnal year, *Dhamma-yatra,* the pilgrimage, instead of *Vihara yatra,* which were taken for amusement by the earlier kings. He is further said to have initiated this tradition by visiting *Sambodhi*, 'Bodh Gaya', where Lord Buddha attained enlightenment (Pande 1965: 12 & 52). Another epigraphic record, which also is significant for the present theme, is Rumandai records, in which he is said to have visited the place of birth of the Lord and felicitated the pilgrimage by constructing monuments (Pande 1965: 189). Sarnath or Mrigadaya, being one of the four places associated with the life of the

Buddha, was certain to have received royal attention. The reference of *Divyadana* is significant, as it records his visits to the Buddhist sites and also donation of buildings. "The Divya (389-94), for instance, mentions Asoka as intimating to Upagupta his desire to visit the places connected with the Buddha's activities, and also to erect stupas there. Thus, he visited Lumbini, Bodhimula, Isipatana, Migadaya and Kusinagara..." (Malalasekera 1995: 325). If this statement is to be relied upon, then the emperor constructed one stupa each at Rishipattana and Mrigadaya. This would also imply that up till the 3rd century BCE, there was no stupa at both these places—Rishipattana and Mrigadaya.

It may be interesting to note that much later, during the 6th century CE, when the Chinese pilgrim Xuanzang had visited Varanasi, he also noticed two stupas. The first one he described away from the Deer Park, which he came across first, while walking from the city of Varanasi on his way to Sarnath. This one was perhaps *Jhaua-jharan*, the one standing at Paharia, near Aktha (Jayaswal 2012: 232-3). If my assertion that Aktha was the Rishipattana of the early Buddhist literature is accepted, then it follows that the stupa of *Jhaua-Jarana* was the one which was first visited by the traveller. The other one was located at the Mrigadaya, where Asoka *Raja* is said to have constructed the Dharmarajika stupa (Beal 1884; Book VII: 45). The traveller also records two other monuments, a vihara, the residence for monks and a pillar erected by '*Asoka Raja*' (Beal 1884; Book VII: 45-46). As was discussed earlier (Chapter 3), the apsidal structure and the pillar bearing Asokan inscription, in front of it, were one unit. The other unit of monument complex of Asokan times was the Dharmarajika stupa and the pillar standing in front of it.

It was also discussed earlier that the inscribed pillar standing in front of the apsidal structure was not seen by the Chinese traveller. And, the one which has been referred by him was perhaps uninscribed and is partly traceable in the fragments of pillar shafts housed under the shed at the site (Chapter 3). Both the units of monuments—the monastery-pillar and the stupa-pillar—were donated by the Mauryan king at Mrigadaya. On

55. Copy of the Asokan inscription on the shaft of the lion capital, Sarnath.

account of the archaeological remains and the literary description, it may be held that Asoka seems to have donated at least three pillars in Rishipattana-Mrigadaya region. One pillar was standing in front of the stupa at Paharia, which itself is located in the periphery of Aktha, the Rishipattana. The other two, as is discussed above, formed part of the monument complexes of the Mrigadaya.

The inscription on the lion capital pillar is in Brahmi script of Asokan time and was originally of eleven lines (Fig. 55), of which the upper three lines are damaged. The intact portion of the epigraph mentions the verdict of the emperor regarding Buddhist Sangha, and is translated as below (Sanhi 1914: 30):

> His sacred Majesty King Piyadasi ... at [Pataliputta] ... the Church is [not] by anyone to be divided. But, whosoever, monk or nun, shall break up the

> Church, shall be made to don white robes and made to dwell in another dwelling. Thus should this command brought to nigh in the order of monks and in the order of nuns.
>
> Thus said his sacred Majesty. One such edict hath been inscribed at the place of assembly in order that it may be near you. And even such an edict ye must inscribe for the laity. And the laity also should come on the Sabbath-days in order to be inspired with faith in this edict. On every Sabbath-day regularly shall each superintendent (of the Law) come to the Sabbath service to be inspired with faith in this order and to learn it.
>
> And as far as your district [extendeth] ye must everywhere make the [edict] known according to the letter thereof. So, too, in all fortified town and provinces, ye must cause it to be made known according to the letter thereof.

There is obviously no mention of donation of any monument in the available passage of this Asokan pillar edict. Whether it was recorded in the missed upper lines of this epigraphs is not certain. But, from the indications of the textual references and also the nature of the earliest group of monuments, King Asoka has been accepted as a generous donor to Rishipattana-Mrigadaya.

Being royal in nature, the donative structures of Asokan times are marked by imperial dictate. As a result, these are large, durable and imposing. Besides being architectural marvels, the carvings exhibit chiselling excellence. To achieve the quality in production, he appears to have taken extra pains for their chiselling by inducting craftsmen and artisans from far-off places. The discovery of a Kharoshthi epigraph of Mauryan times, on one of the sandstone blocks at Chunar hills (Fig. 56), suggests this possibility (Jayaswal 2012: 255-6). It has been argued by me in other publications that this finding in the region conveys more than one historical situation. The middle Ganga plain was using Brahmi script during the Mauryan period. But, use of Kharoshthi, the script prevalent in the north-western part of this subcontinent, when occurs here, even though in restricted manner, needs attention of historians because this evidence

56. Inscription in Mauryan Kharoshti (reading ativaoshah) on the block of Chunar sandstone.

can be interpreted in terms of induction of foreign chisellers/master craftsmen in the middle Ganga plain; particularly, in case of the compositions like Asokan column, which were being prepared under the royal patronage at each of the select location of their erection. The invitee artisans to Sarnath-Varanasi region, therefore, may have come from the Kharoshthi script-using area of north-west, at the invitation of the emperor (Jayaswal 2012: 255-6). The structural offerings at the Buddhist sites initiated by King Asoka not only laid foundation for construction of large religious monuments, which were subsequently followed at large scale by kings and affluent devotees of early Historic and medieval times, but it also raised architecture and sculptural art to the level of classicism.

A group of railing pillars (33), which often are referred to as Sunga creation, have also been assigned to the late Mauryan times by the excavators. Hargreaves, while reporting the findings from Sarnath, mentions 13 inscribed polished capitals, which were donations to the site. He however states that the letters of these inscriptions closely resemble those of the time of Asoka (*Archaeological Survey of India Annual Report 1914-15*: 120). He further clarifies that, "On linguistic considerations too, these are assigned to the end of third or first half of the second century BC" (*Archaeological Survey of India Annual Report 1914-15*: 121). Two names which occur in the epigraphs—Visadeva and Agathi—also confirm the suggested time-bracket. The third name of the donor of the engraving is Hariti. The community which was making these donations was that of merchants, the *Sathavaha* of the inscriptions. That the donors were from different places is testified by the mention of the places Patliputra and Ujjeni (Ujjain) in the epigraphs. The individuals were donating one part of the railing. For instance ... *thamba* was *danam* by ... of '*Ujjeni*'. If Hargreaves' assessment is to be relied upon, then it may be concluded that the practice of donation at Mrigadaya, which was initiated by Asoka, had a following by affluent merchant communities of the succeeding period. That the act was also well organised by this community is clear as the individual offering of various parts of a structure was so planned that complete monument or a major part of a monument could be built successfully. This astonishing feature became much pronounced later during the Sunga and Kanava periods, when stupas were enlarged and encircled with imposing railings and gateways. On account of the evidence at Sarnath, it appears that this practice was initiated during the late Mauryan period.

DONATIONS OF THE SUNGA PERIOD

Taking into account the significance of Mrigadaya to Buddhism, in comparison to sites like Sanchi, Bharhut and Amaravati, the remains of Sunga period are restricted at Sarnath. For, contribution of the period is represented by a group of 53 railing posts, coping stones and cross-bars, about a dozen of which were unearthed by Marshall and Konow not *in situ*, but inset in a mud-brick floor (rectangle in shape and later in date), located in the north-east of main shrine area (Sahni 1914: 208-16). On account of paleography and the style of the carvings of the posts, a date-bracket of 2nd–1st centuries BCE could be assigned to this group. The epigraphs mention the name of the donors in Brahmi script, a practice popular during Sunga times (Fig. 57). The rail stones bearing epigraphs of 2nd century BCE are translated by Marshall and Konow as "The base stone is the gift of the nun Samvahika", and "The railstone of Jamteyika and Siha" (*Archaeological Survey of India Annual Report 1906-7:* 95).

All the Sunga remains were part of a railing. Whether a railing was attached to the Mauryan stupa, *Dharmarajika,* during the Sunga period was also discussed earlier and its possibility was ruled out (Chapter 3) because the stupa was encircled by a low wall, and there is no record that this structure was replaced by a railing in the later period. Instead, that a railing had encircled the sacred place where the Lord had delivered his First Sermon, was submitted as a logical assumption. Perhaps the original wooden railing of the Mauryan times was transcribed in stone around 2nd/ 1st century BCE. Reused in the later times with 3rd/ 4th century CE donation labels, the Sunga railing appears to have gained high reputation, and was reused in the main shrine complex in later centuries. This has been noted by Sahni, who records that some of the pillars were reused as base pillar for lamps in Gupta times with contemporary donors' names (Sahni 1914: 211).

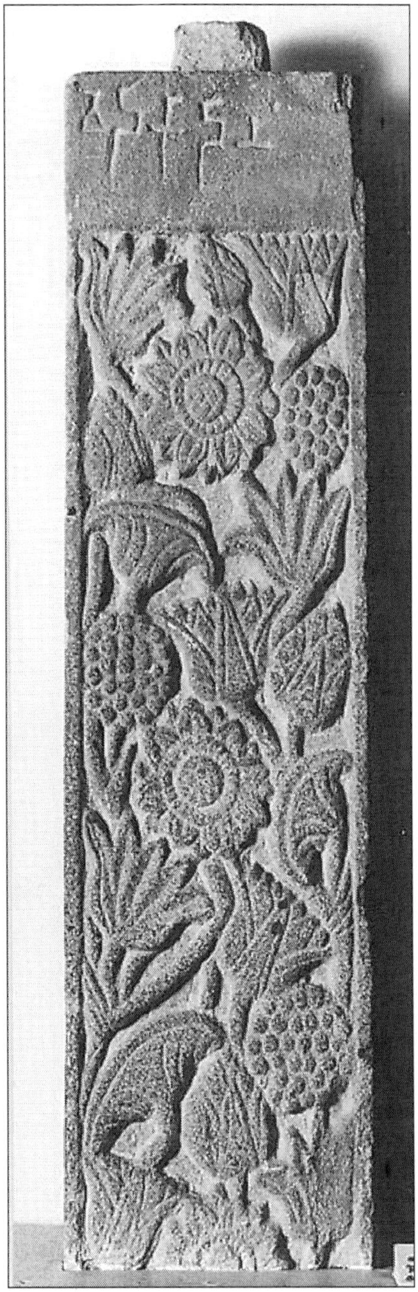

57. Inscription on a Sunga rail-stone in Brahmi script, Sarnath.

DONATIONS OF THE KUSHAN PERIOD

Donation of Buddhist icons at the pilgrim sites was a practice initiated during the Kushan period. Bodhisattva images from Sravasti, Mathura and Sarnath are illustrative examples. The Bodhisattva image of Sarnath is significant for more than one reason. One, that it is inscribed and two, that its medium and style is not indigenous. Cut in red sandstone of Sikari, this colossal image (8′ 1½″ high and 2′10" wide) with tenon base was attached with a large umbrella. Carved in the Mathura style, this image was inscribed both in front and at the back of the pedestal. Besides, the octagonal shaft of the umbrella also retains a 10-line inscription of almost the same content as of the main statue (Fig. 58). The inscription, composed in mixed Sanskrit and Prakrit, has been translated as follows (Sahni 1914: 25):

> In the third year of Maharaja Kanishka, the third [month] of winter, the 22nd day, on this date [specified as] above, was [this gift] of Friar Bala, a master of the *Tripitika* and fellow of Friar Pushyavuddhi [namely an image of] the Buddhisattva and an embrella with a post, erected at Benares, at the place where the Lord used to walk, together with [his] parents, with his masters and teachers, [his] fellows and pupils and with [the nun] Buddhamitra versed in the *Tripitakas*, with the satrap Vanaspara and Kharapallanas, and together the four classes, for the welfare and happiness of all the creatures.

The above epigraph records donation of this image at Benares, where the Lord walked..., by Bala Bhikhu (Pushyavudhi), who was the master of *Tripitaka*s, ... "together with the satrap Vanaspara and Kharapallana, and together with four classes". The date given for this donation is "third year of Maharaja Kanishka" (Sahni 1914: 35). Incidentally, this is the earliest known Buddha image at Sarnath.

The content of this epigraph is particularly important for the history of Buddhist icon making in general and the Varanasi-Sarnath school of sculptures in particular as the date (3rd year of Kanishka = 78+3 CE) 81 CE

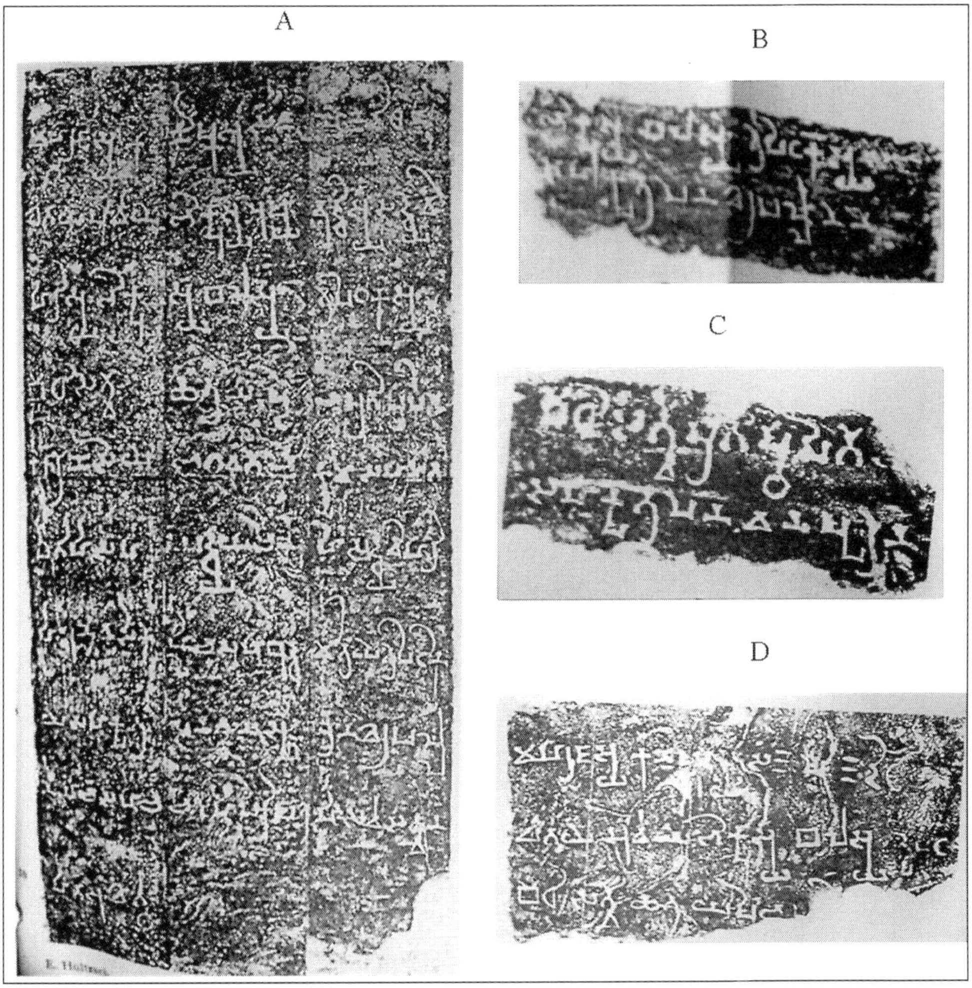

58. Copy of the inscription in Kushan Brahmi on Boddhisattva image donated by Bala Bhikhu, Sarnath.

specifies the beginning of donation and export of Bodhisattva images from Mathura, the sculpture-centre of the Kushans to main Buddhist pilgrimages. The style of carving and the medium of the Bala Bhikhu donational image of Sarnath subscribe the fact that the roots of the Varanasi-Sarnath school of sculptures, which flourished in the subsequent centuries, were in the Kushan images of Mathura. This aspect shall be discussed in the next section with the help of archaeological findings of Varanasi region.

The content of the epigraph under consideration is also noteworthy for determining involvement of the sections of society in causing the installation of donational images during Kushan times. The group of donors mentioned on the Bodhisattva image of Sarnath are a learned monk, two satraps and four classes. The 'Four Classes' are inferred to be the 'monks, nuns, laymen and laywomen' (Sahni 1914: 35). It appears to be a courtesy in which credit is extended to all, or the blessing to be procured by the pious deed of donation is to be shared by all. While two satraps, 'Vanaspara and Kharapallana', are the persons belonging to affluent administrative class of the society, who might have financed the making and installation of the image, the learned monk Bala is said to have supervised the making of the image. Another noteworthy feature is that the learned monk is given priority in the order of the donors in the epigraph. The mention of Bala, the supervisor of the image making/donor as Master of *Tripitakas*, was perhaps to assign authenticity to the icon. It may be recalled that the practice of carving Buddha images had begun in Kushan times. In a situation like this, it is logical to assume that for the acceptance of an icon (produced as one of the earliest samples) by the devotees, it is necessary that its iconography is testified by a reliable religious person, who is well-versed with the scriptures. Bala Bhikhu appears to be one such authority. Since he was a monk, monetary support for acquisition of medium, payment to the sculptor and transportation of the image from Mathura to Sarnath was claimed from the satraps Vanaspara and Kharapallana. If this is accepted, then it may be held that donation of icon at the Buddhist pilgrimage during Kushan times was a joint venture of affluent persons and learned monks.

The offerings made at Mrigadaya became so essential and valued that along with donation of new compositions, a number of earlier structural compositions were also claimed by influential religious sects. The latter tendency is well demonstrated in the epigraphs recording

'Sarvastins'. About half a dozen of late Kushan inscriptions (dating 2nd-3rd centuries CE) have been recorded on pillar, railing posts and staircases.

The shaft of the pillar bearing the Asokan Edict was re-inscribed during the Kushan period (Fig. 40). Some letters of the beginning and end of this epigraph are deliberately rubbed. The remaining label records:

"In the fortieth year of Rajan Asvaghosh, in the first fortnight of winter, on the tenth day ..." (Sahni 1914: 30).

The nature of phrasing of this inscription, though, suggests some kind of donation or claim of a part of already existing monument. It is difficult to ascertain which of the two was recorded in it.

Similarly, two other engravings on the top of the slab of the stone staircases of eastern and southern sides of the Dharmarajika stupa, for instance, have been read and translated by Marshall and Konow (*Archaeological Survey of India Annual Report 1906-7*: 96) as:

> the homage of the Sarvastivadin teacher.

The other two engraved on the Mauryan railing surrounding the stupa in southern chapel of the main shrine (*Archaeological Survey of India Annual Report 1907-8*: 73) were:

> *danam* by the *acharya Sarvastinvadis*

The epigraphs engraved with *Sarvastinvad* is evidence of supremacy of the sect at Mrigadaya in the late Kushan and post-Kushan times (Fig. 59).

59. Inscriptions (Āchāryaṇṁ sarvvāstivā- and dinaṁ parigrāhe) in Brahmi script of 3rd/4th century CE on the Mauryan railing surrounding the southern chapel of main shrine.

Besides, while claiming the earlier monuments, the tendency was also to erase earlier records of donations. Marshall and Konow, for instance, have noted that, "On the right hand side of the sloping edge of the same (east stairs of Jagat Singh stupa) are traces of an earlier inscription deliberately effaced and probably... by the Saravastivadins" (*Archaeological Survey of India Annual Report 1914-15*: 129).

In spite of the above examples, the offerings of idols were being made to Mrigadaya in the late post-Kushan times. A part of an umbrella unearthed from the western side of the main shrine is important. Inscribed in Brahmi script of 2nd/3rd century CE, the language of this composition is Pali (*Archaeological Survey of India Annual Report 1906-7*: 96). Inscription in Pali is rare not only in the middle Ganga plain, but for entire north India. The inscription summarises the principal teachings of Buddha, which was the subject matter of the First Sermon delivered at Mrigadaya. Though the inscribed specimen does not record donation, it is important for religious history and linguistic studies.

DONATIONS OF THE GUPTA PERIOD

The practice of offering of images at Mrigadaya intensified during the Gupta Period. Excavation of the vicinity of the main shrine area particularly was rich as far as recovery of Buddha images is concerned. For example, Hargreaves discovered 44 new inscriptions during 1914-15, in which at least six belonged to the Gupta period (4th–6th centuries CE) (*Archaeological Survey of India Annual Report 1914-15*: 123-27). The names of monk and nun donors were Abhayamitra and Dharmmade. Offering of the image by the nun Dharmmade was made during the later half of the 4th century CE (*Archaeological Survey of India Annual Report 1914-15*: 123). This is estimated on palaeographical grounds.

The monk Abhayamitra donated three images at an interval of three years at Mrigadaya. The earlier image in human size and in *abhaya mudra* was discovered from the southern approach way to the main shrine

(*Archaeological Survey of India Annual Report 1914-15*: 124). The inscription composed in three lines is translated as follows:

> When a century of years increased by fifty-four of the Gupta had passed away and on the second day of the month of Jyeshtha, when Kumargupta was protecting the earth, this image of the Teacher (Buddha), which is unpatrolled for its merits, was caused to be made for worship by Abhayamitra, a monk with mind subdued through devotion. ....

The Gupta Era 154 of this inscription is countable to 473/474 CE. The inscription (Fig. 60) mentions the name of Kumargupta, which as per the genealogy of the Gupta rulers may be identified with Kumargupta II (AD 474), who was ruling the area seven years after the death of Skandhagupta (AD 467) (Majumdar, R.C. 1954: 29).

60. Inscription in Brahmi script recording donation of Buddha image by Abhayagupta, Gupta Period, Sarnath.

Two other offerings made by Abhayamitra are significant to note, since the name of the ruler changes on their engravings. The one is of the standing Buddha on a lotus flower, and the other is an inscribed fragment of a pedestal (*Archaeological Survey of India Annual Report 1914-15*: 124-5). Together these complete the epigraph, which is as below:

> When a century of the year increased by fifty-seven of the Guptas had passed away and on the seventh day of the dark fortnight of Vaisakha, when the lunar mansion was Mula, when Buddhagupta was ruling (the earth), this charming image of one having divided sons (disciples) (Buddha), that is adorned with wonderful art was caused to be made by the Abhayamitra, a Buddhist monk... (*Archaeological Survey of India Annual Report 1914-15*: 125).

These inscriptions are dated in Gupta Era 157, calculated to be 484-5 CE, and mention the name of the ruling king Buḍdhagupta. Silasena was another donor of the 5th century, who appears to have offered an image with an inscription stating:

> Om. Of the Sun's kinsman the Buddha matchless splendour (this) image was caused to be made by Silayasas striving after the highest state of bliss (*Archaeological Survey of India Annual report* 1904-5: 89).

This image of the Buddha offered by him was retrieved from the eastern side of the main shrine (*Archaeological Survey of India Annual Report 1914-15: 126-7).*

Similarly, another image offered during the time by monk Buddhapriya was inscribed (*Archaeological Survey of India Annual Report* 1904-5: 90) and reads as below:

> This is the gift of Buddhist friar Bhudhapriya. Whatsoever merit (there is) in this (gift) let it be for the attainment of supreme wisdom.

Offerings of Shayabhikhu and Dharmasimh may also be added to this list of donors. Bodhisattva images too were being offered during the 5th century CE. The one which is inscribed has been translated as:

> Om. This is the pious gift of the lay-member Surytra the head of a district. Whatsoever merit (there is) in this (gift), let it be to the acquirement of supreme wisdom by all sentient beings. (*Archaeological Survey of India Annual report* 1904-5: 81)

Significance of this specimen is that it records offerings made by an administrator of low rank and a non-Buddhist monk.

Besides the donor epigraphs, there are written records of the Gupta period on the slabs and seals containing Buddhist creed or formula of faith—*dharma-paryaya*. This practice was not in vogue before the Gupta period at Sarnath. The oldest inscribed example of Sarnath, as is reported by Oertel, was found engraved on a broken hand of a Buddha image. This creed is written in the 5th century Brahmi script. There are others of the kind, but are of later date (*Archaeological Survey of India Annual Report* 1904-5: 90). Besides stone inscriptions, the creed was also written on the clay tablets. Oertel has reported at least one such clay tablet of 6th century CE. A clay seal with names of persons like Sri-Guptasimhasya dating to 5th/6th century CE was also found at Sarnath (*Archaeological Survey of India Annual Report* 1904-5: 90).

In the group of epigraphs, which suggests re-donation of earlier parts of the monuments at Mrigadaya, mention may be made of the railing pillars of the Sunga period (Fig. 61). The inscription on this is in Gupta characteristics and it reads:

"This is a pious gift of the devoted worshipper Kirtti, a lamp put up in the Principal Shrine" (Sahni 1914: 211).

There were other lamp-posts excavated by Oertel (*Archaeological Survey of India Annual Report* 1904-5: 66). A four-line inscription of the railing pillar of Mauryan times was engraved in Brahmi of 5th century CE, which reads as follows:

"This lamp (is) the pious gift of the female lay-member *Sulaksmana* at the chief (temple) of the Lord Buddha."

Similar to preceding periods, the tendency to reclaim the earlier offerings by overwriting the donors' signature continued during Gupta

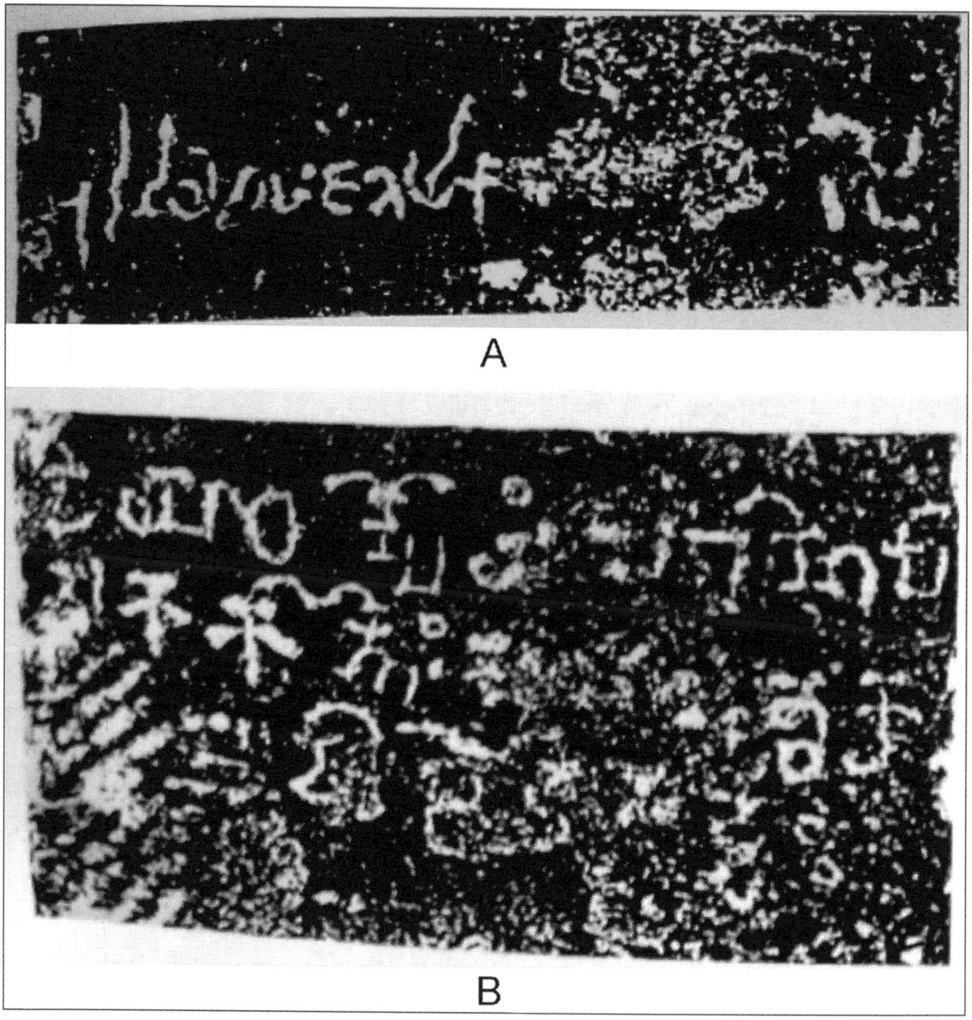

61. Copy of inscriptions on a Sunga railing in Brahmi script of 2nd century BCE and Gupta period, recording donation of the same rail-stone twice.

times. It may be recalled that this practice had started in large way during the late and post-Kushan times. But, in the 4th and 5th centuries CE, it appears to diminish, as the examples of this period are restricted in number. This is particularly noteworthy when one compares it with the donation of inscribed and uninscribed fresh images in large numbers in and around the Mulagandhakuti Vihara.

That the chief temple mentioned in some inscriptions was none but the Mulagandhakuti Vihara too is testified by the written records. Found to the west of the main shrine, the group of seals depicting the event of *Dharmachakra pravartna*, through the *Dharma-chakra* and the deer, was often inscribed. One of the readable epigraphs is: "In the *Mulagandhakuti* of the Exalted one in the illustrious Saddharmachakra." According to Marshall and Konow, "The legend of Saddharmachakra is the name of the whole monastery, which had received this name because it was situated on the spot where the Buddha first turned the wheel (*chakra)* or the good law (*saddharma*)" (*Archaeological Survey of India Annual Report 1906-7:*97).

The palaeography of this seal bears 6th/7th century CE features. Saddharmachakra was the address in use till the 11th century and may be accepted as the old name of Sarnath, popular between Gupta and medieval periods. Their findings in cluster in the main shrine area help in identifying the spot where the Lord sat and turned the Wheel of Law. Needless to mention that this identification is useful for the interpretation of the growth of Mrigadaya in particular and the Buddhist landscape surrounding it in general, which is attempted a little later.

Buildings were also constructed as part of offering at Mrigadaya, during the Gupta period. It has been mentioned earlier (Chapter 3) that the monuments identified of the period at Sarnath are Monasteries II, III and IV, the shrine of the Mulagandhakuti, Dharmarajika, and Dhamek stupas. Chaukhandi stupa may or may not be of the same time. It was also discussed that the first temple structure of Mulagandhakuti Vihara perhaps was constructed following the line of the early Gupta temples, using burnt bricks and stone architectural members. The Gupta temples at Bhitari of the time of Skandhagupta may be accepted as models for visualising the early form of Mulagandhakuti temple. The suggested combination of the brick and stone masonry for the period may also be seen in the ruins of monasteries of the time. Monastery II, north-west of the main shrine at Sarnath, for instance, was identified as an early Gupta structure (Majumdar, B. 1947: 38).

On account of the above, it may be held that by the 6th century CE, Sarnath was strewn with a number of monasteries, stupas and an imposing shrine. Side by side, numerous offerings of idols and carvings further enriched and adorned this pilgrimage. The epigraphs reveal that almost all the sections and followers of different creeds and religions had contributed to this venture. There obviously increased the demand of carvings at Sarnath, which in return helped formation and growth of reputed carving schools in the region. The art schools reached their zenith by the 4th and 5th centuries CE. Some of the Buddha images of the Gupta period of Sarnath have been accepted as masterpieces of Indian plastic art. One of the reasons, perhaps the main one, for the birth of this reputed school of sculpture was the demand of icons by the affluent donors.

THE POST-GUPTA AND EARLY MEDIEVAL DONATIONS

The post-Gupta period, between 7th and 12th centuries CE, indeed witnessed the continuation of offering of icons as well as structures at Mrigadaya, but the proportion of donation inscriptions appears to fluctuate in this long span of time. There distinctively seem to be three divisions: from the 7th to 8th centuries CE, the 9th century CE, and the third between the 10th and 12th centuries CE.

The inscriptions of the 7th and 8th centuries at Sarnath are restricted in comparison to the preceding period, the Gupta times. If this was due to the nature of reporting or was a reflection on the patronage of the establishment due to unstable politico-social conditions is a significant issue, which shall be discussed later. Also, offering of idols did continue during this period, though lesser in number. An image found from the north-west of the main shrine is inscribed in the character of 8th century CE. The epigraph is translated by Marshall and Konow (*Archaeological Survey of India Annual Report 1907-8:* 75) as:

> This is the pious gift of the Buddhist Friar, the *sthavira*... Whatever religious merit there is herein let it be for the acquisition of unsurpassed knowledge for all beings ...

Similarly, the two clay seals reported by Hargreaves bear inscriptions in 7th and 8th centuries CE (*Archaeological Survey of India Annual Report 19014-15:* 127):

"In the illustrious Mulagandhakuti of the Holy One, at the celebrated Saddharmachakra..."

Most of the inscribed records of 9th century CE belong to clay tablets, which mention the Buddhist creed. Oertel has reported at least 17 such examples, most of which he has dated to the 9th century. But, in a couple of cases these are said to bear 8th/9th century CE characteristics (*Archaeological Survey of India Annual Report 1904-5:* 103-4). In this category was another example, which is said to bear 9th/10th century CE features. This 18-line inscribed clay tablet with a stupa in the centre according to Hargreaves contained a Buddhist *mantra* (upper 14 lines) and Buddhist creed (lower 4 lines) (*Archaeological Survey of India Annual Report 19014-5:* 128).

But, three inscriptions which are engraved on stone in the characteristics of 9th century CE are significant. All the three are donations by Amritapala. Two of these are reported by Hargreaves (*Archaeological Survey of India Annual Report 19014-15:* 127-28) and have been translated as below:

> Om. (This structure) was caused to be made by Amritapala having reference to his father...

> Om. With reference to (his) maternal uncle, Amritapala caused (this structure) to be made.

The third one has been reported by Marshall and Konow (*Archaeological Survey of India Annual Report 1907-8:* 75), which has been translated as follows:

> Visvapala. By the merit which has been acquired by me after having caused ten chaityas to be made .... Of Sri-Jayapala has been made with reference to those (chaityas) by Amritapala.

Jayapala has been identified as the father of the king Vigrahapala while Jayapala's father Visvpala was a younger brother of King Dharmapala, who lived in around 861 CE. This genealogy helps in assigning the date when a number of structures chaityas and viharas were perhaps offered by Amritapala at Sarnath.

The clay tablets inscribed with Buddhist creeds were common offerings in the area of the main shrine during the 10th to 12th centuries CE. Marshall and Konow have found at least seven such pieces (*Archaeological Survey of India Annual Report 1907-8:* 75).

The offering of inscribed stone images appears to intensify between the 10th and 12th centuries CE. Mention may be made of the recorded gift, which was made in the 11th century CE by Rajputra Hatharideva, son of Rajputra Najunadeva (*Archaeological Survey of India Annual Report 1907-8:* 76). There are also two other inscriptions reported by Marshall and Konow. Similarly, the lower part of an image, which mentions donation by a layman Mabhuka, too is noteworthy (*Archaeological Survey of India Annual Report 1906-7:* 100). Perhaps the shortest inscription, which has been dated to the 12th/13th century CE (*Archaeological Survey of India Annual Report 1914-5:* 128), is said to be:

> ...the pious gift of the mother (or mothers) of the illustrious Jasamana Udayana and Vikrama (who is) a female disciple...

Mention may also be made of the six fragments of inscription, which were found from the monastery called 'Hospital' (*Archaeological Survey of India Annual Report 1906-7:* 101).

> In the [happy] victorious reign of the [Parambhattaraka Maharajadhiraja Paramesvara], the devoted worshipper of Maheshwara, [the lord of Triklinga, who by his own arm] had acquired the title of lord over three Rajas the illustrious Karna(deva), [who meditated at the feet of the] Paramabhatta[raka

> Maharaja]dhiraja Paramesvara, the illustrious Vama[deva], in [Kalchuri] Samvat 810, on the fifteenth day of the bright fornight of Asvina, on a Sunday. Here, in the big Vihara called Saddharmachkrapravarttana, of the order of the friars, the Sthaviras... and Manorathgupta were caused to give their blessing.

Though, the name of the donor is not available, the date of this record is intact. Dated in Kalchuri Samvat 810, on the 15th day of the bright fortnight of Asvina on a Sunday, it has been calculated by Kielhorn as 4th October 1058 CE (*Archaeological Survey of India Annual Report 1906-7:* 100). The other important fact which is known from this epigraph is that as late as the 11th century CE, the main monastery at Sarnath was known as *Saddharmachkrapravarttana*. This was the complete version of the name occurring partly on the seals and the Mahipala inscription. It further suggests involvement of the lay followers in the uplift of Mulagandhakuti.

The characteristic trend of the donation of medieval period at Mrigadaya was perhaps detailed recording of donation of monuments. This was accomplished by long epigraphs. These records are most valuable for the history of dynasties, as well as for acquiring the details of the donations. A well-documented construction of Monastery I, by Kumaradevi, the Buddhist queen of Govindchandra (114-1154), is an example of monumental donation at the site by a Hindu follower of Dhamma (Majumdar, B. 1947: 36-37). Found on a rectangular slab excavated to the north of the Dhamek stupa, it was lying over the Gupta monastery (Fig. 62). Engraved in Nagri script, it is composed in 26 verses by the poet Srikunda and was engraved by Silpi Vamana *(Archaeological Survey of India Annual Report 1907-8:* 76-80). Besides mentioning the family ties, this inscription elaborates donation by the queen at Sarnath. It is mentioned in Verse 21, for instance, that a vihara was constructed here.

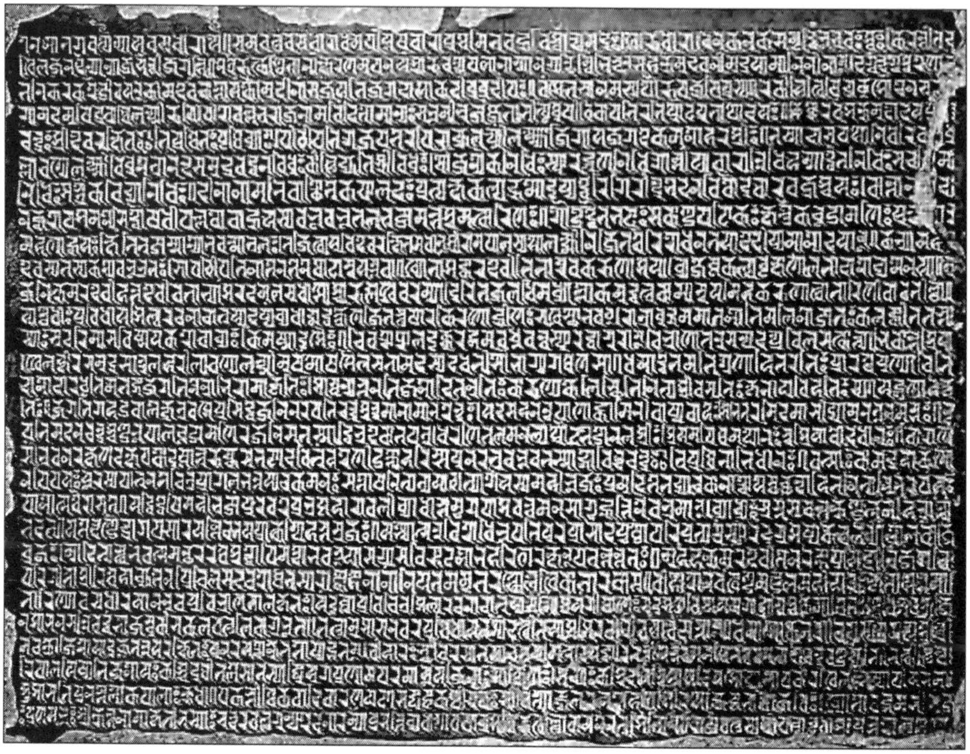

62. Inscription of Gahadvala Queen Kumaradevi recording donation of monuments at Sarnath.

> This Vihara, an ornament to the earth, the round of which consists of nine segments, was made by her, and decorated as it were by Vasundhara herself in the shape of Tarini, and even the Creator himself was taken with wonder when he saw it accomplished with the highest skill in the applying of wonderful arts and like to (the palaces of) the gods.

The mention of a copper grant and the aim to construct the monastery, the *sri-Dharmachakra-jina vihar*a, of Verses 22 and 23 too are of historical value.

> Having prepared that copper-plate grant which was connected with the teaching of the *sri-Dharmachakra-jina*, and having given it to *Jambuki,* the foremost of all *pattalikas,* for so long a time as moon and sun endure on earth.

63. Inscriptions in Brahmi of 11th century CE recording donation and restoration of monuments at Sarnath by Sivapala and Vasantapala, Sarnath.

> This Lord of the Wheel of the Law was again restored by her in accordance with the way in which it existed in the days of Dharmasoka, the ruler of men, and even more wonderfully, and this Vihara for the sthavira, was elaborately erected by her, and might be placed there stay there as long as moon and sun (endure).

It is also clear from the above inscription that there was an old image of the Lord Buddha, which was addressed as 'Dharmachakrajina', and the shrine where it was placed was known as 'Dharmachakra-Jina Vihara'. It may be recalled that the Chinese traveller Xuanzang mentions a large copper image of the Lord when he visited Mrigadaya in 7th century CE. He records (Beal 1884. Book VII: 46) that:

> In the middle of the *Vihara* is a figure of Buddha made of *teou-shih* (native copper). It is size of life, and he is represented as turning the wheel of law (preaching).

Whether the image was installed in the temple, which was restored by Kumaradevi, or it was another idol of a later period would remain uncertain in the absence of written and archaeological records. But, it may be held that the image of the preceding deity, the Buddha in the main shrine for number of centuries was of copper, while the offering of the other idols at this site were carved in stone.

Incidentally, the donation of Kumaradevi also testifies to the fact that among the devotees who contributed to Sarnath there were also followers of the Brahminical pantheon. This was not the lone example; another inscription engraved on the pedestal of a preaching Buddha of 11th century CE (Fig. 63) mentions that the donors Shirapala and his brother Vasantapala (of Bengal), had also established in Kashi the temple of Ishan/Siva and Chitraghanta/Durga, and built the shrine of *Gandhakuti,* at Sarnath. The inscription also records restoration of two principal monuments of Mrigadaya (Sahni 1914: 88-89).

5

SCULPTURING WORKSHOPS AND THE SARNATH SCHOOL OF ART

Sculpturing Workshops and the Sarnath School of Art

Offering of the 'pious gift', the idol of Buddha, at Mrigadaya in its history shows a rising curve with regard to the quantum, from Kushan to the medieval times. The evidence for this was discussed in detail earlier (Chapters 3 & 4). The import of an image, from elsewhere, such as Mathura, a practice of the early Kushan times, was unable to meet the increasing demand of carvings of the subsequent periods. The logical way to meet this situation was to produce carvings locally. In the archaeological findings of Varanasi-Sarnath region of the last decade, this cause-effect relationship between sculpturing centres and the quantitative demand of icons at Sarnath is well reflected. The stone carving workshops which were rural in nature were located close to Sarnath. Easy accessibility of raw material was an added advantage. Located at some distance (2 to 3 km) from the consumer centre Sarnath, these had close producer-client relationship with each other. This close socio-economic tying up of the artisans and the clients certainly was a major factor, which had extended boundaries of the Buddhist landscape of Rishipattana-Mrigadaya beyond its nucleus.

ARCHAEOLOGY OF SCULPTURING WORKSHOPS

After about a century of the initial discovery of Sarnath, intensive archaeological investigations were conducted around the site in 1994. These investigations were to identify supporting settlements of this religious establishment. The density of population, both of the inhabitants and the devotee visitors, as is suggested by the Buddhist scriptures and the archaeological remains, was to be viewed in terms of large demands of day to day, as well as ritualistic articles at Sarnath. "Sarnath is spoken of as though it may have been a city of itself", was the assessment by Sherring on account of the Ceylonese records (Sherring 1868: 325). If the population density here during ancient times was as large as a city, then the geographical and ethnological models of cities appeared a logical indication to plan the discoveries of supporting sites in this region. Accordingly, it was hypothesised that the peripheral region of the Sarnath monument-complex was the most likely area for the existence of satellite settlements. In view of this assumption, Sarnath was investigated.

It was mentioned earlier that the concentration of ancient remains at Sarnath was within the area bounded on east, north and west by *tal*s or the palaeo-access-pools (Chapter 3). The opposite banks of these water reservoirs were the first target of our search. A series of mound-like formations were noticed opposite the 'Deer Park' bank of Sarang-tal. The modern village Khajuhi, located to the north, is situated on a raised ground. The natural erosions and the human non-archaeological diggings indicated that the entire deposit here was composed of compact yellow clay with occasional occurring of iron palettes, which is a typical formation of natural soil of the region.Similar observations were recorded during exploration of the area around other villages—Ghuhurpur, Singhpur, Madarpur and Hasanpur (north and north west of Khajuhi) (Jayaswal 1998: 112). However, a small trench was excavated in the eastern side of Khajuhi. It was confirmed that the northern bank of the Sarang-tal is devoid of ancient remains. The western and southern sides of the Buddhist remains at Sarnath are low lying and, to the best of my knowledge, have not so far revealed traces of ancient sites. The eastern periphery of the monument complex is more or less similar to the north. The raised grounds in this case are not only devoid of archaeological remains, but appear to be accumulation of earth during the construction of Sarnath railway station. The search for feeding centres of Sarnath, therefore, had to be diverted to the other area.

Banks of two water channels—the Aktha-*nala* and Rajapur-*nala*—which encircle a wider peripheral region of the Sarnath monument-complex, appeared promising for retaining satellite sites. These water channels along with the main rivers, Varuna (for Aktha-*nala*) and Ganga (for Rajapur-*nala*) in which these discharge water, form a circuit of about 3-4 square kilometres, wherein the monument-complex occupies the small northern part of it. The area drained by both these streams was investigated.

Aktha-Narokhar-*nala*, originating from the Sarang-tal, connects the Buddhist pilgrim site with Ganga via the river Varuna (Jayaswal 1998: 110). Two ancient sites—Aktha and Paharia—were found to be located here. Excavation of Aktha revealed an independent and older settlement than Sarnath, while Paharia is a stupa mound. As is mentioned above, this site could be identified as Rishipattana of the Buddhist texts. Our exploration of the banks of Aktha-Narokhar-*nala*, although was very rewarding otherwise, failed to locate a single supporting settlement of Sarnath.

An ancient channel which connected Ganga and Sarnath was traced during our field survey. This dried-up rivulet, Rajapur-*nala*, was dotted with a chain of small rural settlements, where icons and stone blocks were carved (Jayaswal 1978). The main sites discovered were Asapur, Kotwa and Rajapur. The former two were excavated. However, due to high density of modern occupation on the mound, Rajapur could not be dug. Another site which was excavated on the bank of Rajapur-*nala* was Tilmanpur. This is a protected site of the Archaeological Survey of India. The chrono-cultural sequence of this site fell between the Mauryan and the Late Kushan times (Jayaswal 1998: 119-174). But, no trace of stone chiselling was unearthed here. This was perhaps a resort on the ancient land route of north India.

Highly damaged by modern brick kilns, Asapur was perhaps a workshop of post-Gupta times. The cultural sequence at this site, which was found preserved in a very small part of the mound, however could be ascertained to fall within Kushan and post-Gupta times (Jayaswal 1998: 175-83). Early to my investigations on the site, an image of Surya, the Brahmanical deity, bearing stylistic features of 8th century CE, was found from a non-archaeological digging. The image is housed in Bharat Kala Bhavan, the museum of the Banaras Hindu University (Biswas & Jha 1985). The other carved stone specimens noted at the site were architectural parts, half finished, semi-finished with post-Gupta motifs. The chiselling debris of earlier periods—Kushan and Gupta—were not distinct. The surface finds of Asapur appear to be reminiscent of the chiselling activities of the Gupta and post-Gupta periods.

The small mound at Kotwa, however, was quite intact and revealed almost a complete sequence of stone carving of early Historic times. The modern village of Kotwa (Long. 83°03′15" E & Lat. 25°20′20" N) is a small settlement situated on the left bank of Rajapur-*nala*, a palaeo-channel stream of the Ganga, a little away from the confluence of the *nala* and the main course of the river. Except for a small part (to the west), which is under cultivation, the mound at Kotwa (with an extension of 250 m x 75 m) is extensively inhabited. The mound was identified as a small ancient village of stone sculptors and was excavated extensively (Jayaswal 1998: 208-10) in 1994. As a result, four ancient stone carving floors were exposed. On and around the floors rested a huge accumulation of stone debris, indicating large-scale chiselling of sandstone. The rural nature of the site with the predominance of chiselling-refuse was quite distinctive. Associated with these were potsherds and broken pieces of carvings. On account of the typology of the pots, and the style and subject of the carvings, a time-bracket between *c.* 1st/2nd century BCE and 11th/12th century CE could be ascertained for this site. The three periods identified at this site were Kushan, Gupta and post-Gupta/early medieval. It is not without significance that this time span by and large corresponds with the history of stone images, which have been obtained from the Buddhist pilgrimage of Sarnath.

ARCHAEOLOGY OF THE LITHIC RESOURCE AREA

One of the major factors for the growth of sculpturing centres, besides the demand, was the accessibility to good quality medium, the sandstone, in desired quantity. Similar to other cities of the middle Ganga plain, in the Varanasi-Sarnath region also the choice of the chiselling medium throughout the historical period was the Vindhyan sandstone. Chunar hills, which are composed of Vindhyan formations, retain fine quality sandstone, topping the large portion of this hilly terrain. Ancient quarrying operations recorded here, though measuring 10 sq. km, were not exhaustive. Archaeological findings suggest that large quantities of sandstone blocks, in a number of hues, were being quarried from these hills, between 3rd century BCE and 12th century CE (Jayaswal 1998).

Ancient quarries in the hills around Chunar township were identified in 1990 by Prof. P.C. Pant and myself (Pant & Jayaswal 1990). The hill-top of Chunar (Long. 82°02′ E & Lat. 25°04′N) is littered with a number of cylindrical blocks of sandstone. Scattered randomly on the plateau-like flat terrain, in and around the dug rock formations and slope of hills, these large blocks were also found lying in the depressions and *nalas* and submerged in the Ganga. A detailed investigation conducted around Baragaon village between the years 1990 and 1993 indicated that there were a number of undressed and half-dressed blocks, and heaps of chiselling debris around the dug formations of live sandstone beds (Fig. 64). On account of the appearance, local folktales, and the discovery of epigraphs, it was possible to identify these as abandoned quarries. As many as 452 ancient quarries containing marks of extraction of stone blocks, chiselling debris, undressed, half-dressed and completely dressed cylindrical blocks, and records of the blocks in the form of count marks were recorded. A total number of 1128 cylindrical blocks were noted, out of which 112 dressed blocks were also inscribed. Bearing inscriptions dating

64. View of ancient quarry at Chunar.

between 3rd century BCE and 13/14th century CE, these blocks were found lying inside and at the outer periphery of the quarries, slopes and in the valley in clusters (Jayaswal 1998). The palaeography of the inscribed blocks suggests that sandstone was being quarried from the hills of Chunar from Mauryan times up to the medieval period. The practice of exploiting these hills for raw material continued in the middle Ganga valley, through out the historical and modern times.

The evidence obtained at Chunar convincingly demonstrates the entire mechanism of stone extraction, its transportation to the construction sites, and the management system controlling these operations during ancient times. The abandoned quarries of the Chunar hills were of various dimensions. In most of the cases, one thick sandstone layer was extracted. As a result of this mode of operation, the quarries in general had an average depth of two to four metres, and they were abandoned after removing the upper formation. Each quarry was utilised only once, or in the case of repeated utilisation, it was carried out in

65. Cylindrical sandstone blocks in and around the quarry, Chunar.

close succession. This is because the Upper Vindhyan formation is characterised by an extensive stretch of sandstone bed right at the top of the plateau-like formation. Further, the quality of the composition of the sandstone here is finely textured and is particularly suitable for fine chiselling (Wadia 1957: 133).

The quarrying operations in ancient and in modern times were more or less similar, except for changes in the modes of transportation. The introduction of the automobile for transportation has changed the form of exported stone blocks from Chunar hills. *Patia*, the flat slab, is the modern form of blocks, which are transported from Chunar to various parts of the middle Ganga plain. The ancient blocks, however, were cylindrical in shape. Given their heavy weight, these blocks were transported first by surface and then through navigation (Fig. 65). For surface transportation, it was imperative to chisel these blocks into a cylindrical form. A block when detached from its parent bed was dressed right there by chiselling the circumference. The dressing was done to provide these blocks a circular periphery and a cylindrical form, convenient for rolling them down the hills. The advantage of having surface without prominent ridges and depressions

66. Cylindrical sandstone blocks in the process of transportation, Chunar.

on the blocks enabled the blocks to roll down with little damage. The cylindrical shape was thus not chiselled simply for the construction/ carving of pillars but also to facilitate the transportation of the big blocks.

It was evident from the survey of Chunar hills that the first part of the journey of the extracted blocks was performed by rolling the blocks down the hills. For this operation, perhaps help from elephants was also sought. I am inclined to believe so, because in one of the rock-shelters at the Durga-khoh there are engravings of elephants tied with chains. Pushing of heavy block of sandstone by elephant, in every likelihood, would have considerably facilitated the surface transportation of the extracted stone blocks. The gentle slopes and even the *nala* beds, which also follow the descending contour of the hilly terrain, were used for this purpose (Fig. 66). This mode was followed until the blocks reached the main course of the Ganga, from where these were navigated up and down streams with the help of wooden rafts. The submerged blocks which failed to be loaded on rafts and fell in the main course of the Ganga near Chunar and

67. Evidence for navigation of sandstone blocks through Ganga.

Varanasi were recorded by us (Fig. 67). This provided supporting evidence for holding such a hypothesis.

The small streams, like Rajapur-*nala*, connected the main course of the Ganga with the workshop sites. These sites were located on the banks of this palaeo-channel, and away from the main channel of the Ganga (Fig. 68). I have demonstrated elsewhere that an effective mechanism of transportation of large sandstone blocks was already devised and was in practice between Chunar hills and settlement of ancient Varanasi from the time of Asoka, the Mauryan king. It is thus logical to conclude that this system had continued in the Kushan and later times also (Jayaswal 1998), as even today Chunar slabs are transported to the city of Varanasi through navigation. It may not be a mere coincidence that the workshop sites, in the form of small village settlements, were located on Rajapur-*nala*. A smooth route of transportation of huge blocks of stones was formed by this stream and the connecting Ganga (main route of transportation), on the side of which is located Chunar hills. Also the quarrying operation at Chunar hills commenced at the time of Asoka, when donation of monuments using sandstone was initiated at Sarnath.

UNDERSTANDING ANCIENT CARVING THROUGH MODERN SCULPTURING WORKSHOPS

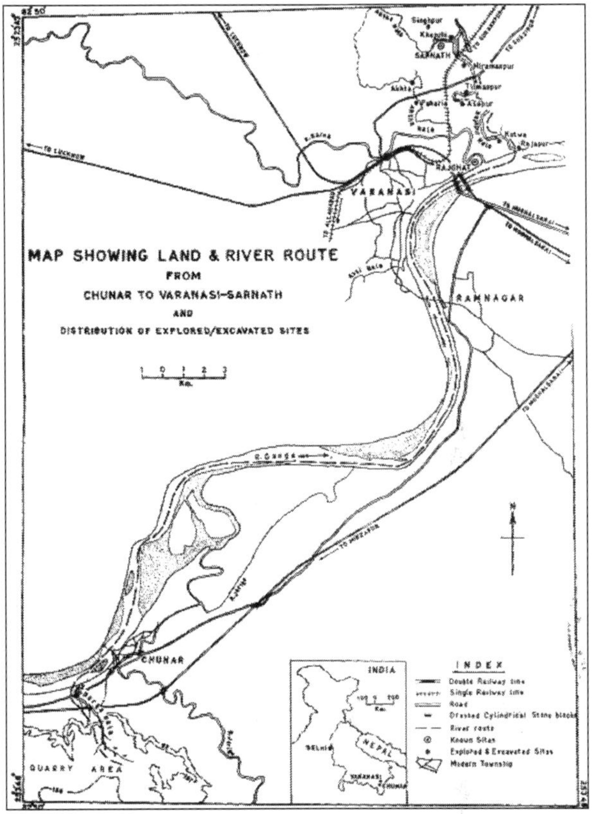

68. Map showing route of transportation from Chunar to Varanasi.

With a view to understanding the sculpturing craft, icon-making workshops of Varanasi city were studied. The modern carving centres are of two categories: one: where portraits of important persons are modelled, while at others images of divinities are produced. It is the latter category which has relevance to the present theme, as their format represents traditional carving. In modern times, Jaipur, Rajasthan has a reputation for icon carving. Following the Jaipur style of sculpturing, the present-day workshops of Varanasi city cater to the local needs as well as those neighbouring small townships, like Mirzapur, Jaunpur, Gazipur, Chunar, etc. (Jayaswal & Singh 1998: 232-137), where images of gods and goddesses are required. Ethnographic information was gathered from one of the most famous and active centres of icon making, Lallapura, by visiting and interviewing the craftsmen in the year 1993.

Jaipur Murty Kendra is located in Lallapura mohalla, a densely populated area of Varanasi city. The main produce of this workshop is the images of gods and goddesses carved primarily on white or grey marble, the medium popular in modern times in north India. But sandstone and other soft stones are also used at times. The choice of medium depends mostly on the demand of the customers, while the images are made following the Jaipur style, a modern tradition of sculpturing which has in recent years gained popularity in north India. It has been observed that most of the idols installed in modern Hindu temples of northern India are carved in Jaipur style. The name of the centre under consideration appears to claim direct rapport with the earned reputation of Jaipur region famous for making images of divinities. We were informed that at the initial stage, a couple of sculptors were actually brought to Varanasi from Jaipur, who established the Jaipur style at this workshop.

The workshop under study is an enclosed open space, where raw material and carved sculptures are accumulated in heaps at the periphery, while carving activities are performed in the centre, which is kept more or less spacious and empty (Fig. 69). Owned by Ram Sewak Prasad, who himself supervised the entire chiselling operation, a team of 25 to 30

69. General view of modern sculpture carving workshop, Varanasi city.

craftsmen worked here from dawn to dusk. Each craftsman specialised in one type of work, e.g., primary dressing, chiselling of the physiognomic details, rubbing the surface, colouring, etc. Three to five persons are engaged in each category of work. But, there was only one master-craftsman named Bachau, who is actually responsible for the formulation of the composition and execution of the finer details. It was his artistic amplitude and skill which is mirrored through the entire produce of this icon-making workshop.

Our study revealed that sculpturing processes at Lallapura workshop are initiated by the chief sculptor, Bachau. He would first draw the composition over the selected suitable block of stone. The carving theme is sketched along a vertical line and the entire composition, from top to bottom, is arranged. The figurative form in this case, thereafter, is drawn in accordance with the traditional way of relative measurement units, which are also recommended in ancient texts (Gopinath Rao 1968: 3). For instance, the entire length of a standing figure is divided into four equal parts or *bhangas*. At Lallapura centre, each of the

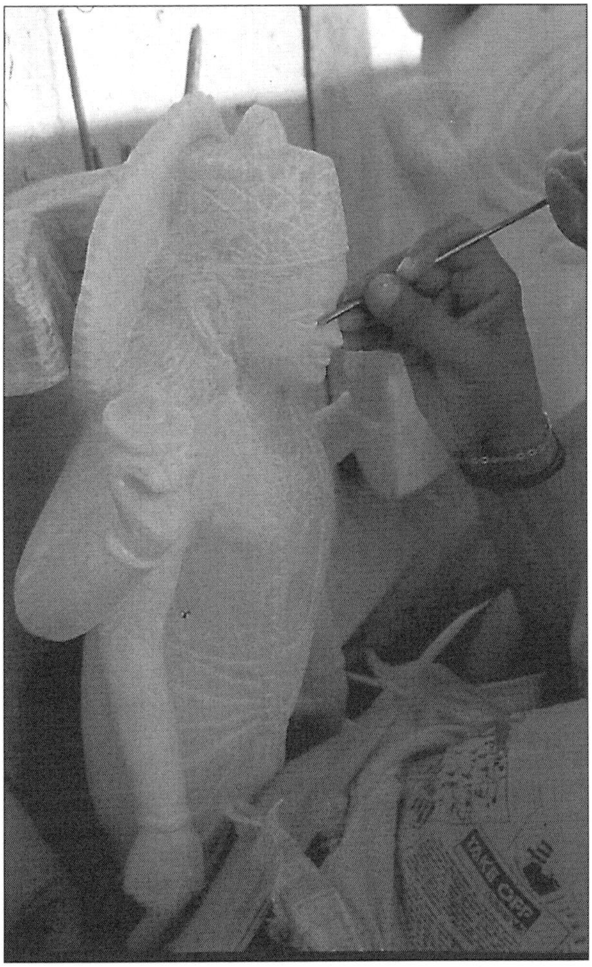

70. Master craftsman at work, at Lallapura, Varanasi.

71. Initial dressing of an image, Lallapura, Varanasi.

measuring units, from top to bottom, are: crown to neck, neck to nave, nave to knee and knee to the bottom of the feet. Similarly, width of different parts of the body is determined by using various combinations of this unit. The centre of the forehead, tip of the nose, middle of the chin, and nave of the central figure fall invariably on this centrally drawn main line of the composition.

Chiselling of an image is done in two to three stages. The first stage of chiselling is confined to the primary dressing of the select block of stone. Using *takani* and *tipani* (local names for broad edged chisels), the stone cutter, not the master sculptor, knocks out the extra mass of stone from the drawn composition (Fig. 71). The primary dressing operation is carried out by a select few chisellers. In the second stage, general shape of various parts of the composition is brought out. Rough form of parts of the body like, hand, crown, ornaments, etc. are carved out. The same group of chisellers, who perform primary dressing, execute chiselling of the second stage. In the third stage, when details of human anatomy, hair dress, ornaments, dress, etc. are carved, the task is performed invariably by the chief craftsman. Various types of fine-edged chisels are used for careful carving at this stage. For example, the round-edged chisel, *takuli*, pencil-pointed chisel, *kaudena,* etc. are used for executing minute details like the pupil of eyes, brows, nostrils and details of ornaments, hair style, etc. It is this stage which is responsible for denoting the stylistic features to the sculpted figures.

The final stage of finishing of the image includes rubbing and at times even colouring. In order to remove the chisel marks and smoothen the surface of the carving, a laborious task is performed. The carved surface is rubbed by *kurum* stone (a type of porous hard stone) by sprinkling water over the surface from time to time. Unskilled persons, the sons of the stone cutters and chief sculptors' family are usually engaged in this task. In case of painted images, oil colours are applied over the rubbed and finished surface by the painters.

It was also possible to calculate counts of images, which a workshop with one craftsman and his team of about two dozen assistants can produce. Carving of a medium-sized (2-3' high) elaborate figurative form, on soft variety of marble stone is produced in two to three months. Whereas, the production period of a large idol (6' high) takes five to six months. In the entire production time, the labour put in by the master-craftsman is almost half. On an average, one chief sculptor produces 10 to 12 medium-sized or 3 to 4 large-sized images per annum (Jayaswal & Singh 1978: 235). If this statistic is worked out further, 400 to 500 small-sized or 100 to 150 large-sized icons are carved by the master sculptor in his entire workmanship life because, in general, the craftsmanship period of an individual lies between 20 and 60 years of age (about 40 years). These ethnographic observations help interpreting the origin, growth and produce quantities of the ancient sculpture workshops of Sarnath School of Art.

SARNATH SCHOOL OF ART IN ARCHAEOLOGICAL PERSPECTIVE

The archaeological horizons at Kotwa correspond, by and large, with the history of stone sculptural art of the Varanasi–Sarnath region, as the three periods identified at Kotwa are the Kushan, Gupta, and post-Gupta/early medieval.

It may be clarified that the earliest stone sculptures, the lion capital and some other specimens stored in Sarnath Museum date back to Mauryan times, 3rd century BCE (Sahni 1914: 28-31). Though these examples are also chiselled on Chunar sandstone, the medium used mostly for the production of ancient carvings in Varanasi, these cannot be accepted as products of local craftsmanship. I have shown elsewhere that these examples were modelled under the direction of royal dictate, and may not be accepted as the workmanship of local stone-cutting tradition (Jayaswal 1998: 208). There is also no impact or continuity of these carvings in the succeeding stage, Sunga period (1st/2nd century BCE), which also appears to yield only a couple of stone sculptures—Aktha Yaksha and parts of railing, now stored in Sarnath Museum (Lin-Bodien 1981; Sahni 1914: 32). Not only is the number of specimens restricted but there is no archaeological finding to support that sculpture making was an indigenous practice in Varanasi at this point of time.

Beginning of Common Era witnessed the dawn of stone carving in Varanasi. It is interesting to note that the images of this time (Kushan period, between 1st and 3rd centuries CE), which are stored in Sarnath Museum, comprise both local produce and the imported ones. For example, out of nine Kushan images described by Sahni, three are carved of Sikari sandstone, the medium used at the Mathura centre of carving while the remaining six have been carved from Chunar sandstone (Sahni 1914: 37-41). Sahni also concludes that the later images were modelled by a local sculptor, who copied the Bodhisattva image made at Mathura centre, particularly the one which was donated by Bala Bhikhu, discussed above.

It is also testified from the chiselling debris of workshop sites, as the one at Kotwa, that chiselling had started during first occupation—Period I,

72. Exposed Kushan chiselling floor at Kotwa.

dated to Kushan times (Fig. 72). The demand of icons for religious monuments and rituals in this period appears to be confined primarily to Buddhism and were also limited in amount in the Varanasi-Sarnath region. Another noteworthy aspect is that as large blocks of stone were required for carving of colossal independent figures of Bodhisattva, quarry and transportation of the medium from Chunar hills to the workshops in Varanasi was special in nature. The desirable large blocks once loaded on the logs near Chunar hills were navigated downstream to Varanasi and the chiselling spot had to be at the bank of the navigational channel functioning as the route of transportation. Kotwa had this advantage. Since the demand of the icon during this period was restricted, existence of one workshop may be visualised for the time. This may perhaps also explain why chiselling debris of Kushan period was not present at Asapur, though it was inhabited during this period.

The succeeding period, coeval with the dynastic rule of the Guptas, is the stage of excellence in the history of sculpturing art of Varanasi. The culmination of carving art of the time is marked by an impressive proportion of figurative forms, mastery of composition of the theme, and divine expression of the images, which is so characteristic of the classical Indian art. Numerous masterpieces donated to the Buddhist establishment at Sarnath (Sahni 1914) are illustrative examples of the fine execution of the Varanasi school of sculptures. Archaeological findings suggest that the

73. Exposed Gupta chiselling floor at Kotwa.

earlier workshops continued. Period II of Kotwa, which is of Gupta period, testifies this. For, at this site Gupta chiselling debris rest just above a Kushan chiselling floor (Jayaswal 1998). But, besides continuation of the earlier carving workshops, many new settlements were at work.

The post-Gupta period also experienced large-scale stone cutting for both image making and decorative architectural panels by master craftsmen of the region (Fig. 73). This is evident from the large collection of carvings at Sarnath (Sahni 1914).

Continuation of the earlier workshops, and with additions of some other new centres, were catering to the needs of the early medieval demands of Sarnath and Varanasi. The remains of Period III, at Kotwa, are dated to the same period. Survey of Rajapur-*nala* has brought to light sites like Rajapur, Asapur, etc., which form part of new workshop sites of Gupta and post-Gupta times. It is also evident from the Surya image that at some of these workshop sites, idols of Brahmanical deities were also been carved.

SARNATH SCHOOL OF ART: ORIGIN & DEVELOPMENT

The title 'Sarnath School of Art' is for the excellent carvings of Buddha and Bodhisattva images of the Gupta period, which were unearthed from Sarnath. A good part of these are housed in the Sarnath site museum. However, some were transported to the other places, both in ancient and modern periods (Chapters 3 & 4). Nonetheless, the collection of Sarnath Museum has images, which ascertain a much wider time span—Maurya to Early Medieval—for the sculptural art of the Sarnath-Varanasi region. In this group one can identify a number of segments, which may not be in true sense representative examples of the school of sculpture under consideration. Take, for example, the Maurya-Sunga group, which though obtained from the excavations of Mrigadaya belongs to the pre-Sarnath school of sculpturing because the Mauryan specimens, the lion capital and the other fragments with Mauryan polish were the products under the direction of King Asoka. The Sunga railing pillars and cross-bars, too, are not representative of local chiselling. Even then the group, particularly the carvings of the Mauryan times, contributed to the Sarnath Shool of Sculpture by preparing a stable ground in terms of choice and acquisition of suitable raw material. Full utilisation of lithic resource area and the mode of transportation of large sandstone blocks from Chunar to Varanasi region was the contribution of the Mauryan period to stone carving of the middle Ganga plain, where King Asoka had caused to erect many pillars (Fig. 74). Similarly, the early medieval sculptures of Sarnath may not form part of the referred-to school. But, the group is significant for the end and later continuation of some of the Gupta characteristics.

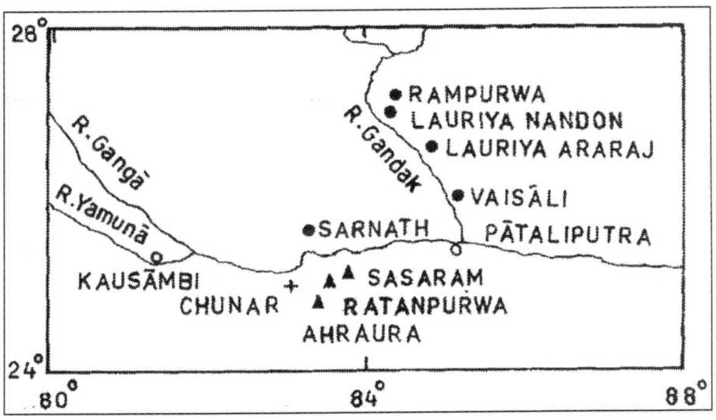

74. Map of Asokan pillars of the middle Ganga Plain.

The earliest stone carving in an organised way in our

region of study, on archaeological and epigraphic grounds, may be dated to Kushan times. It was mentioned earlier that the local copies made of Mathura products of Bala Bhikhu Bodhisattva image, housed in the Sarnath Museum, have been identified as the first regional carvings. The original model carved out of Sikari sandstone was replicated in Chunar sandstone (Figs. 46 & 48). As mentioned earlier, the mechanism for acquiring raw material for replicating the Sikri sandstone model with Chunar sandstone was already known for some time, and must have been followed without difficulty. But, who was the master sculptor? A local or an invitee craftsman of Mathura? The answer to this question can be given on account of our ethnographic observation and some of the established historical facts.

Historical evidence indicates that during the Kushan period, there were important icon producing centres in north India, like Taxila, Mathura, etc. Sarnath had yet to rise up to the status of an image making centre of repute. The donation demand of Sarnath was fulfilled by importing images from the famous and nearby centre Mathura. Import of Bodhisattva icons from Mathura to Sarnath is attested by the epigraphical records, which were discussed above. When the demand for icons increased, there was need to produce images locally. This need was fulfilled by making copies of the Mathura style of compositions at Varanasi. This is apparent from the other contemporary Bodhisatattva images made of Chunar sandstone at Sarnath. There is no doubt that such an initiation marked the beginning of icon production in the area of our study. But, the question is whether the copies made in Varanasi were products of local artisans or were creation of a workshop headed by the master craftsman from Mathura.

Clues for answer to this lie in the ethnographic instance. It was shown above, for instance, that image making in modern Varanasi was initiated by bringing master craftsmen from Jaipur, which is the main icon producing centre of north India. This was after Varanasi had lost the past glory of sculpture chiselling in the last century. A speedy growth of the craft is possible in this situation. Also a team of local persons receive training in this process. It may be held that a similar process had taken place during

Kushan times also, which established stone carving as one of the main crafts of Varanasi because, in the following centuries this craft could reach the status of world-famous carving tradition under the banner of 'Sarnath School of Sculpture'. Moreover, it may not be an overstatement that the main reason for the growth of the Sarnath style was the continuous and successive increase in demand by the donors.

The hypothesis held for quite some time by the art historians is (Williams 1983: 76; Huntington 1985: 201) that roots of the Sarnath School of Sculpture was buried in the Kushan modelling. This is also supported by our ethnographic and archaeological recordings. It has been elaborated that adoption of Gupta idiom at Sarnath was under the influence of Mathura style, which was an outcome of spontaneous growth of the earlier sculpture making tradition, viz. Kushan (Saraswati 1957: 134). It has been further suggested that the Sarnath centre in mature form came into existence during the later half of the 5th century (William 1983: 76; Huntington 1985: 201), when compositions were marked by classicism. The depiction universality and the lack of individualism, which are much apparent in the stone sculptures of Gupta period Sarnath, perhaps are reflective of the same mechanism which was noticed at Lallapura. That is, a team of craftsmen with a chief sculptor as the head was at work here for a number of generations in succession. If this presumption is accepted, then a rough estimate of the quantum of produce from Sarnath centre can also be determined. It has been established on the basis of the historical evidence that the production at Sarnath in a major way had started around the third quarter of the 5th century (William 1983: 76; Huntington 1985: 201). Though the carvings continued in the post-Gupta periods, the prevalence of classical Gupta idiom appears to have continued by the end of the 6th century CE (Asher 1980: 7-8).

A total span of about 150 to 200 years may thus be calculated as the production time of the Sarnath School of Sculpture, on account of the stylistic characteristics borne by the collection obtained from Mrigadaya. If the above-mentioned statistics of the individual production rate of the images (400-500 for medium and 100-150 for the large sized), on account of the craftsmanship-span of the present day chief sculptor (about 40 years), is applied for the Gupta collection of Sarnath, it can be argued that a single workshop in one-and-a-half centuries to two centuries was able to supply 500-600 large-sized images or about 1000-1500 medium-sized images. A total number of about 200 to 250 large and about 1000 medium images could easily be carved at one workshop. Four to five generations of chief sculptors with their team of craftsmen in this hypothesis would be at work. This quantitative count has direct bearing on the available images of the Sarnath style. For, it has been recorded that about 400 Buddha-Bodhisattva images of Gupta period are stored presently at Sarnath (Williams 1983: 79; Sharma, 1988; Sahni 1914). If the loss incurred from the scavenging operations at Sarnath in the later times for acquiring building material (Sahni 1914: 9 & 12), and time to time export of icons from this centre (Asher 1980: 31-32) is taken into

75. General view of mound at Kotwa, with rich chiselling debris.

76. Split cylindrical sandstone block for carving two images.

consideration, then the quantity of sculpture produce by Sarnath School of Sculpturing workshop of the Gupta times would not be very far from the above-mentioned estimate. A model for a single or at most two workshops, each with one chief sculptor, would therefore be a logical deduction for the production of Buddha-Bodhisattva images during the Gupta period for Sarnath.

It may well be summarised that the proposed workshops of the Sarnath School was located on the bank of Rajapur-*nala*. The archaeological findings suggest that Kotwa could be one such centre, which not only had stone carving tradition prior to Gupta period, but was also on the route of the transportation of block of stones from Chunar. It may be mentioned that a block was found submerged on the confluence of Rajapur-*nala* and the Ganga near Rajapur village. Also, a cylindrical block of sandstone was found half broken at Kotwa during our exploration. The quarries at Chunar hills suggest that the transportation of raw material for carving of Gupta compositions was in the form of cylindrical blocks. The average size of these blocks measured one metre to one-and-a-half metres. From one such block raw material for carving two images could be obtained. Composed in fine laminations, the Chunar sandstone blocks could easily be split into two, from the centre (Fig. 76). The split blocks,

77. Back view of Buddha image, Sarnath.

straight-convex in section and large enough in length (5′ to 6′ long), were apt for composing a standing Buddha image in high relief. It may be recalled that most of the standing Buddha and Bodhisattva images of Sarnath collection are characterised by flat back but with complete contours of the frontage (Fig. 77). The nose, which in most cases was the highest projecting point of the idols, in this case was placed on the circular surface, near the top of the length of the select block, from where the chiselling of the image was initiated. The hand of the images in *abhaya mudra* or *varad-mudra,* raised from the elbow, when protruding out of the main mass of stone block, were carved separately and affixed with iron clamps to the main image. There are many examples where such a joint can be noticed.

It is also revealed by our ethnographic studies that the master craftsman draws the entire composition following the middle line in accordance with the iconographic norms. Though iconography of Bodhisattva and Buddha images perhaps were not crystallised during the Kushan period, by the Gupta period the main deities under worship in all the Indian religions had acquired iconographic features, and Buddha-Bodhisattva images were no exception. Thus, it is logical to hold that the

Buddha and Bodhisattva images produced in the Sarnath School of Sculpture were carved following the iconographic norms.

Acceptance of single workshop hypothesis is also helpful in explaining the indigenous elements within a style of a period. The Sarnath School was an offshoot of the Gupta style. Governed by the general iconographic norms and the style of depiction, "figures in *bhanga,* transparent drapery, lessening the physiological details, and ornaments," images of the Sarnath centre went ahead in providing spiritual appearance and serene look to its products (Figs. 78 & 79). Lowering and almost closed eyes, the divine smile and wet transparent drapery, are some of the typical features, which are unmatched, and are marked by classicism (Fig. 80). Prevalence of these features uniformly in the entire collection of Sarnath Buddha does subscribe

78. Standing Buddha image, Gupta period, Sarnath.

79. Buddha bust with classic Gupta features, Sarnath.

to a one workshop hypothesis because only when one chief craftsman is responsible for the execution of all the compositions of a centre—creation to carving details of the physiology, uniformity of features and diagnostic stylistic traits—can come up as the demarcating features of a school of art. This fact had come to my notice in the ethnographic instance of Lallapura also, which was discussed above. Change in the craftsman would be reflected in some minor details of the icons. Every forty to fifty years, which is the accepted work-span of a master craftsman, one may expect change in the execution of images. The collection of Buddha images of Sarnath, if studied with this view, would also show the changes.

That some of the above-mentioned workshops situated on the Rajapur-*nala* were producing by and large carvings of Buddhist themes is suggested by some Jataka stories. The narration of *Babbu-Jataka* (No. 137), for instance, elaborates that Bodhisattva was born a stone cutter in Kashi, who used to quarry and shape stones in a rural set-up (Cowell 1884: 294-96), suggesting that stone carving was an established craft in Kashi in ancient times. It would also suggest that the primary theme of stone carving was Buddhism. It is because of this stone carvers were

80. Buddha head of Gupta Period, Sarnath.

highlighted by induction in this Jataka story. It is true that the theme of Jatakas relate to the remote past. But, it is also significant to note that the date of the Jatakas, though a matter of debate, is assigned mostly between the Sunga and Gupta periods (Winternitz 1933: 116-15). Moreover, the ambience of the story under consideration somewhat corresponds with the archaeological findings of Kushan and Gupta chiselling workshops located near Sarnath. Identification of Kotwa as one of the major workshops of the Sarnath School of Sculpture, therefore, is a plausible deduction, but in the present state of our knowledge perhaps a debated one.

The follow-up of the Guptas up to the early medieval periods crystallised the stylistic characteristics, as well as existence of numerous carving workshops feeding Mrigadaya. The mushroom growth of stone sculpturing workshops in the vicinity of Sarnath is also indicative of migration of a number of artisans in the region from other regions. The increase in the demand of products, and fulfillment of it by masters with high artistic amplitude of carvings, might have helped the workshops earn high reputation. This reputation would likely have prompted export of images to other pilgrim sites, resulting in the further increase in demand and production of masterpiece compositions. Besides icons, carvings were also utilised for adorning structures. The carved slabs on the Dhamek stupa are characterised by classical Gupta floral panels and are examples of skilled carving of the time.

Desertion of the Buddhist establishment of Sarnath, sometime around 12th/13th century CE, appears to have uprooted the long flourishing sculpturing tradition of Varanasi. There appears to be desertion of sculptors' settlements in the region, and a sudden lowering proportion of ornate monuments. My ethnographical study indicates that after a long gap of about seven to eight centuries, stone sculpturing in Varanasi was reinitiated afresh in the twentieth century. Lallapura is a living example of it. But, it lags behind the compositional skill, which was attained by the Sarnath School of Sculpture during Gupta times.

6

THE INTANGIBLE BOUNDARIES DRAWN BY THE JATAKAS

The Intangible Boundaries Drawn by the Jatakas

Jatakas are stories of the previous lives of Buddha. In each story, a Bodhisattva takes birth as a member of different section of society. His portrayal as one or the other member of the animal kingdom too occurs. The Jatakas, a rich section of Indian mythology, assume to mirror society and the geo-physical environment of ancient times. But, the time of the narrated events or situations, and the compilation of the Jataka stories, are quite apart from one another. The concept of Jataka stories takes one much beyond the sphere of the presence of historical Buddha (6th century BCE) because these are stories of his many previous births, through which he transcended. Though the time of the narrated events or situations is the remote past, the ambience or the backdrop of these stories are comparatively very recent because the compilation of Jataka stories is much later in date (c. 3rd century to 5th century CE), than the historical Buddha.

There are numerous references to Varanasi in the Jataka stories. In the general manner in which these stories open is: "Once upon a time, when Brahmadatta was king of Benares" or "when Brahmadatta reigned Benares", "the Bodhisatta was born", (Cowell 1895-1905. Vols. I-V). The mentioned illustrative examples help one to draw the inference that the Buddhist mythology, in the form of Jatakas, had adapted the city of Varanasi as its backdrop. It may also be important to note that the Buddhist literature is silent about Buddha's visit to this city. But, Varanasi occurs numerous times in the texts, as "Rishipattana-Mrigadava was said to be located near Benares" (Woodword 1927: 101, 111 & 112), suggesting that the Lord went directly to Rishipattana-Mrigadaya, Aktha-Sarnath, the area not only close to the capital city, but also located within its boundaries (Jayaswal 2009: 9). Moreover, Varanasi as a territorial unit is mentioned in the Buddhist texts (Rhys Davids & Carpenter 1903: 146), with nomenclature 'Kashi' for the Janapada and 'Varanasi' for its the capital. It was this city which was the nucleus of the mythological stories under consideration.

To understand the relationship of the city, the place of happenings of the Jataka stories, the origin and growth of Buddhist pilgrimage Sarnath and the composition of numerous mythological stories, the date of three events, the time of Gautama Buddha, antiquity of Varanasi, and the time of the composition of the stories are to be taken note of. The events narrated in these stories of course are difficult to assess because these are supposed to have taken place in the remote past, implying great antiquity and their date of uncertainty. Archaeological discoveries help ascertain a somewhat reliable time-bracket for the city, the historical Buddha and the ambience of the Jataka stories.

The archaeological horizon of the middle Ganga plain, which could be identified as being contemporary to Buddha, is the Northern Black Polished Ware (NBPW). It was discussed earlier that prevalance of this deluxe lustrous ware is credited with the establishment of Mahajanpadas and the emergence and growth of cities. The traditional date-bracket assigned to this techno-cultural period is accepted to be c. 600–200 BCE (Narain & Roy 1976: 23). According to the Buddhist sources, the Mahajanpadas, which are listed to be sixteen (*sodasha*), flourished around 550 BCE. This is close to the calculated time of the date of the *Mahaparinirvana* of Gautama Buddha (487/88 + total lifespan 80 = 567/568 BCE) (Pathak 2002: 28). The archaeological horizons contemporary to the Lord therefore would be the above-mentioned proposed time-bracket of the NBPW period. Kashi is listed among the *Sodasha*-Janpadas, and Varanasi was its capital at this time.

The territorial recognition of Kashi Janpada in the list of *Sodasa*-Mahajanpadas leaves no doubt that when Buddha came to Rishipattana-Mrigadaya to deliver his First Sermon, Varanasi was the capital of Kashi kingdom. Incidentally, the excavation of Kashi-Rajghat suggests that the identified capital of Kashi Janpada was occupied about a couple of centuries prior to the arrival of the Buddha in this region. For, the first habitation, the lowest deposit of Period IA of Kashi-Rajghat, rested over a swampy land, on the left bank of the Ganga, on its confluence with Varuna in around 800 BCE (Narain & Roy 1976: 23). It was the succeeding period, IB, which has yielded remains of NPBW culture. On account of the C_{14} date of 490±100 BCE, this phase is countable to c. 6th/5th to 4th centuries BCE (Narain & Roy 1976: 24), which makes it contemporary to the Buddha. The date of 8th century BCE for the lowest habitation floor is also confirmed by the recent MS dating on Rajghat which was collected during reexcavation of the site under supervision of B.R. Mani and me. This would imply that the settlement history of Varanasi city was at least two centuries older than the origin of Buddhism. If the earliest date of Aktha is taken into account, then the habitation in the nucleus of the Kashi Janpada can easily be pushed back another thousand years. This antiquity would certainly match with the 'remote past' suggested in the Jatakas.

Composed in Pali language, the Jatakas read, "Once upon a time, when Brahmadatta was king of Benares" (Jatakas Nos. 151, 152, 153, etc.) (*The Jataka.* Vol. II. 1895), and the other "the Brahmadatta reigned Benares" (Jatakas Nos. 178, 182, 180 etc.), "the Bodhisattva was born" (*The Jataka.* Vol. II. 1895). These references are significant for more than one reason because within this political background the Bodhisattva is placed in various forms, in his different births. The important examples are: member of a Brahmin family (*Akitta-Jataka.* No. 480), 'as Chaplain' (*Uddalaka-Jataka.* No. 486), 'a stone cutter' (*Babbu-Jataka.* No. 137), 'in potter's family' (*Kumbhakara-Jataka* No. 408), '...an Elephant' (*Mati-Jataka.* No. 455), '...in the family of a certain village of Kasi an only son' (*Takkala-Jataka.* No. 446), etc. These occurrences indicate that not only a large section of

Varanasi society received focus in Jataka stories, but contemporary fauna was also selected as the theme. Needless to say, such occurrences shed significant light on ancient Varanasi and provide a base for the interpretation of various unknown socio-economic aspects of the city. But there is another hidden clue in the Jatakas, that is the adaptation of the cultural milieu of an entirely diverse socio-religious system. For instance, the city of Varanasi was and still is a prominent Brahmanical settlement (Jayaswal 2011). In the Jatakas, not only the social structure of this city is accepted as the backdrop, but even diagonally opposite religious format like 'Brahmin family' has been inducted. This certainly is an instance when Buddhist mythology flourishes over the infrastructure of a multi-layered cosmopolitan city.

The adaptive and inductive nature of the Jataka stories can be demonstrated through some select stories, which represent three major facets: the Bodhisattva in the backdrop of the major crafts of early historic Varanasi, the Bodhisattva in non-Buddhist socio-religious background of Varanasi, and the Bodhisattva in the geo-physical setting of the city of Varanasi.

The significant Jataka stories in which the Bodhisattva is portrayed as craftsman are, *Kachhapa-Jataka* (No. 178) and *Babbu-Jataka* (No. 137). The translation of *Kacchhapa-Jataka* (No. 178) after Rouse reads (*The Jataka.* Vol. II. 1895):

> Once upon a time when Brahmadatta was reigning in Benares, the Bodhisata was born in a village as a potter's son. He plied the potter's trade ....
>
> At that time there lay a great natural lake close by the great river of Benares. When there was much water, river and lake were one; but when the water was low... they were apart....
>
> Now fish and tortoises know by instinct when the year will be rainy and when there will be a drought. So at the time of our story the fish and tortoises which lived in that lake knew there would be a drought; and when the lake without of water they swam out of the lake into the river. But, there was one tortoise that would not go into the river, because, said

he, "here I was born, and here I have grown up, and here is my parents' home: leave it I cannot ......

Then in the hot season the water all dried up. He dug a hole and buried himself, just in the place where the Bodhisata was used to come for the clay. There the Bodhisata came for some clay; with a big spade he dug down, till he cracked the tortoise' shell, turning him out on the ground.

Some noteworthy points in the above quoted passages are:

- That the Bodhisattava was born in a potter's family.
- That for the earthen pots clay was obtained from the dried bed of ponds.
- That there were traders who indulged in the trading of earthen pots.

Archaeological findings of Ramnagar are comparable with the description given in this Jataka story. Situated on the right bank of the Ganga, Ramnagar (83°17' E & 25°16' N) is a small settlement known for the fort of the Maharaja of Banaras. The ancient habitation of Ramnagar has a widespread stretch of about 3 kilometres between the fort (located on the northern end of the mound) and the Shastri bridge (on the national highway). But, the ancient settlement appears to be confined to the bank and does not extend beyond half a kilometre from the river side (Fig. 81).

81. View of Ramnagar mound from Ganga.

During archaeological investigations conducted at Oriyaghat (Ramnagar), it could be ascertained that this region was under occupation between Janapada and Late Kushan periods (Jayaswal & Kumar 2006). The location of this site and the cultural remains exposed give a clear indication that this was a trade-based settlement. For, being located on the bank of the Ganga river, it was well connected with various parts of the Ganga plain on one hand and on the other by the side of the main land route, connecting the middle Ganga plain with the Deccan.

Kachhapa-Jataka says that the Bodhisattva was born as a potter's son and was indulging in the trade of pottery. Oriyaghat was a pottery producing settlement, according to archaeological deductions, and has a direct bearing on the present discussion. Digging of the peripheral area of Oriyaghat mound (Trench C'2) exposed a pottery producing workshop. Not only were NBPW potsherds found in very large numbers, but these evinced a range of colours resulting from various types of firing conditions. Also, thick layers of whitish ash bands were found in succession in which some half-baked potsherds were embedded. Traces of pottery kilns exposed during excavations confirmed production of earthen pots and pan (Fig. 82). This locality thus was identified as the production centre of

82. Exposed NBPW workshop at Oriyaghat, Ramnagar.

83. NBPW shards found at Oriyaghat, Ramnagar.

the deluxe (NBPW) ware (Fig. 83). It is further logical to visualise that these workshops were owned by potters.

The main produce of the workshop exposed at Oriyaghat was the deluxe ware or the NBPW. It has been accepted that this pottery was traded. Evidence unearthed at Ramnagar also confirms this assumption (Fig. 84) as inscribed potsherds were found in good quantity at this site. The likelihood that the NBPW after preparation was marked or labelled before being exported to the contemporary cities is strong. It may be interesting to note that the settlement at Oriyaghat was not using this deluxe ware. For, the number of NBPW potsherds found from the habitation here is restricted. Contrary to this, Varanasi (Kashi-Rajghat), the capital city of Kashi Janpada, was using this deluxe ware in large quantities, but perhaps was not producing it locally. Pottery with graffiti marks comparable to Ramnagar have been reported from Kashi-Rajghat

84. Engraved NBPW shards, Oriyaghat, Ramnagar.

in considerable proportion (Narain & Roy 1977: 115-116: Pl. XXVIII). Likewise, there could be other settlements where pottery from Ramnagar might have been imported. If this was the case then traders in pottery were perhaps prominent members of society in Varanasi during early Historical times, and this Jataka story mirrors it.

That there was a large natural pond near the mighty river Ganga is another important reference, which can be drawn from the *Kachhapa-Jataka*. Location of a pond by the side of the Ganga at Oriyaghat (Ramnagar) was identified during field studies. The main trench, which was dug up to the depth of 10 metres, revealed that the earliest cultural layer, the lowest Layer 16, was overlying a dried pond bed (Jayaswal & Kumar 2006). This assumption is based on the sampling and testing of sediments of natural soil lying at the base of the occupation layers. This Aeolian deposit of soil blown from the Vindhyas covered the dried pond before it was occupied for dwelling. This indicated that there was a long time gap between the drying of the pond and the occupation of its bed for habitation. Incidentally, the earliest archaeological horizon at this site, which comes from a metre thick deposit (Layer 16), is dateable to 18th to 14th centuries BCE, implying that the existence of the pond and its drying up were old events. How old is a question which needs to be addressed by further studies.

A complete sequence of sediments of the Ramnagar bank of Ganga could be prepared (Jayaswal & Kumar 2006, and Shukla & Raju 2008). Shukla has also investigated other parts of Varanasi and has studied the deposits of Varanasi with a view to reconstruct the history of the water channels in general and the Ganga river in particular. Evidence for tectonic movements has been recorded in the region, which happened around 7000 BCE (Srivastava & Shukla 2009). It resulted in the uplifting of the banks of the Ganga river to attain the present form. Not only was the channel trapped between the left and right banks, but also ponds located on the banks drained out. The deep gullies and dissects of the bank at Ramnagar are reminiscent of this event. Thus, draining/drying of the pond at Oriyaghat may also be accepted to be part of this geological event, which took place thousands of years before the place was colonised. The pond, abode of the tortoise (*Kachhapa*) of the *Kachhapa-Jataka,* also accords that the theme of this Jataka story was a very old incidence, which travelled in the memory generations together up till compilation of the Jatakas under consideration.

The second assertion, that with good rains the water level of the river used to rise up to the level of the pond, is indirectly supported by the archaeological findings of Oriyaghat, as a massive platform/ embankment was exposed at this locality (Fig. 85). In the periphery of the mound (Trench C'3), an imposing platform made of rammed brick bats, potsherds and *kankar* was encountered at the depth of 4.30 m. This 0.78m thick structure was superimposed by eleven layers, assigned to Late Northern Black Polished Ware and Kushan periods. Below the platform

85. Profile of embankment, Oriyaghat, Ramnagar.

lay five distinct layers (12-16). Occurrence of good quality NBPW in layers 13-15 suggests that a platform was constructed some time during the Late NBPW period.

This platform served as a protective device to the settlement from the rising water from the Ganga river. Evidence for floods was also unearthed from the adjoining area (Trenches C'3 and B'2-C'2 at depth of about 5 metres below the surface). Similar evidence was also unearthed from the deposits of Period IB, at Kashi-Rajghat, which has been interpreted as: "...it was a clay embankment which served to prevent the scouring of the banks and also to stop the flood water entering the habitational area" (Narain & Roy 1976: 23). The settlements of Ramnagar and the city of Varanasi, therefore, were experiencing frequent floods. Incidentally, the topography of the Kashi-Rajghat mound is similar to Oriyaghat, Ramnagar, as both are located on the cutting side of the river and over a thick alluvial deposit. Traces of pond at Kashi-Rajghat have not been recorded, while its existence is attested at Oriyaghat, Ramnagar. It may be held that though at the time of the settlement the pond had dried up completely, the old situation in which water of the river and pond could be one possibly remained in the memory being circulated in the form of a folktale.

The above account reveals that the theme of *Kachhapa-Jataka* was based on a situation similar to the geomorphology and culture of the NBPW phase (c. 6th to 4th century BCE) of Ramnagar.

Bodhisattva as a stone artisan is portrayed in *Babbu-Jataka* (No. 137), translated version (*The Jataka*. Book 1. Vol. I. 1895: 294-96) of the relevant portions of which reads as:

> Once upon a time when Brahmadatta was reiging in Benares, the Bodhisattva was born a stonecutter, and growing up became expert in working stones. Now in the Kashi country there dwelt a very rich merchant who had amassed forty crores in gold. And when his wife died, so strong was her love of money that she was re-born a mouse and dwelt over the treasure. And one by one the whole family died, including the merchant himself. Likewise the village became deserted and forlorn.
>
> At the time of our story Bodhisattva was quarrying and shaping stones on the site of this deserted village; and the mouse used often to see him as she ran about to find food. At last she fell in love with him; and, bethinking her how the secret of all her vast wealth would die with her, she conceived the idea of enjoying it with him. So one day she came to Bodhisattva with a coin in her mouth, to buy meat for her and for him. And this went on, the mouse giving the Bodhisattva a coin every day, and he in return supplying her with meat.
>
> The story further goes on, as how Bodhisattva saves her from cats. And ever after the grateful mouse brought the Bodhisatta two or three coins instead of one as before, and by degree she thus gave him the whole of the hoard.

The narration of *Babbu-Jataka* is particularly noteworthy for the following:

- Bodhisattva was born in a stone cutter's family.
- As he grew up, he turned into an expert stone cutter.
- He was quarrying and shaping stones.
- The site where he was chiselling was a deserted village.
- The mouse, wife of a merchant in her earlier birth, was paying him gold coins for buying food (meat). Ultimately, the mouse gave him the gold coin hoard.

A clear reference to stone chiselling activity in a non-urban context is mirrored in this description. I have discussed in detail the archaeological findings of Chunar, the quarry area, and the stone chiselling workshop earlier (Chapter 5). Here it is sufficient to repeat that stone craft was a flourishing and famous tradition in Varanasi during the Early Historic to Medieval period. The quarrying of stone and carving of shape near a deserted village, which is referred to in the above story, implies that the artisan Bodhisattva was part of some crafts village, which was in the vicinity of some old affluent settlement which had been deserted. It may be interesting to note that the excavation of chiselling horizons at Kotwa and Asapur also indicate small rural setting of stone cutters. It may also be recalled that a number of the small settlements, like Aktha and Tilmanpur, which were on the trade route of north India, were deserted around the 3rd century CE. Further archaeological evidence suggests, that stone carving as a local craft in Varanasi region was initiated around the beginning of the comman era. Another important reference of *Babbu-Jataka* is the use of gold coin for purchasing food. Coins in gold were initiated during the Kushan period and continued in the Gupta period. All these facts would suggest that the narration of *Babbu-Jataka* is referring to Late Kushan or Early Gupta period, when Varanasi was known for stone carving craft and was also a city enriched by the traders/merchants.

The description of the *Akitta-Jataka* reads (*The Jataka*. Vo. III. 1901: as follows:

> Once upon a time, when Brahmadatta was king in Benares, the Bodhisattva was born in the family of a Brahmin magnate, whose fortune accounted to eighty crores. They named him Akitti ... a sister was born and they gave her the name Yasavati. The Great Being proceeded at the age of sixteen years to Benares, where he completed his education and then returned. The story further runs as, after death of his parents, at the age of sixteen he and his sister decided to become ascetic....
>
> So leaving the house with all its gold and precious metal, he and his sister departed. And the gate of Benares by which they went was Akitti Gate, and the landing stage they went down to the river, this also was called the Quay of Akitti.

In the above quoted passages, the following points are of particular significance:

- That the Bodhisattva Akitti was born in a Brahmin family.
- That he went to receive education at Varanasi, which was not the place where he resided.
- That the gate and the quay of the settlement through which he departed was named after him.

The ancient settlement of Aktha, which has been identified as Rishipattana, and discussed in detail earlier (Chapter 2), also provides backdrop for *Akitta-Jatakas* (Jayaswal 2013). It may be recalled that the significance of this settlement was recognised up till the Mauryan period. But, its desertion by the Late Kushan period would indicate that the religious significance of this settlement perhaps was erased from the minds of the people by the Gupta period. Finding of the Aktha Yaksha statue from the periphery of the site would further suggest that the inhabitants here were following Brahaminical and folk religion up to at least 1st/2nd centuries BCE. However, the following archaeological assertion of Aktha is relevant for the present theme.

The comparable features of the narration of *Akkita-Jataka* with the archaeological findings of Aktha reveal close affinity of the two. Like other Jataka stories, the tale of Bodhisattva Akitti, too, is of a previous birth of Buddha, indicating remote antiquity of the event. It is not without significance, that the earliest occupation of Aktha is dated between 1800 and 1400 BCE. This date is more than thousand years older than historical Buddha. Thus to the compiler of the *Jataka-Akitti*, the antiquity of Aktha would be a suitable backdrop.

In the second assertion from the story, Akitti was born in a Brahmin family. The archaeological contexts do suggest that Aktha was predominantly a Brahmin settlement. The habitation floors of all the four periods of Aktha—Later Vedic, Janapada, Maurya-Sunga and Kushan—retained traces of fire ritual performances (Jayaswal 2009). Association of ritual earthen pots, the pottery-discs (*kapalas*), is another indication of performance of Vedic rituals at this site, as a regular practice. Intense ritual activities at Aktha were recorded during 1st century BCE to 3rd century CE.

It is also mentioned in the story that the Bodhisattva Akitti went to receive education at Varanasi. From his native settlement Aktha, he proceeded to Kashi-Rajghat (ancient identified city of Varanasi) to receive education. On account of archaeological investigations, it can logically be held that the settlement of Aktha was not only separate from Kashi-Rajghat, but it was also located at a distance from the city. The archaeological history of settlements in Varanasi region testifies that in the first stage only Aktha was occupied. While in Janapada times (about 800 BCE), the confluence of the rivers Ganga and Varuna, Kashi-Rajghat region was also inhabited. Aktha survived contemporary to Kashi-Rajghat till Late Kushan times. Thus, these two—Aktha and Kashi-Rajghat—were separate settlements between Janapada and Late Kushan times (c. 800 BCE–3rd century CE).

A gate and the quay were named Akitti, after the name of the Bodhisattva Akitti. The name Aktha of the modern village, where the ancient site is located, sounds alien to this region. The name of the rivulet Aktha-*nala* is also unique. For, to assign one name to a settlement and also to a water channel is not a common practice in this part of the country. It is mentioned in the Jataka that due to the Bodhisattva, the gate to Varanasi and the quay, for going down the river, were named Akitti. Is it not possible that the name of the settlement and also the rivulet of the modern times is remembrance of one such old event, which gets focussed in *Akitta-Jataka*?

Whether the events actually happened or were imagined may be difficult to ascertain. It may be mentioned that in case of *Akitta-Jataka*, the canvas on which the story was elaborated was the ancient settlement of Aktha. Not only its remote antiquity and nature, predominately a Brahmin settlement, inspired the story, but the strong influence of Buddhism in this region too was a contributory factor. The close vicinity of Sarnath, where the Buddha had preached his First Sermon, over the centuries was a centre of attraction for many—the monks and devotees of various sections of society, which also includes non-Buddhists.

Ancient Varanasi also appears to be famous as an education centre. In several Jatakas, glimpses of world reputed teachers or gurus imparting education to a large number of students are available. For instance, according to the *Musika-Jataka* (Jataka No. 373), Bodhisattva, who was born in a Brahmin family, became a teacher of world fame (Cowell 1897; Vol. III: 142). Similarly, in *Durajana-Jataka* (No. 64), the famous teacher of Benares, the Bodhisattva, was teaching 500 students, which also included foreign students (Cowell 1895; Vol. I: 159). The description of *Labha-Jataka* (*The Jataka*. Vo.II. 1895; Jataka No. 287) elaborates even the mastery of the knowledge of a teacher. The Bodhisattva born in the family of Brahmin, "when he grew up to the age of sixteen years, he had already mastered the three Vedas and the eighteen accomplishments; and he became a far famed teacher, who educated a body of 500 young men" (*The Jataka*. 1895; Vol. II: 287). That education was closely associated with religion is also reflected from the description of this Jataka story. The youth after receiving education "...praised the quality of religious life; and straight became a hermit, and craved alms with righteousness, cultivating attainments, until he became destined to Brahman's world". The education centres of the time were perhaps in the form of *ashramas*, each meant to impart teaching of one guru. Material remains of these centres would logically follow the format of hermitage settlements, which are difficult to survive, hence not easily found in an archaeological context.

It can be logically held that mythological stories like the Jatakas were being woven within the cultural environments of some ancient settlements, which had great antiquity, rich culture make-up and were also places of religious repute.

The Benares of these stories was not only a city or a settlement, but a geographic unit, which comprised a city supporting craftsmen villages, forests, hills, etc. Three instances quoted above, for instance, 'the Brahmin' (*Akitta-Jataka*. No. 480), 'stone cutter' (*Babbu-Jataka*. No. 137), and 'potter' (*Kachhapa-Jataka*. No. 178), were prominent crafts-production groups and the caste of the early Historic society of Varanasi, which like many others embraced Buddhism. There appears an effort to induct main facets of socio-religious forms of the city in these mythological stories. It was also apparent from the above deduction that the composition of many of the Jatakas with focus on Varanasi took place around the time of Kushan and Gupta periods. It is only logical to visualise that part of the citizens were also followers of the Dhamma, but there might have been times when conversion to Buddhism was a regular practice. Bodhisattva himself is said to be born a number of times as a Brahmin. But he possessed qualities of the Buddha. Circulation of these stories certainly was to erase difference of religious followings from the masses.

A list of names is available for Varanasi in the Jatakas stories. Ramma, as mentioned above, is referred to as a city in *Yuvanjaya-Jataka*, Sudassana city in the Culla-sutasoma birth (Jataka No. 525) (*The Jataka.* Vol. V. 1905), Surundha in Udaya bhadda birth (Jataka No. 458) (*The Jataka.* Vol. IV. 1901), Brahmavaddhana in Sona-ndana birth (Jataka No. 532) (*The Jataka.* Vol. V. 1905), and Pupphavati in the Khandahala birth (Jataka No. 542) (*The Jataka.* Vol. I. 1895). "In this manner its name changes on each several occasion" (Rouse 1901: 75-76 in *The Jataka.* Vol. IV). The list of names mentioned in the Jataka stories for ancient Varanasi raises such questions as, whether these were different names for one settlement, ancient Varanasi? Or, were there different settlements/localities within the boundaries of ancient Varanasi region? In the light of the above, it may be held that the shifting settlement pattern of ancient Varanasi appears to be reflected in the Jataka stories by a number of names (Jayaswal 2013). But, in the present state of knowledge, the listed names of this text are difficult to identify in totality. It does, however, suggest that almost all the localities of Varanasi city had been included in the theme of the Jatakas. It is therefore possible to conclude that the city of Varanasi, though a cosmopolitan settlement during the historical period with a large section being non-Buddhist, was the ground for the Buddhist mythology. The fact also remains that so far there is no distinct material remains of Buddhist followings from the ancient city area. I would therefore like to conclude that the Jatakas suggest an extent of intangible boundary of Buddhist landscape to Varanasi city, which was not just the concentration of dense population, but was a geo-physical unit with satellite and supporting settlements composed of people of diverse religious following.

7

THE BUDDHIST LANDSCAPE OF VARANASI

Origin, Growth and Shrinkage

The Buddhist Landscape of Varanasi: Origin, Growth and Shrinkage

Archaeological investigations conducted in and around Sarnath in the last century and recent times have unfolded many facets of the history of the Buddhist landscape of ancient Varanasi, which have been embodied in this book. The scrutiny of archaeological findings of Aktha and Sarnath, for instance, distinctively revealed that these two places may logically be identified as Rishipattana and Mrigadaya. Supplemented by the Buddhist scriptures, it was further possible to conclude that these twin settlements were not only the earliest locales of the sacred landscape under study, but formed the nucleus of the Buddhist establishment. The large following of Buddhism, which was ever increasing in the succeeding centuries after the delivery of the First Sermon, naturally attracted the devotees to the places of major events of the life of Gautama Buddha. These places immediately became auspicious pilgrim sites. The visits of devotees and the offerings made at the Buddhist establishments resulted in large demands of daily utility items, including the ones ritualistic in nature. One such pilgrimage was Mrigadaya, which met the great quantum of demand locally. The mushroom growth of satellite settlements in the peripheral area of Mrigadaya were villages specializing crafts and resorts. Lying between Mrigadaya and the city of Varanasi, these might have been serving feeding centres to both.

However, their proximity and specialisation of the produce suggest that their existence was deep-rooted into the demands of the Mrigadaya. It is thus logical to accept that the workshop and other resort sites on Rajapur-*nala* and Aktha-*nala* demarcate the expansion of Buddhist landscape of Varanasi, beyond its nucleus. The boundaries of this landscape were further enlarged and crossed over to the other sacred landscape of Varanasi, when the events of Buddhist mythology, recorded in the form of the Jatakas, adapted the socio-cultural scenario of the Varanasi city and the Kashi region. This expansion was obviously in the form of intangible boundaries. Details of all these facets were elaborated in the previous chapters of this tome. The summary of the findings are presented below, in view of interpreting historical growth and the decline of the Buddhist landscape of Varanasi.

THE BACKDROP: RISHIPATTANA AND THE *RISHI*-CULTURE

It was elaborated in Chapter 2 that the main reason for selecting Mrigadaya as the place of First Sermon by Gautama Buddha was its vicinity to Rishipattana, which both as per archaeological findings and the scriptures was the abode/resort of *rishis*. It was also shown that the main reason for the establishment of Aktha (Rishipattana) in the Later Vedic period appears to be the movements of Vedic people from north to south-east forming the northern land route. It is also identified as the route of migration of communities from the west (Saraswati Valley) to the east (banks of Sadanira in north Bihar). Located by the side of this route, this small settlement perhaps became the resort of *rishi*s and sages who were frequently going up and down from the Himalayan region to various parts of the middle Ganga plain. As a result, the place soon earned fame as the port of the sages, and thus came to be known as Rishipattana. That these visitors were followers of Vedic religion is also attested by the nature of the exposed habitation floors and associated antiquities. The floors with the use of fire and *kapalas* (the containers of the Vedic sacrifice), for instance, are indicative of prevalence of *rishi* culture at Aktha.

It was also noted earlier (Chapter 2), that the hermitage format of Aktha was the oldest horizon among all the ancient settlements of Varanasi. On account of the C_{14} dating obtained from Period I of Aktha, the beginning of Rishipattana is dated to 18th century BCE, while its continuity lasted till 3rd/4th century CE. It was also conjectured that the visit and stay of the sages and the learned ones, at least thousand or twelve hundred years earlier than the advent of the Lord, helped Rishipattana gain reputation of being a centre of wisdom. Such a place of reputation would have certainly attracted Gautama Buddha, who was eager to preach his wisdom and learning to mankind. The challenge for acceptability of his teaching by the inhabitants of such a centre appeared promising. For, if his teachings were accepted here, then it would be recognised by a large section of society. The confident Gautama took this challenge and was successful in establishing his teachings for the benefit of mankind.

Another advantage might have been the geographical location of Rishipattana. Since Rishipattana/Aktha was located en route a major connective system of the Indian subcontinent, it was also suitable for the spread of a new ideology to distant places. It may thus not be illogical to summarize that establishment of the Vedic culture in the Varuna Valley of Varanasi paved the way for Buddhism. And also since Rishipattana was located in Varanasi region, Gautama Buddha selected Mrigadaya near Rishipattana for his First Sermon, even though he attained wisdom at Bodh Gaya.

ORIGIN AND GROWTH OF THE LANDSCAPE

In the light of the archaeological discoveries and narrative accounts, it may be held that the nucleus of the Buddhist landscape of Varanasi was the Mrigadaya, which could be identified as Sarnath. Situated a little away, Rishipattana provided a background for the makeup of Mrigadaya, and receded to the background after the First Sermon. The material remains of Sarnath evidence a steady growth from the natural habitat of deer into a flourishing Buddhist pilgrimage of repute (Chapter 3). History of this religious establishment is dated between 6th century BCE and 12th century CE. Adorned with intricate carvings and large numbers of structures, Sarnath testifies to a well-established nucleus of the most sacred landscapes of Buddhism.

It was noted that, the main factor for the origin and growth of sarnath was the generous patronage of the donors. The earliest group of structures and sculptures—monastery, Dharmarajika stupa and the lion pillar of the time of Mauryan king Asoka, for instance, to the vihara of the medieval period which was constructed by Queen Kumaradevi—are donations to this Buddhist establishment. The offerings of independent icons at this site during Kushan times also was not of less significance as this practice initiated donation of images of Buddhist divinities at Mrigadaya. This practice in turn became one of the major factors for the origin and development of stone carving and the 'Sarnath School of Art'. As a result of this, by the Gupta period, Sarnath had earned the reputation of one of the most productive and artistic icon carving centres of India.

The Gupta period was the stage when not only the nucleus of Buddhist pilgrimage widened, but also the landscape of Sarnath expanded towards the southern axis, up to the Ganga (about 5 km). This was due to the demand of stone carvings at Sarnath that gave impetus for the growth of craft centres on Rajapur-*nala*, which was well connected with the resource area—the Chunar hills. Besides the heavy demand of icons at Sarnath from donors, there were other supporting factors which helped this region to become one of the world famous centres of sculpture production in ancient India. Easy availability of good quality sandstone in the neighbouring hills of Chunar and natural facility for the transportation of the medium through navigation (Jayaswal 1998) were the other added advantages. The archaeological findings of Chunar and Varanasi-Sarnath regions throw significant light on the entire mechanism of sandstone carving and also revealed interrelationship of the main consumer centre, the Buddhist establishment of Sarnath, with the craft villages/workshops (Kotwa) and the resource area (Chunar). The entire mechanism of lithic craft developed and continued on the grounds of the nature and quantum of demand of donors of the idols and the monuments.

Besides the above-mentioned geo-cultural demarcation of Buddhist landscape, considerable part of the Brahminical landscape of Varanasi appears to be accepted by the Buddhists. For, the nucleus of many of the Jataka stories is Kashi and Varanasi. In view of material remains, though, Varanasi may be accepted as being part of a Brahminical settlement, and the intangible boundaries of the Buddhist landscape appear to embrace this city also.

SHRINKAGE AND FORGOTTEN LANDSCAPE

In around the 13th century CE, the flourishing Buddhist establishment of Sarnath appears to have lost its glory. One notices that by the 12th century CE, offerings were made to Mulagandhakuti Vihara and its vicinity even by devotees having faith in Brahmanism. Take for example the royal members of Pala and Gahadavala dynasties, whose offerings are recorded in epigraphs mentioning their faith in Saivism. Early medieval Brahmanical images of Sarnath were obtained from this very site, but their proper context is not known. Whether power of the Brahmanical followers was the cause for the uprooting of this Buddhist establishment is difficult to ascertain. Decline in Buddhist following is evident in the archaeological records of Sarnath. So is the case with the stone carving sites, like Kotwa, which indicate that the demand for images had ceased to exist by c. 13th century CE in this region, as a result of which these craft centres were abandoned. In about a couple of centuries, the sacred landscape of Mrigadaya-Sarnath was completely abandoned and was also erased from the minds of the people after a while. It then was discovered as an archaeological site in the 20th century.

Varanasi, already a reputed place of wisdom with great antiquity, was further enriched in spirituality and a new ideology to experience the truth of life, which was promoted by Buddhism.

The cultural canvas of Varanasi became particularly vibrant with a balanced combination of spirituality and excellence of material expressions. On one hand, the growth of Buddhist pilgrimage at Sarnath provided an impetus for quantitative and qualitative development of arts and crafts in Varanasi region. On the other, the region attracted saints, sages and monks, who had attained wisdom and spirituality. It has been mentioned earlier that the city of Varanasi, according to Jataka stories, became a centre for education and learning, where religious conducts were also imparted to the youth. The very fact that the Lord in his previous births is shown to excel, in Jatakas, in a number of craft and art traditions, is suggestive of appreciation for skills of techno-artistic heritage by the contemporary society. It was also apparent from the details on archaeological remains of Sarnath that every following generation showed concern to keep earlier parts of monuments and icons, which were offered at Mrigadaya (Chapter 3). One wonders if this ancient socio-cultural scenario is not very relevant for modern society, when we look for a balance between morality-spirituality and technological development along with appreciation for our culture heritage, which is inclusive of tangible and intangible arts and traditional knowledge.

Bibliography

Agrawala, V.S. 1964. *The Wheel Flag of India: Chakra-Dhvaja* (Being a History and Exposition of the Meaning of the Dharma-Chakra and the Sarnath Lion Capital). Varanasi.

Altekar, A.S. 1937. *History of Benares.* Banaras Hindu University, Varanasi.

Archaeological Survey of India Annual Report 1904-5. 1908. (Reprinted 2003). F.O. Oertel 'Excavations at Sarnath'. Archaeological Survey of India, New Delhi: 59-104.

Archaeological Survey of India Annual Report 1906-7. 1909. (Reprinted 2002). J.H. Marshall and S. Konow. 'Sarnath'. Archaeological Survey of India, New Delhi: 68-101.

Archaeological Survey of India Annual Report 1907-8. 1911. (Reprinted 2002). J.H. Marshall and S. Konow. 'Sarnath'. Archaeological Survey of India, New Delhi: 43-80.

Archaeological Survey of India Annual Report 1914-15. 1920. (Reprinted 2002). H. Hargreaves. 'Excavations at Sarnath'. Archaeological Survey of India, New Delhi: 97-131.

Archaeological Survey of India Annual Report 1921-22. 1924. (Reprinted 2002). D.B. Spooner (Ed.). Archaeological Survey of India, New Delhi: 42-44.

Asher, F.M. 1980. *The Art of Eastern India, 300-800.* Oxford University Press, Delhi.

Beal, S. 1869. *Travels of Fah-Hian and Sung-Yun Buddhist Pilgrims from China to India (400 AD and 518 AD).* (Reprinted 2003). Asian Educational Services, New Delhi: 134-137.

——. 1884. *Si-Yu-Ki. Buddhist Records of the Western World. Translation from the Chinese of Hiuen Tsang (AD 629).* Vol. II. Book VII. (Reprinted 1980). Asian Educational Services, New Delhi: 44- 61.

Biswas, T.K. & B. Jha. 1985. *Gupta Sculptures.* Bharat Kala Bhavan. Banaras Hindu University, Varanasi.

Bajpai, K.D. 1989. 'Bodhisattva and Buddha: The Early Iconic Forms'. In *Buddhist Iconography.* Tibet House, New Delhi. Sambhota Series II: 60-68.

Cowell, E.B. (Ed.). 1895-1905. *The Jataka or Stories of the Buddha's Former Births.* Vols. I-VI. (Reprinted 1990). Munshiram Manoharlal, New Delhi.

Cunningham, A. 1871a. 'Benaras, Sarnath'. *Archaeological Survey of India. Four Reports Made During the Years 1862-63-64-65.* Vol. I. XXV. (Reprinted 2000). Archaeological Survey of India, New Delhi: 103-130.

——. 1871b. *The Ancient Geography of India I. Buddhist Period (*Including the Campaigns of Alexander, and the Travels of Hiuen-Tsang). (Reprinted 1996). Low Price Publications, Delhi.

Dharmadhikari, T.N. 1989. *Yajnayudhani (An Album of Sacrificial Utensils with Descriptive Notes).* Tilaka– Maharastra – Vidyapitha. Vaidika Samsodhana Mandala, Pune.

Eggeling, Julius (trans.). 1882. *The Satapatha-Brahmana. According to the Text of the Madhyandina School.* Vol. V. The Sacred Books of the East (SBE 44). (Reprinted 1990). Atlantic Publlishers & Distributors, New Delhi.

Ganguly, D.C. 1957. 'The North India During the Eleventh and Twelfth Centuries'. Ch. II. *The History and Culture of Indian People: Vol. V: The Struggle for Empire*. Bharatiya Vidya Bhawan, Bombay: 52-54.

Gaur, R.C. 1983. *Excacations at Atranjikhera. (Early Civilization of the Upper Ganga Basin)*. Motilal Banarsidass, New.

Ghosh, A. 1973. *The City in Early Historical India.* (Reprinted 1990). Indian Institute of Advanced Study, Simla & Munshiram Manoharlal, New Delhi.

Gopinath Rao, T.A. 1914. *Elements of Hindu Iconography*. Vol. I. Part. II (Second Edition. (Reprint 1985). Motilal Banarsidass, Delhi.

Gupte, R.S. 1980. *Iconography of the Hindu Buddhists and Jains.* Taraporevala Sons & Co. Pvt. Ltd., Bombay.

Harle, J.C. 1986. *The Art and Architecture of the Indian Subcontinent.* The Pelican History of Arts. Middlesex.

Havell, E.B. 1905. *Beneras, The Sacred City*. London.

Horner, I.B. 1951. *The Book of the Discipline (Vinaya-Pitaka).* Vol. IV. (Mahavagga). (Reprinted 1982). The Pali Text Society, London.

——. 1954. *The Collection of the Middle Length Sayings (Majjhim-Nikaya).* Vol. I. (Reprinted 1995). Pali Text Society, Oxford.

Indian Archaeology 1992-93: A Review. Archaeological Survey of India, New Delhi: 99.

Huntington, S.L. 1985. *The Art of Ancient India: Buddhist, Hindu, Jain.* Weather Hill, New York.

Jayaswal, V. 1998. *From Stone Quarry to Sculpturing Workshop: A Report on the Archaeological Investigations around Chunar, Varanasi & Sarnath.* Agam Kala Prakashan, Delhi.

——. 2001. *Royal Temples of Gupta Period: Excavation at Bhitari.* Aryan Books International, New Delhi.

——. 2003. 'Aktha: A Satellite Settlement of Sarnath, Varanasi (Report of Excavations Conducted in the Year 2002)'. *Bharati.* Bulletin of the Department of Ancient Indian History, Culture & Archaeology, 2000-2002. Vol. 26. Banaras Hindu University, Varanasi: 61-180.

——. 2004. 'Asokan Pillars: Medium, Chiselling & Composition'. *The Andand-vana of Indian Art.* Dr. Anand Krishna Felicitation Volume (Eds. N. Krishna & M. Krishna). Indica Books, Varanasi: 35-46.

——. 2009. *Ancient Varanasi: An Archaeological Perspective.* Aryan Books International, New Delhi.

——. 2009a. 'Antiquity of Varanasi as Revealed by Excavations at Aktha (2008-9)'. *Puratattva.* Bulletin of the Indian Archaeological Society. Vol. 39: 141-46.

——. 2011. *Adikashi se Varanasi Tak.* (Hindi). Aryan Books International, New Delhi.

——. 2012. 'Mauryan Pillars of the Middle Ganga Plain: Archaeological Discoveries of Sarnath-Varanasi and Chunar'. (Eds. P. Olivelle, J. Leosho & H.P. Ray). *Reimaging Asoka: Memory and History.* Oxford University Press, New Delhi: 229-257.

——. 2013 'Jataka-stories and Archaeology: A Case Study of Varanasi'. *Varanasi: Myths and Scientific Studies* (Ed. Vidula Jayaswal). Aryan Book International, Delhi: 71-89.

——. 2013a. 'Early Archaeological Cultures of the Middle Ganga Plain: Unity in Diversity'. *Cultural Unity of India (Phase I).* International Seminar, Ramakrishna Mission Institute of Culture. Kolkata (Jan. 16-18, 2013).

Jayaswal, V. & I. Singh. 1998. 'Sculpturing Process: A Study of Past and Present'. In *From Stone Quarry to Sculpturing Workshop: A Report on the Archaeological Investigations around Chunar, Varanasi & Sarnath.* Agam Kala Prakashan, Delhi: 232-37.

Jayaswal, V. & Manoj Kumar. 2006. 'Ramnagar: Discovery of a Supporting Settlement of Ancient Varanasi'. *Puratattva*. Bulletin of the Indian Archaeological Soceity. Vol. 36: 85-92.

Jayaswal, V. & Meera Sharma. 2006. 'Pottery-disc: The *Kapala* of the Vedic *Yajna'. Purabharati: Studies in the Early Historical Archaeology and Buddhism* (Commemoration Volume in Respect of Prof. B.P. Sinha). Eds. B.R. Mani and S.C. Saran. Sharda Publishing House, Delhi: 38-47.

John, S.S. 1989. *The Legend of King Asoka: A Study and Translation of the Asokavadana.* Motilal Banarasidass, New Delhi.

Jones, J.J. 1949. *The Mahavastu*. Voulme I. Translated from the Buddhist Sanskrit. (Reprinted 1987). Pali Text Society, London.

Kane, P.V. 1973. *History of Dharmashastra. (Ancient and Medieval Religious and Civil Law).* Vol. IV. Second Edition. Bhandarkar Oriental Research Institute. Poona.

Kashyapa, J. (Ed.). 1958. *The Dighanikaya (2 Maha Vagga)*. Pali Publication Board, Bihar Government: 9.

Krishna, A. 1982. 'The Gupta Style of Sculpture from the City of Varanasi'. *Rupa Pratirupa* (Alice Boner Commemoration Volume). Ed. A. Krishna. Bible Impex Private Ltd., New Delhi: 87-88.

Lalji, 'Shravak'. 2003. 'Chini Yatriyon ke Yatra-vivran Main Mrigday (Mrigdav) Van Vihar' (Hindi). *Research Journal, Faculty of Arts.* Vol. 8. (2002-03). Banaras Hindu University, Varanasi: 52-66.

Law, B.C. 1951. 'North India in the Six Century BC'. Ch. I. *The History and Culture of Indian People: Vol. II: The Age of Imperial Unity*. (Reprinted 1968). Bharatiya Vidya Bhawan, Bombay: 1-17.

Lin-Bodien, C.G. 1981. 'An Early Yaksha from Aktha near Sarnath (Varanasi, U.P.)'. *Chahavi* (Rai Krishnadas Felicitation Volume). Vol. 2. (Ed. Anand Krishna). Bharat Kala Bhavan, Varanasi: 294-97.

Majumdar, B. 1947. *A Guide to Sarnath*. (2nd Revised Edition). The Manager, Government of India Press, Delhi.

Majumdar, R.C. 1954. 'Rise of the Guptas'. Ch. I. *The History and Culture of Indian People: Vol. III: The Classical Age*. (Reprinted 1970). Bharatiya Vidya Bhawan, Bombay: 1-32.

Malalasekera, G.P. 1937. *Dictionary of Pali Proper Names*. Vol. I. (Reprinted 1995). Munshiram Manoharlal, New Delhi.

Marshall, J.H. 1922. 'The Monuments of Ancient India'. *The Cambridge History of India, Vol. I*. Cambridge University Press, Cambridge.

Meister, M.W., M.A. Dhaky & K. Deva (eds.). 1988. *Encyclopaedia of Indian Temple Architecture: North India*, Foundations of North Indian Style c. 250 BC-AD 1100. American Institute of Indian Studies, New Delhi.

Mookerji, R.K. 1968 (Rep.). 'Asoka, The Great'. Ch. V. *The History and Culture of Indian People: Vol. II: The Age of Imperial Unity*. Bharatiya Vidya Bhawan, Bombay (4th Edition): 88-89.

——. 1968a. 'The Fall of the Magadhan Empire'. Ch. IX. *The History and Culture of Indian People: Vol. II: The Age of Imperial Unity*. Bharatiya Vidya Bhawan, Bombay (4th Edition): 95-100.

Narain, A.K. & T.N. Roy. 1968. *The Excavations at Prahladpur (March-April 1963)*. Banaras Hindu University, Varanasi.

——. 1976. *Excavations at Rajghat (1957-58; 1960-65)*. Part I. The Cutting, Stratification & Structures. Banaras Hindu University, Varanasi.

——. 1977. *Excavations at Rajghat (1957-58; 1960-65)*. Part II. The Pottery. Banaras Hindu University, Varanasi.

Narain, A.K. & P. Singh. 1977. *Excavations at Rajghat (1957-58; 1960-65)*. Part III. *Small Finds*. Department of Ancient Indian History, Culture & Archaeology, Banaras Hindu University, Varanasi.

Narasimhachar, Vidvan So. 1944. *The Srauta Sutra of Apastamba with the Bhasya of Dhurtaswami and The Vrtti of Ramagnicit Prasnas 1-5*. Government Oriental Library, Mysore.

Oldenberg, H. (Trans.). 1886. *The Grihya-Sutras: Rules of Vedic Domestic Ceremonies*. Vol. 1. *Sacred Books of the East:* Vol. 29. (Reprinted 1990). Atlantic Publishers & Distributors, New Delhi.

Oldenberg, H. & Max Müller. 1892. The *Grihya*-Sutras: Rules of *Vedic Domestic Ceremonies*. Vol. 2. *Sacred Books of the East:* Vol. 30. (Reprint 1990). Atlantic Publishers & Distributors, New Delhi.

Pande, G.C. 2001. *Vedic Samnskriti* (Hindi). Lokbharati, Allahabad.

Pande, R. 1944. *Ashok ke Abhilekha* (Hindi). Gyan Mandal Ltd., Kashi Hindu Vishwa Vidyalaya, Varanasi.

Pant., P.C. and V. Jayaswal. 1990. 'Chunar Stone Quarries Raw Material for Sculpture and Architecture'. *Marg.* A Magazine of the Arts. Vol. XLII. No. 1. National Centre for the Performing Arts, Bombay: 59-61.

Pathak, V.S. 2002. 'Date of Buddha's Mahaparinibbana and Inscriptions of Asoka'. *Bharati.* The Bulletin of the Department of Ancient Indian History, Culture & Archaeology. (Ed. V. Jayaswal). Vol. 26: 5-28.

Pusalkar, A.D. 1971. 'Traditional History from the Accession of Parikshit to the End of the Barhadratha Dynasty'. *The History and Culture of Indian People: Vol. I: The Vedic Age*. Bharatiya Vidya Bhawan, Bombay.

Rhys Davids, T.W. & J. Estlin Carpenter. 1982. *The Digha Nikaya*. Pali Text Society, London.

Rhys-Davids, T.W. 1903. *Buddhist India*. (Reprinted 1970). Indological Book House, Delhi.

Rouse, W.H.D. 1901. *The Jataka*. Vol. 4. (Ed. E.B. Cowell). (Reprinted 1990). Munshiram Manoharlal, New Delhi.

Sahni, D. 1914. *Catalogue of the Museum of Archaeology at Sarnath.* Calcutta.

——. 1933. *Guide to the Buddhist Ruins at Sarnath.* Calcutta.

Saraswati, S.K. 1957. *A Survey of Indian Sculpture.* Calcutta.

——. 1954. 'Art: Architecture'. Ch. XIX. *The History and Culture of Indian People: Vol. III: The Classical Age*. (Reprinted 1970). Bharatiya Vidya Bhawan, Bombay: 1-32.

Satvalekar, S.D. 1983. *Atharvaveda ka Subodha Bhashya* (Hindi). Part II (Khanda 4-6). Valsad.

Settar, S. 2003. *Footprints of Artisans in History: Some Reflections on Early Artisians of India.* General President's Address. Sixty-fourth Session of the Indian History Congress. Bangalore.

Sharma, Meera. 1988. 'Sarnath ke Vishesh Sandarbha main Purvi Uttar Pradesh aur Bihar main Buddha Pratimaon ka Vikas'. (Ph.D. Thesis in Hindi). Banaras Hindu University Library, Varanasi.

Sherring, M.A. 1868. *Benares: The Sacred City of the Hindus in Ancient & Modern Times.* (Reprinted 1990). Low Price Publications, Delhi.

Singh, B.P. 2004. *Early Farming Communities of the Kaimur (Excavations at Senuwar 1986-87, 89-90).* Vol. I. Publication Scheme, Jaipur.

Singh, P. 1994. *Excavations At Narhan (1984-89).* Department of Ancient Indian History, Culture & Archaeology, Banaras Hindu University, Varanasi.

Sinha, K.K. 1967. *Excavations At Sravasti – 1959*. Monograph of the Department of Ancient Indian History, Culture and Archaeology. Banaras Hindu University, Varanasi.

Sircar, D.C. 1968. 'North India After the Kushanas'. Ch. XI. *The History and Culture of Indian People: Vol. II: The Age of Imperial Unity*. Bharatiya Vidya Bhawan, Bombay (4th edition): 159-76.

——. 1968. 'The Kushanas'. Ch. IX. *The History and Culture of Indian People: Vol. II: The Age of Imperial Unity*. Bharatiya Vidya Bhawan, Bombay (4th edition): 136-53.

Swaminathan, C.R. (ed.& trans.) 1997. *Kanvasatapathabrahmanam.* Vol II. Kalamulasastra Series. (General editor Kapila Vatsyayan). Indira Gandhi National Centre For The Arts, New Delhi and Motilal Banarsidass, Delhi.

Thapar, B.K. 1957. 'Maski 1954: A Chalcolithic Site of the Southern Deccan'. *Ancient India. Bulletin of the Archaeological Survey of India*. No. 13. New Delhi: 4-142.

The Dighanikaya (2 Maha Vagga). 1958. (Gen. Ed. Bhikkhu J. Kashyapa). Pali Publication Board, Bihar Government: 9.

The Jataka. 1895. Tr. R. Chalmers (Ed. E.B. Cowell). Vol. I. (Jataka Nos. 1-150). (Reprinted 1990). Munshiram Manoharlal, New Delhi.

The Jataka. 1895. Tr. W.H.D. Rouse (Ed. E.B. Cowell). Vol. II. (Jataka Nos. 151-300). (Reprinted 1990). Munshiram Manoharlal, New Delhi.

The Jataka. 1897. Tr. H.T. Francis & R.A. Neil (Ed. E.B. Cowell). Vol. III. (Jataka Nos. 301-438). (Reprinted 1990). Munshiram Manoharlal, New Delhi.

The Jataka. 1901. Tr. W.H.D. Rouse (Ed. E.B. Cowell). Vol. IV. (Jataka Nos. 439-510). (Reprinted 1990). Munshiram Manoharlal, New Delhi.

The Jataka. 1905. Tr. H.T. Francis (Ed. E.B. Cowell). Vol. V. (Jataka Nos. 511-537). (Reprinted 1990). Munshiram Manoharlal, New Delhi.

The Jataka. 1907. Tr. E.B. Cowell (Ed. W.H.D. Rouse). Vol. VI. (Jataka Nos. 538-547). (Reprinted 1990). Munshiram Manoharlal, New Delhi.

Wadia, D.N. 1957. *Geology of India.* (Third Revised Edition). London.

Williams, J.G. 1983. *The Art of Gupta India: Empire and Province.* New Delhi.

Winternitz, M. 1933. *A History of Indian Literature.* Vol. II. (Reprinted 1987). Munshiram Manoharlal, New Delhi.

Woodword, F.L. 1927. *The Book of the Kindred Sayings (Snyuktta-Nikaya) or Grouped Sutta*. Part IV. (Reprinted 1996). The Pali Text Society, Oxford: 101, 111 & 112.

Vogel, J. Ph. 1906. 'Buddhist Sculpture from Benares'. *Archaeological Survey of India Annual Report 1902-04.* New Delhi: 212-26.

Index

Abhayamitra 110, 136-38
Abhaya mudra 94, 96, 136, 172
Aeolian deposit 185
Agathi 130
Agiabir 14
Agni 32
Agni-kund 35
Agnishomau 32
Akbar 109
Akitta-Jataka 180, 189-90, 192-93
Akitti 190-92
Aktha 15-18, 21-23, 25-31, 36-38, 41-52, 87, 126-27, 152, 164, 179-80, 189-92, 196-98
Aktha Yaksha 164, 190
Aktha-*nala* 15, 25, 152, 191, 197
Altekar, A.S. 2, 5
Amaravati 130
Amra fruit 111
An-mo-lo-mango 115
Anda 66, 90
Anga 3, 7
Apastamba 32
Areca-nut shaped bead 46
Arrow-heads 48
Aryan culture 5, 7
Aryan homeland 6
Asapur 17, 152-53, 165-66, 189
Ashramas 193
Ashta-Kapala 32
Ashvamedha-jnana 99
Asoka(n) 11, 16, 22, 26, 60, 62, 64-66, 68-69, 71, 73, 75, 78, 80, 83, 86, 88, 91, 98, 115-16, 122-23, 125-30, 158-59, 167, 199
    column 68, 70, 73, 78, 80, 82, 90-91, 108, 113, 129
    pillar 70, 73-75, 83, 86, 91, 108, 128
Assi 7, 9
Asvina 145
Atharvaveda 30
Atranjikhera 42-43, 46-47
Auguttar-Nikaya 2
Ayas 48
Ayodhya-Patna 49
Ayodhya-Vaisali 49

Babbu-Jataka 174, 180-81, 188-89, 193
Bachau 161
Bala Bhikhu 88, 93-94, 98, 132-34, 164, 168
Ballia 2, 49
Banaras/Benares 5, 16, 22, 49, 54-55, 95, 132, 153, 178-82, 188, 190, 192-93
Baragaon village 154
Beal, S. 9, 58, 65, 68-69, 112, 115-17, 120, 126, 147
Bengal Asiatic Society 60
Bhanga(s) 161, 173
Bharat Kala Bhavan 153
Bharhut 81, 130
Bharsivas 87
Bhitari 47, 103-05, 110, 114, 141
Black Slipped Ware 34, 37-38, 40-41, 43-44
Black-and-Red Ware 34, 37-38, 40-43
Bodh Gaya 22, 125, 198
Bodhimula 126
Bodhisattva 18, 88, 93-95, 97-98, 116, 120, 132-34, 138, 164-65, 167-68, 170-74, 178, 180-81, 183, 188-93
Brahaminical 190
Brahmadatta 5, 178, 180-81, 188, 190
Brahmanism 200
Brahmaputra 99
Brahmi (script) 85, 127-28, 131, 136, 139
Brahmin/Brahmanical 9, 18, 81, 148, 180-81, 190-93, 200
  deities 166
  habitat 19
  landscape 200
  magnate 190
  pantheon 148
  settlement 181, 191-92
Buddha 2-6, 8, 12, 14-15, 18-19, 22-23, 26, 50, 52, 54, 62, 64, 85, 87-88, 93-95, 97, 100, 107-12, 114-16, 120, 123-26, 132, 134, 136-39, 141-42, 147-48, 150, 167, 170-74, 178-80, 191-93, 196-98
Buddhagupta 63, 111, 114, 138
Buddhapriya 138
Buddhist 2, 5, 7-13, 15-16, 18-20, 22-23, 25-26, 52, 54-55, 59-60, 63-65, 68-69, 80-81, 86-88, 104, 106, 108-11, 114, 120, 122-24, 126-27, 129, 132-34, 138-39, 141, 143-45, 150-52, 154, 165, 174, 176, 178-79, 181, 192, 194-97, 198-201
  mythology 19, 178, 181, 194, 197
  remains 18, 68, 151
  Sangha 127
Buxar 49

Cave No. XI of Ajanta 102, 106
Central and Western Asia 49
Chaitya-griha 79, 106
Chakra 97, 141
Chalcolithic 33, 42, 48
Chambal 99
Champa 3
Chandodar 57
Chandra-tal 57
Chandragupta 99
Chandragupta II 99-101, 110, 112

Chatai 30
Chaukhandi (mound/stupa) 56-58, 60, 101, 108-09, 113, 117, 141
Chetganj bazaar 59
Chhatravali 67, 77, 89, 98
Chitraghanta 148
Christian cross 110
Chunar 17, 59, 94-98, 104, 128, 154-59, 164-65, 167-68, 171, 189, 199, 200
  sandstone 96-98, 104, 164, 168, 171
Cidasi 32
Close kiln 39-40
Cowell, E.B. 2, 13, 19, 174, 192
Culla-sutasoma 193
Cunningham, A. 10, 54, 56-60, 106-08, 119

Danam 130, 135
Darsapurnamasa-kapalopadhana sacrifice 32
Dashashvamedha 87
Deccan 183
Devalayas 9
Dhamek (stupa) 10, 56, 58-61, 63-64, 100-01, 106-07, 113, 116, 141, 145, 176
Dhamma 4, 64, 87, 124, 145, 193
Dhamma-yatra 125
Dharma-chakra 141
Dharma-paryaya 139
Dharmachakra-Jina Vihara 92, 101, 117-19, 122, 146-47
Dharmachakra pravartna 141
Dharmapala 144
Dharmarajika (stupa) 59-60, 64-67, 75, 78-79, 81, 83-84, 86, 88-89, 92, 98, 101, 108, 113, 116, 122, 126, 131, 135, 141, 199
Dharmasi 32
Dharmasimh 138
Dharmasoka 146
Dharmmade 136
Dhartramasi 32
Dhruva 36
Dhurvamasi 32
Digha Nikaya 6
Divya-vadana 16, 126, 65
Durajana-Jataka 192
Durga 148, 157
Dvadasa-Kapala 32

Early Gupta (times) 84, 86, 88, 101, 105
Early Medieval (period/times) 17-18, 66, 109, 114, 116-17, 120, 122, 175
Edge ground potsherd 33
Eggeling, J. 32-33
Ekadasa-Kapala 32

Fa Hien 99, 101, 112-14
Fau poh 117
First Sermon 5, 12, 15, 19, 22-23, 64, 83, 85, 123-24, 131, 136, 180, 192, 196-98
Friar Bala 132
Friar Pushyavuddhi 132

Gahadavala(s) 5, 11, 64, 200
Gamesman 33

Ganas 3
Gandhakuti 148
Gandhara 7
Ganga (river) 3-5, 7, 9, 13, 17, 23, 25, 33-34, 37, 42, 46, 51-52, 79, 86, 104, 108, 114, 124, 128-29, 136, 152-58, 167, 171, 179-80, 182-83, 185-87, 191, 197, 199
  plain 3-4, 7, 23, 33-34, 42, 46, 51-52, 79, 86, 104, 114, 124, 128-29, 136, 154, 156, 167, 179, 183, 197
  Valley 3, 5, 37, 155
Ganguly, D.C. 11, 64
Garbhagriha 111
Gaur, R.C. 34, 42, 47
Gazipur 18, 159
Geometric potsherd 33-36
Ghata 44, 46
Ghuhurpur 151
Gopuram 118
Gorakhpur-Allahabad 49
Govindchandra 11, 64, 145
Grihas 29
Gupta(s) (period/dynasty) 5, 13, 18, 26, 54, 64, 73, 84, 86-88, 90-92, 95-97, 99-114, 116-17, 119-20, 131, 136-39, 141-42, 145, 153, 164-67, 169-73, 175-76, 189, 193, 199
  Style 95, 107, 173

Hall, Fitz-Edward 61
Hargreaves 79, 114, 129-30, 136, 143
Hariti 130
Hasanpur 151
Hastinapur 5, 47
Hermika 66-67, 83, 89, 98
Himalayas/Himalayan 3, 16, 23, 51, 99, 197
Hindu temples 160
Historical Buddha 2, 4, 22-23, 178-79, 191
Xuanzang 9, 58, 65, 68-70, 73, 75, 78-79, 109, 111, 115-16, 120, 126, 147
Hopscotch 33
Horn, C. 61
Horner, I.B. 11, 16, 55, 124
Humayun 109
Hunas 100, 114

Indian Museum 60-62
Indian mythology 178
Indra-Agni 32
Inverted firing technique 39-40
Ishan 148
Isipatana 16, 23, 124, 126

Jagat Singh stupa 56, 59, 64, 71, 93, 136
Jain faith 18
Jaipur 159-60, 168
Jakhera 35-36
Jambuki 146
Jamteyika 131
Jamuna 99
Janapada(s) (period) 2, 3, 5, 12, 26-27, 49-50, 125, 179-80, 183-84, 191
Jasamana 144
Jata-Juta 50
Jataka(s) 2, 13-14, 19, 174-75, 178-82, 181, 185-86, 190, 192-94, 197, 200-01

Jaunpur 159
Jayapala 144
Jayaswal, V. 3, 5, 13-16, 18-19, 25, 27-28, 31, 34, 38-39, 41, 45, 47-48, 50, 69, 79, 82, 87, 94, 103-05, 110-11, 114, 126, 128-29, 151-55, 158-59, 163-64, 166, 179, 181, 183, 185-86, 190-91, 194, 199
Jhaua-jharan 27, 126
Jhusi 14
Jones, J.J. 16, 23
Ju-lal 115
Juhu 36

Kabis 39
Kachhapa-Jataka 181, 183, 185-86, 188, 193
Kalchuri 145
Kanava 81-82, 85, 130
Kane, P.V. 32, 36
Kanishka 81, 86-89, 93, 97, 132
Kanpur 2
Kanvasatapathabrahmanam 36
Kapala 19, 31-33, 35-37, 46, 51, 191, 197
Karn phul 59
Karna(deva) 144
Kashi 2-3, 5-7, 12, 14, 19, 49, 125, 148, 174, 179-80, 184, 187-88, 191, 197, 200
Kashi Janpada 12, 49, 180, 184
Kashi-Rajghat 7, 12, 14, 125, 180, 184, 187-88, 191
Kaudena 163
Kaushambi 3, 5-6
Khajuhi 151
Khandahala 193
Kharapallana(s) 132, 134
Kharoshthi (epigraph/script) 128-29
Kielhorn 145
King Piyadasi 75, 127
Kirtti 139
Kittoe, Markham 61
Kolkata 60-62
Konow 62, 65-66, 72, 83-84, 88, 97, 108, 116-17, 120, 130-31, 135-36, 141-44
Kosala 3, 5
Kotwa 17-18, 152-53, 164-66, 171, 175, 189, 200
Krishna, K. 38-39
Kumar, Manoj 13
Kumaradevi 11, 63-64, 99, 117, 122, 145, 147-48, 199
Kumargupta I 99-100, 103-04, 110-11, 114
Kumargupta II 63, 137
Kumbhakara-Jataka 180
Kurum 163
Kushan (period) 5, 13, 26-27, 45, 50, 64, 73, 79, 81-82, 84, 86-88, 90-94, 97-100, 102, 108, 111, 122, 132-36, 140, 150, 152-53, 158, 164-66, 168-69, 172, 175, 183, 186, 189-91, 193, 199
  style 97
Kusinagara 126

Labha-Jataka 192
Laity 128
Lal, B.B. 47
Lallapura 159, 161, 169, 174, 176

Late Kushan (period/time) 26, 45, 92, 152, 183, 190-91
Late Maurya (period) 63, 79, 81-82, 130
Late NBPW period 187
Later Vedic 7, 25, 27-30, 37-39, 41-42, 45-50, 191, 197
  communities 16
  people 7
  period 27-28, 38-39, 41-42, 47-50, 197
  Samhitas 28-29, 48
Law, B.C. 2-3
Li 2
Lichhavis 99
Lin-Bodien, C.G. 27, 164
Loha-ayas 48
Lu-ye 115
Lumbini 126

Mabhuka 144
Mackenzie, Colonel C. 60
Madarpur 151
Magadha 3, 5, 7, 99
Mahajanpadas 2-4, 179-80
Mahaparinirvana 124, 179
Maharaja of Banaras 182
Mahavastu 11, 16, 22, 58
Maheshwara 9, 144
Mahipala 145
Maitreya 107-08, 112, 116
Majumdar, B. 22, 60, 66, 79, 82-83, 88, 91-92, 99, 101-04, 107-09, 111, 117-19, 142, 145
Malagandhakuti Vihara 101
Malalasekera, G.P. 16, 22, 126
Mandi 14, 27
Mani, B.R. 11, 125, 180
Manorathgupta 145
Marshall, John 62, 65-66, 68-70, 72-74, 80, 83-84, 88-89, 92, 97, 108, 116-17, 120, 130-31, 135-36, 141-44
Marutamsardhah 32
Maski 36, 43
Mathura 88, 94-95, 97-98, 132-34, 150, 164, 168-69
  School 98
  Style 95, 98, 132, 168-69
Mati-Jataka 180
Maukharies 5
Maurya(n) (period/times) 17-18, 26, 63-64-65, 70, 74-75, 77-83, 90-92, 107-08, 124, 128-31, 139, 155, 164, 167, 190-91
Maurya-Sunga 26, 82, 167, 191
Megalithic 36-37, 42
  burials 37
  deposits 36
Megaliths 43
Middle Ganga (plain/valley) 3, 37, 51, 79, 104, 124, 128-29, 136, 154-56, 167, 179, 183, 197
Mirzapur 159
Monarchical states 87
Mookerji, R.K. 11, 49, 64, 81
Mortuary rituals 37, 43
Mrigadaya 10-11, 16-17, 22-23, 52-55, 58-59, 63-65, 79-83, 86, 88, 94, 100, 108, 114-15, 122-28, 130, 134-36, 139, 141-42, 145, 147-48, 150, 167, 169, 175, 179-80, 196-201
Mula 138

Mulagandhakuti Vihara 80-81, 84-86, 90-91, 93-94, 96-97, 99, 101, 108-11, 113-15, 117, 140-41, 143, 145, 200
Munjavan 7
Musika-Jataka 192
Mythological stories 179, 193

Naga rule 87
Nagri script 145
Narain, A.K. 12, 34, 47, 125, 179-80, 185, 187
Narhan 42-43, 46
Narmada 99
Narokhar-*nala* 15, 25, 27, 152
Naya Tal 58
NBPW 3, 13, 179, 183-84, 187-88
Neolithic-Chalcolithic 48
Nigam 12, 14
Nirvana 22
Non-Aryan region 6-7
Norakhar *nala* 57
North India 3, 16, 87, 109-10, 136, 152, 159-60, 168, 189
Northern Black Polished Ware 3, 13, 27, 34, 52, 74, 124, 179, 186

Oertel, F.O. 11, 62, 66, 68, 71, 83, 93-94, 96-97, 107-09, 113, 139, 143
Oriyaghat 183-86, 188

Paharia 25, 27, 126-27, 152
Painted Grey Ware culture 36
Pale-Red-Gritty Ware 45
Pali 136, 180
Pande, G.C. 28, 30, 49
Pant, P.C. 154
Parimitas 30
Patia 156
Patliputra 3, 99, 130
Pattalikas 146
Pattana 49
Phusa 29-30
Pipal tree 97
Post-Gupta 64, 92, 104, 111, 120, 142, 153, 164, 166, 169
Post-Northern Black Polished Ware 13
Pottery-disc(s) 28, 30-31, 33-37, 191
Pradakshina patha 66, 90, 108
Prahladpur 47
Pratyeka-Buddhas 22
Pre-Asokan 64, 80, 109, 123, 125
Pre-Buddhist 12, 26
Pre-*Dharmachakra-pravartana* 123
Pre-Mauryan 79, 123-25
Pre-Northern Black Polished Ware 13
Pual 39, 45
Pupphavati 193

Rajan Asvaghosh 135
Rajapur-*nala* 17-18, 25, 152-53, 158, 166, 171, 174, 197, 199
Rajasthan 159
Rajghat 7, 12, 14, 43, 47, 125, 180, 184, 187-88, 191
Rajgriha 49
Rajputra Hatharideva 144
Rajputra Najunadeva 144
Ramanagar 12
Ramma 193
Ramnagar 13-14, 27, 182-88
Red Ware(s) 34, 37-38, 41, 44-45

Relic casket(s) 59-60, 66, 88-89, 107-08
Republican 3, 87
Rhys Davids, T.W. 2, 5, 179
Rig Samhitas 28, 48
Rishi culture 197
Rishipattana 15-17, 21-23, 25, 27, 47, 50-52, 58, 87, 123-24, 126-28, 150, 152, 178-80, 190, 196-98
Rishis 22-23, 25, 30, 46, 49-51, 197
Rivett-Carnac 62
Rock Edict VIII 125
Roy, T.N. 12, 34, 47, 125, 179-80, 185, 187
Royal Asiatic Society 73
Rumandai records 125

Sabbath-day 128
Sadanira 50, 197
Saddharma 141
Saddharmachakra 54, 141, 143
Saddharmachkrapravarttana 145
Sahi, M.D.N. 35
Sahni, D.R. 11, 18, 63, 69, 73, 75, 80, 94-97, 130-32, 134-35, 139, 148, 164-66, 170
Saiva followings 9
Saivite 7-9
Sakas 99
Saketa 49
Sala-sukta 30
Salas 30
Sambodhi 125
Samudragupta 99
Samvahika 131
Samvat 145
Sanchi 81-82, 110, 130
Sandstone of Sikari 132
Sangha 80, 123-24, 127
Sangharama(s) 18, 58, 112, 115, 117, 120, 124
Sangkar 59
Saragganatha 54
Sarang-tal 7, 25, 54, 57, 64, 151-52
Sarangnath 101, 113
Saraswati Valley 50, 197
Saravastivadins 136
Sarnath 7-8, 10-12, 14-19, 22-23, 25-27, 53-64, 66, 68-73, 75, 80-83, 86-94, 96-98, 100-02, 104-09, 111-14, 116-17, 120, 122-26, 129-30, 132-34, 139, 141-42, 144-45, 148-52, 154, 159, 163-76, 179, 192, 196, 198-201
  Museum 18, 27, 68, 164, 167-68
  Railway station 152
  School of Art 150, 163-64, 167, 199
  School of Sculpture 88, 93, 97, 132-33, 167, 169, 171, 173, 175-76
  Style 98, 169-70
Sarvastins 135
Sathavaha 130
Satapatha-Brahmana 32
Satvalekar, S.D. 7
Shakya Muni 3, 5, 123
Shakyas 3
Shayabhikhu 138
Sherring 61, 151
Shikhar 111, 115
Shirapala 148
Siha 131
Sikari sandstone 97, 164, 168

Silasena 138
Silpi Vamana 145
Singh, B.P. 35
Singh, Jagat 56, 59-60, 64, 71, 93, 136
Singh, P. 42, 46
Singh, Raja Cheta 59
Singhpur 151
Sinha, A.K. 11, 80
Sinha, K.K. 47
Siva 9, 27, 54, 87, 101, 103, 148
Siva temples 9
Skandhagupta 100, 103-04, 110, 114, 137, 141
Sodasa-Mahajanpadas 2-4, 180
Springle-whorl 46-47
Sravasti 47, 49, 132
Sri-Guptasimhasya 139
Srikunda 145
Srivastava, Ajai 11, 125
Sthavira 143, 145-46
Sudassana 193
Sulaksmana 139
Sunga (period) 26, 64, 81-85, 98-99, 129-31, 139, 164, 167, 175, 191
Surundha 193
Surya 153, 166
Surytra 139
Swaminathan, C.R. 36

Takani 162
Takkala-Jataka 180
Takuli 163
Tandulkar-Jataka 2
Tarini 145
Tathagat 123
Taxila 49, 168
Tectonic movements 186
Teou-shih 147
Thakur, N. 48
Thamba 130
Thapar, B.K. 36
The Jataka 180-81, 188-89, 192-93
Thomas, E. 61
Tilmanpur 18, 47, 152, 189
Tipani 162
Triklinga 144
Tripitakas 132, 134
Triratna 97

Udaya bhadda 193
Udayana 144
Uddalaka-Jataka 180
Ujjeni 130
Upabhrt 36
Upagupta 126
Upamitas 30
Urna 97
Ushnisha 97

Vaisakha 138
Vaisali 3, 49, 69, 99
Vama[deva] 145
Vanaspara 132, 134
Varad-mudra 172
Varanasi 1-3, 5-10, 12-14, 18-20, 23, 49, 52, 60, 86-88, 94, 97, 124, 126, 129, 132-34, 150, 154, 157-60, 164-69, 176, 178-81, 184-87, 189-201
Varanasi-Sarnath school 132-33
Varuna 7, 9, 25, 27, 50, 61, 108, 115, 152, 180, 191, 198
Vasantapala 148

Vasundhara 145
Vatsa 3
Vedic
  culture 198
  patra 31
  practice 37, 99
  religion 51, 197
  rishi 50
  rituals 23, 31, 33, 36, 191
  sacrifice 51, 197
  Samhitas 28-29, 36, 48
  yajna 19, 31
Vigrahapala 144
Vihara 18, 65, 79-81, 84-86, 90-94, 96, 97, 99, 101-03, 106, 108-10, 112-13, 115, 117-20, 122, 125-26, 140-41, 145-47, 199, 200
Vikrama 144
Vimanvatthu 124
Vinaya-Pitaka 124
Vindhyas/Vindhyan 154, 156, 185
  formation 154, 156
  sandstone 154
Visadeva 130
Vishvabhyah 32
Visvpala 144
Vriji 3

Wadia, D.N. 156
Wheel of Law 55, 115, 122, 124, 141, 147

Yajna 19, 31, 35-37
Yantramasi 32
Yasa 124
Yuvanjaya-Jataka 193